Absent with Cause

D1249163

Routledge Education Books

Advisory editor: John Eggleston
*Professor of Education
University of Keele*

LB
3081
.W45

Absent with Cause
Lessons of truancy

Roger White

WITHDRAWN

#18.00

EBS 6-23-81

Routledge & Kegan Paul
London, Boston and Henley

First published in 1980
by Routledge & Kegan Paul Ltd,
39 Store Street,
London WC1E 7DD,
9 Park Street,
Boston, Mass. 02108, USA and
Broadway House,
Newtown Road,
Henley-on-Thames,
Oxon RG9 1EN
Printed in Great Britain by
Redwood Burn Ltd, Trowbridge & Esher
© Roger White 1980
No part of this book may be reproduced in
any form without permission from the
publisher, except for the quotation of brief
passages in criticism

British Library Cataloguing in Publication Data

White, Roger, b. 1948

Absent with cause
1. Bayswater Centre
I. Title
371.9'3   LC145.G7   80–40630

ISBN 0 7100 0665 9

This book is dedicated to:

Val, who enabled the Centre to start

Hilary, who shared the struggle to start it

Rog and Chris, who have demonstrated that those difficult days were worth the struggle

Dave, whose friendship inspired it

But most especially, to Lizzie, who has shared all the difficulties, and whose love has given me the strength to go on striving for a cause we believe in.

Contents

Acknowledgments

To the many people who have helped develop the Bayswater
Centre since its first conception in 1975 I would like to express my gratitude. A special thank you must go to those
who give us support in the day-to-day running of the centre:
Bill and Pam Davies who help us maintain the building in
working order; Mrs Hodges and her staff who ensure we
don't suffer from malnutrition; our support group of Anne
Hewer, Sally Hogg, Lynn Goswell, Andrew Bird, Philip
Darley, David Davies, Chris Neubert, John Tuckett, Dan
Watkins and Hugh Coulsting, who have given us the professional and moral backing so crucial to staff morale and the
healthy development of the centre; the Director of Education and his staff in Avon House North who have oiled the
wheels for us at various stages and who provide the administrative and advisory support essential for the functioning
of the centre; past students from Bristol University and
Bristol Polytechnic who have encouraged us with their fresh
ideas and enthusiasm in a reciprocal learning process; and
of course all pupils, past and present, who have proved
that the work is worth doing.

To those who hosted me so warmly on visits to different
schools, units and centres in different parts of the country;
to Pat Bayliss, Dulcie Worsfold and Thelma Easterby for
typing the manuscript; and to Val Saunders and Dave Davies
who read the drafts and offered appropriate criticism I owe
a very special debt, because without their help these experiences would never have appeared in book form.

Abbreviations

CSE	Certificate of Secondary Education
CSV	Community Service Volunteers
DES	Department of Education and Science
D of E	Duke of Edinburgh's award scheme
EWO	Educational Welfare Officer
HMI	Her Majesty's Inspectorate
ILEA	Inner London Education Authority
LEA	Local Education Authority
MSC	Manpower Services Commission
TDA	Taking and Driving Away
VSO	Voluntary Service Overseas
YOP	Youth Opportunities Programme
'TES'	'Times Educational Supplement'

Introduction

The attendance of some youngsters at their local comprehensive schools is zero. A row of noughts fills the ten spaces in the register each week. At fifteen, after ten years of schooling, some youngsters have gained almost nothing from the experience on offer.

Three years ago, in a national survey conducted for the DES, it was estimated that in just one week, 800,000 pupils had been 'absent without good cause'. The irony of those inverted commas should not be lost on those of you who work with truanting children, and know that very often there is plenty of cause for their absence. It shouldn't surprise anyone who glances – even just occasionally – at articles in the educational press.

Since the Second World War many erudite studies have analysed the problem of truancy and under-achievement, and suggested various symptoms and causes.

Research in the 1950s and 1960s, for instance, concentrated on demographic educational studies that correlated attainment and performance with factors outside the school such as social class. In the late 1960s researchers like Hargreaves shifted the emphasis to a study of what was actually happening within the school to influence attainment. The de-schoolers like Illich and Freire used such material to suggest that, since schools were so harmful to so many kids, they should be abolished. De-schooling as an ideal became the slogan of the 'radical' educationalists of the early 1970s.

The situation in 1980 is that, however laudatory and reasonable are the arguments and ideals of the de-schooler in theory, the existing school model is too solid an edifice to be demolished overnight with just a simple re-distribution of resources.

1

Perhaps what needs to be done instead is to consider practical ways in which the school system can be amended and
supplemented to enable those who are gaining little from it at
present to enjoy more of its facilities and the vast per capita
sum invested in their schooling.   To this end, without accepting the de-schooling model completely, it is worth considering practical approaches that can be drawn from the
study of alternative educational programmes, such as free
schools, truancy centres, adventure playgrounds and work
experience units, which operate outside the 'normal' educational precincts, and yet which appear to provide a meaningful educational context for the young people who attend.
   This book concentrates on such alternative models of provision of schooling for truant children, and discusses their
implications for mainstream education.
   From observations of a unique experiment operating in
north Denmark, and from observations of some of the alternative projects operating in this country (concentrating in
depth on one particular unit, the Bayswater Centre, in Bristol) this book attempts to draw out ideas and approaches that
could hold possibilities for re-structuring 'normal' schools.
   Bayswater Centre now provides full-time education for
'phobic', 'disruptive' and 'maladjusted' 14- and 15-year old
adolescents who have stopped attending ordinary comprehensive school, and for whom the alternative may be home tuition or residential provision in community homes or assessment centres.
   The Centre began life as a privately funded experiment in
1974 - one of the many alternative schemes that mushroomed
in the early 1970s in Britain.   Despite the pervading atmosphere of financial restraint that followed local government
re-organisation, it had won considerable support from the
local authority within a year.   It was no doubt helped by
being regarded as an aspect of special education at a time
when there were few units in schools dealing with 'vulnerable' pupils.
   Part of this book describes Bayswater Centre during its
early days, when resources were limited in terms of buildings and equipment, and when the staff were struggling to
establish a credible identity and base for the Centre.   Those
of you who have ever been associated with such an enterprise
will know about the isolation and the weariness and the
depression often felt by the staff in the 'development' stage.
You will know that what keeps things going is an eternal optimism that 'something will turn up' and a personal commitment

buoyed up by memories of those moments of elation when the 'drop-out' kids you're working with do something that moves you to tears. By describing what actually happened in a documented year with a whole intake of youngsters, the intention is to probe beneath the labels of 'failure', 'phobic' and 'maladjusted', to show that a meaningful educational programme can be offered and accepted, despite disastrous home backgrounds or a previous history of complete failure at school.

Interviews with the youngsters after they had left the Centre, comments from their parents, and perceptions of the students who helped at the Centre, all give valuable insight into what really are appropriate curricular models and structures for adolescent school children.

By pointing to the success of an ethos that redefines the three Rs as Responsibility, aRticulation and Relevant education, and actually gives young people a real opportunity to participate in planning their own education, and by reference to other projects working along similar lines, the intention is to discuss the implications for state provision.

This is a book about what actually happened at the Centre in a year, rather than just a polemic about possible theoretical approaches. It endeavours to show how labels like 'school phobic' and 'maladjusted' just conceal a whole host of causal problems which must be taken into account, at an individual level, in educating children. It highlights some of the problems that kids have to cope with, and shows that 'failures' can succeed (even at academic subjects) if the educational provision is relevant in their terms and given on an adult basis.

Since units and schools like the Bayswater Centre are criticised for their comparative per capita expenditure and for the impossibility of replicating their ideas and approaches within the state system on a large scale, then part of their function must be to refute this criticism by pointing out practical, enabling ways in which this can take place.

'Absent with Cause' attempts to do just that.

Chapter 1

Danish lessons in practical education

A CHANCE MEETING

It was one of those rare February days when the muffled
deadness of winter promises to evaporate into a still, blue
sky. There is hope of spring. You cease to clutch your
coat quite so tightly, and can afford to linger and notice the
new life around you.

We had recently occupied new premises – a rambling old
abandoned primary school that was much too large for our
purposes. In two of its downstairs classrooms we were at
least able to base our school.

One of the rooms had originally served as a staff room,
but all that remained was a sink, a work-top and a beautifully sanded pine floor that had last seen polish a year before.
The off-white light shades on the ceilings were cracked or
gone.

The second room was larger. Echoes of banging desk
lids and ink wells being collected and filled by the duty moni-
tor still lingered in the initials carved on the wide window
sills, the tattered National Savings posters and the 'Daily
Telegraph' map of the Empire in faded pink that remained
stuck to otherwise bare walls. A circle of tables occupied
one end of the room, protected by a line of large cupboards
and a wardrobe, pulled across to divide the room into sections. In the remainder of the room, a woodwork bench, a
record player, a sewing machine, and various kinds of art
materials jostled for a place of prominence. Only the dart
board in the corner seemed inviolate.

The playground outside was normally a barren, tarmac
wilderness: lifeless except for the odd torn crisp bag and a
wrecked 1956 Anglia, which represented the extent of an un-
consummated car mechanics project.

4

That particular February day, though, was different. As
we pushed open the cast-iron gates that shielded the school
from the outside world, we were greeted by the sight of a
brightly decorated forty-five seater coach, of uncertain vin-
tage but clearly functional, parked beside our paint-spattered Anglia.

Milling around were dozens of casually dressed young
people engaged in a communal unloading exercise and shouting directions and messages in a strange language. Sleeping bags, boxes of food, guitars, rucksacks, kitbags, suit-
cases all emptied from the bus into the building we were
using as a school.

We stared in amazement like Rip Van Winkle awaking from
his slumber. Had we been evicted whilst asleep?

A familiar face loomed in front of us; Lester (one of our
kids) was panting under the weight of a grey kitbag.

'Bloody nuts this lot,' he informed us, 'All the way from
Denmark just to stay in this dump!' They was here when I
got here half an hour ago.'

What d'you mean? Who are they? Why are they here?
Where are they staying?'

Lester shrugged and disappeared through the doorway,
followed by a couple of blond Danish boys. Their questions
to him in lilting, musical English resonated from the corridor. Curious to learn more, we approached the group by
the bus.

Lester was right! They were from Denmark - a group of
thirty pupils and half a dozen teachers from a school in the
north of Jutland. The 'trip' was part of the organised curriculum for the whole school. All the students and teachers
were currently visiting different foreign cities in groups
like this one. A similar busload had gone to London, another to Cork. The school, Tvind (described by the Danes
as an 'after-school'), catered for youngsters between the
ages of 14 and 16. Rather like our own, it was concerned
predominantly with youngsters who didn't fit into the normal
school system.

After-schools are a long-established tradition in Denmark.
They exist as alternatives to the state high schools, yet by
Danish law are still eligible for statutory funding, assuming
they fulfil various basic educational requirements. It is
possible to establish a residential school in Denmark and receive government support to the tune of 85 per cent of the
expenses. All that is required is a 'supporting group' of
at least fifty people who can testify to the need, a curriculum

framework drawn up that satisfies fundamental educational criteria, and a headmaster and teachers whose credentials the state will accept ... and a lot of commitment.

Tvind was such a school and with a mix that was roughly 70 per cent working class and 30 per cent middle class, its 120 pupils were drawn essentially from low-income families. The pupils could stay until 16 when, as in England, they were legally entitled to leave school (having then completed nine years' education). (1) Though the curriculum embraced fundamental academic work that enabled all pupils to sit for the common state exams at the end of their final year, its emphasis was on learning through practical experience.

This visit to England was in line with that philosophy – designed to further the students' knowledge of English and English society through direct experience.

During their two-week stay, using the large, unheated rooms above us as a base, they visited schools, factories, offices, youth clubs, and such like. Through interviews and discussions with English people, they collected a wealth of information which was pooled every night at a common meeting where reports were written up and the events of the day discussed and recorded.

Right from the start we were impressed by the group's self-discipline. The Danish youngsters were no older than ours and their backgrounds in many cases were remarkably similar. Yet whereas we, as teachers, would probably have experienced difficulties of organisation and control – and motivation – if we'd arranged such a visit, there seemed to be no such problems with the Danish group.

Without any fuss, or arguing, or coercion – but with plenty of discussions – they would organise themselves into groups for the day and structure their own programme of activities. From their cramped, cold base above us they arranged a full programme for that fortnight, with the pupils apparently participating very willingly at every stage.

Inevitably, because we were downstairs, there were many occasions for coffee and chat. On their last evening we arranged a party for them and invited friends linked with our own school to come along. Though the Danes all refused the proffered alcohol (since one of their rules was no drinking) they joined in with enthusiasm.

What was noticeable in all these exchanges between the Danish youngsters and our own group of kids was an apparent difference in maturity. In self-assurance and awareness the Danes were streets ahead, and their discussions – even using the foreign English language – were often at a more complex level, in both language and concepts, than our youngsters could match.

It became clear during the Danes' brief stay that Tvind not only embodied all the principles we believed in, but was actually practising them. Self-determinism, participation and enthusiasm were liberally sprinkled with humour and warmth. There was no feeling of antagonism between 'staff' and 'pupils', and plenty of commitment to the communal 'survey' of England with which the groups were engaged.

Our observation of their activities during that fortnight stay, coupled with discussions and a study of their self-descriptive literature, presented a kind of Utopian picture of their school. The factual information alone was impressive enough.

Tvind itself is a complex of three schools in a very rural area of north Jutland. As well as the 'after-school' which these youngsters attended, there is a teacher's training school and what they refer to as a 'folk high school' – a kind of further education college, where the only entrance qualifications are that an applicant is over 18 and not a drug user'.

The folk high school system is uniquely Danish. Inspired by the ideas of the poet-clergyman Grundtvig in the mid-nineteenth Century, they were developed initially to prepare the common people for the transition from absolute monarchy to universal suffrage. Their educational framework accepted the reality of peasant life and thinking as the basic starting point. The cultural ideals were intended to be those of Denmark (its history, literature and language), not those of a foreign culture like Greece or Rome. The schools still retain much of the original simplicity of concept, and the organisation is centred very much round that of a co-operative residential community, where jobs are shared and interchangeable, and where democratic participation is a basic feature. (2)

The after-schools in Denmark are also an integral part of the Danish system. Many are religious-based schools, rather like our own church-aided private schools, but some like Tvind are founded on principles of communal decision-making and self-reliance.

There are no non-teaching staff at Tvind. Everything – the office work, the building maintenance, the cooking, cleaning, washing, farming, painting, vehicle maintenance and so on – is carried out by the students and teachers.

Organisation in Tvind is decentralised. The students and teachers together determine their own programme. At common meetings matters of finance and planning are decided through discussions and debate until agreement is reached. Such issues as the buying of new vehicles, the arrangement for a weekend visit by parents, the founding of a new job group, would be issues for debate at such meetings. The emphasis throughout is on linking theoretical learning with practical experience and to this end the pupils are all allocated (by consent) to one of eight 'job-groups' in which they stay for two or three months at a time. The job-groups – clerks, printers, mechanics, farmers, journalists, energy technicians, cooks and builders – must devise their own programmes centred around the demands of the particular job, and the ideal is that theoretical learning of subjects like Danish and mathematics will be linked in relevant ways to the practical work required by the job.

The school is residential and conforms to the normal pattern of terms followed by the state schools. The pupils spend every third weekend during term away from the school, so giving the teaching staff an opportunity to discuss policy and educational issues amongst themselves.

Tvind is financed in much the same way as all Danish schools, with the state providing 85 per cent of teachers' salaries and certain standard equipment, while the pupils' parents make up the remaining 15 per cent in fees (though many are grant-aided by their local authorities).

At the after-school the pupils spend one or two years, depending on whether they arrive during their eighth or ninth year of education – but all take the common state exam even though they have generally been discouraged from sitting exams in their former schools. In this aspect alone Tvind's achievement is remarkable. Since its inception in 1973 few pupils have failed the exam. Given the cross-section of intake and Tvind's professed emphasis on a <u>practical</u> education programme, this is quite a success story.

In life-style it seemed and sounded rather similar to that of an idealised Chinese commune, with democratic, non-hierarchical self-government, and job rotation and sharing amongst staff and pupils. Their educational philosophy of 'Learning by Doing' which incorporated the crucial elements of shared commitment, responsibility and resources, reflected the ideals espoused by Nyerere for Tanzania in his pamphlet 'Education for Self-reliance'. (3)

There seemed nothing comparable in England and we decided we must visit the school. With 80,000 visitors a year our request must have seemed quite routine to them, but we wanted to do more than visit; we wanted to be involved with the school in an exchange that was more than just a zoo-like, spectator experience.

We had read their literature; we had talked with people who'd visited already and knew something of the work, so we knew their basic principles, but there were many other things we wanted to know.

For instance, about the curriculum: how did they actually relate the theoretical work to practical work in such a way that the pupils were still able to pass state exams, which like our own English exams necessitate learning a large slice of purely academic knowledge? How did they decide the content of the lessons bearing this in mind? How did they decide the method of presentation once they'd agreed on content – and who decided? Was it the teachers, or pupils, or both?

And about the structure and organisation: how did they select the pupils who came? Was it really as simple as 70 per cent working class and 30 per cent middle class on a first-come-first-served basis? And how were they able to motivate such youngsters, who'd rejected ordinary schooling, to accept the discipline necessary to succeed at state exams? And how was it they had reached the point where self-determinism amongst the pupils actually worked, where the rules were not only agreed on with the youngsters but enforced by them as well?

And what of their 'graduates': what happens to them when they leave? Was Tvind successful in helping them obtain satisfying and appropriate employment?

We wanted to know whether Tvind really worked or was the glossy successful image present to the outside world merely one side of the story – with the real truth about structure and organisation well concealed. (4)

We sailed to Denmark in June, shortly before their summer term finished.

THREE DAYS AT TVIND

After a nineteen-hour boat trip and a four-hour train journey we reached Ulfborg in the early evening. Reassured by a passing resident that the elaborate dialling tone of the nearest telephone negated the 'WIRKER IKKE' sign hanging outside, we rang the school for further directions.

'Take the road for Hostelbro and Tvind is only five kilo-
metres away ... you could catch a taxi.'
'We'll walk....'
'OK, ask for Marianne when you arrive.'
Actually we hitched a lift from a friendly Dane! Though
he worked many miles away, he was as interested in the
school as we were. The windmill of which we'd heard and
read loomed above us as he drove into the gravel car park
that had presumably been built to accommodate some of the
80,000 visitors they'd hosted that year already.

As a symbol for all that Tvind stands for - self-help,
self-sufficiency, theory linked to practical endeavour, relevant co-operative work and study - it is simply and magnifi-
cently impressive. (5) Most of the 80,000 visitors to Tvind
in 1978 came because they had heard about the largest windmill in the world - built by a team composed largely of unpaid
and unskilled volunteers. It has become a live political
weapon within Denmark for those resisting the introduction
of nuclear power. 'Atomkraft? Nej Tak!' is a slogan supported by a majority of Danish people, whose combined opposition prevents the building of atomic reactors.

The blades were still.

It was the time of evening between afternoon and night,
when even the birds have fallen silent, resting before their
dusk chorus.

Then gently but steadily, a humming grew to a sighing, to
a rushing, to a swishing. Above us the blades had started
to turn. We stared fascinated as the 40-foot diameter stro-
boscope whirled powerfully 180 feet up.

'Just testing,' the Dane explained.
'Does it work?' we asked.
'Not yet, but it will,' he affirmed.
'Will it?' There was some doubt in our voice, which he
must have detected.
'It must - it has to,' he declared quietly. 'There is too
much to lose.'

With that we shook hands and he drove off leaving us alone
with the towering concrete mill. This monument of a tangible alternative to nuclear reactors had to succeed. The
blades slowed and finally stopped. Silence again.

We walked towards the hut that Marianne had directed us
to over the phone.

The first impression of the site was reminiscent of a red-
brick English university campus: people ambling at a leisurely pace in multi-coloured shirts and denim jeans; sitting

and talking quietly on the grass; an atmosphere of calm, un-
hurried purpose.

A girl approached us down the gravel drive - an orange
headband holding back flowing blonde hair.

'Hello,' she smiled warmly. 'I'm Marianne - it's good
you have arrived.'

We introduced ourselves, and she led the way to a large
terrapin-style hut - the 'information house', which we subsequently learnt was the nerve centre of the whole school.

Over tea and biscuits she explained something about herself and the school, confirming what we'd read in various
articles and what we'd personally observed with the group in
Bristol. Marianne, suspended from school at 15 for disruptive behaviour, who'd argued and fought with teachers in a
high school in her hometown of Aarhus, and who'd been labelled as unmanageable and difficult, was now leading a discussion about the methods and merits of alternative schooling
with two quizzical Englishmen - in excellent English and with
plenty of reference to her own experience of that country
(Marianne had in fact been one of the group who'd visited
Bristol). She was now 16 and had just passed the 'real'
exam, the exam all Danish pupils take after ten years of
schooling, and the exam which her old school in Aarhus had
judged her incapable of passing.

For an hour she talked with us, showing no sign of disin-
terest or irritation at what to her must have seemed some
very odd questions. At seven o'clock she pointed to the
time.

'We shall eat now and you can meet Annie' (the headteacher
recognised by the ministry). Marianne led the way to a
large dining hall; 120 bodies - the whole of the after-school
- were already half-way through their meal. 'Just take
what you want and we'll find a place in there.' Marianne
pointed to an adjoining room and proceeded to gather up
quarter-empty trays of meat and vegetables.

Half a dozen of Marianne's friends joined us next door.

'Who cooked this?' we asked.

'The cook's group, it always happens this way. They
prepare all the food for the school.'

We munched red cabbage and pork, plenty of it, well
cooked and seasoned.

'Hello Roger, hello David.'

We turned to face a smiling, gentle-faced woman - Annie -
looking very different from the fur-coated muffled figure
we'd last met in Bristol.

'We made it at last.'

'At last,' she laughed. 'Any longer and we would have gone! But it's good to see you. Tonight we have a party – it's the end of exams, but tomorrow we'll have plenty of time to talk....' Annie broke off to answer a couple of boys who were anxiously trying to attract her attention. Much gesticulating, much laughter, much shaking of heads. One of the boys pointed in our direction and spoke a few words of Danish. 'Nils wants you to help him gather wood for their bonfire!' explained Annie.

'Well, once we've finished eating....' The rest of our reply was drowned by a chorus of emphatic 'NEJs' from Marianne's friends. Nils shrugged and departed.

'They say "no" because Nils should have done it already. He's had all day to get wood – it was his job and he's just been lazy today.'

'How will he manage then?'

'He will do it.' Annie sounded quite confident. 'Everyone is expecting a bonfire. Nils will collect the wood – certainly he will.'

We smiled and wondered.

The 'party' was a real celebration. Every group had prepared some contribution, with its own performance or activity. In one of the large classrooms cleared of furniture we watched two 15-year-old girls give a demonstration of jitterbugging – Olga Korbut style – with backward leaps and plenty of cartwheels. The backing music and vocals were provided by a scruffy combo of Danish boys who see-sawed into the rhythm with polished expertise and plenty of laughter.

The enthusiasm was infectious and both girls had soon stimulated the whole room of spectators into following their steps. Five-year-old kids, downy-chinned adolescents, and adults, swayed and bumped and leapt around on the dance floor. And Annie, beautifully unprepossessive, moved with the rest, a figure of enjoyment, absorbed in the circle of life around her.

Between sequences the two girls explained the steps and at these moments there was no need to call for silence – 150 people went quiet, without any prompting apart from that of the quiescent combo on the platform.

We stood at the side, understanding absolutely nothing of what was going on, but at one with the atmosphere in the room. We smiled and laughed too, entranced by the enthusiasm of the dancers. Behind us, little children, offspring of the teachers or the students of the travelling folk high school, hung through the open windows, too small to get in, but too big to miss the fun.

Age meant absolutely nothing.

Over the children's heads, across the darkness and on the far side of the huts, orange sparks crackled into the night air. The bonfire was alight.

Next morning we sat in the sun on benches outside the huts. Sounds of rattling plates and running water indicated breakfast preparations in each of the four blocks that accommodated the whole after-school. Groups of kids drifted past - mostly ignoring us, or, less often, smiling a greeting. A girl we'd spoken to the night before, Leila, came across to join us.

'Hello! Have you had breakfast?'

We shook our heads.

'We'll go over in a few minutes then.' She sat on the edge of the seat, leaning back to soak up the sun.

'Leila, have you been here long? How did you come here?'

She explained about leaving school at the ninth grade without taking exams because the school had suggested it wasn't worth it. She'd had no job and was drifting around until she heard about Tvind, where she came for a visit and, liking it, had been able to join the school where she'd now been for just a year. Like the others in the tenth grade she'd just finished her exams - which she'd passed. 'But my old school was probably right - if I'd stayed there I'd have failed I'm sure - it was so different. Here I could work.'

A shout from across the courtyard interrupted her explanation. Marianne waved a greeting and walked across.

'We eat now and then I'll show you round - OK?'

'That would be very good....'

We followed her to her block and entered the communal dining room, where most of thirty others were already sitting eating. A few smiled a greeting and one girl waved us to some seats.

The groaning boards: Tyk milk and brown sugar. Cream cheese and mounds of hard Danbo cheese adorned with caraway seeds to go with the sliced black rye bread. Honey and jam for those with sweeter taste buds. All washed down by mugs of tea filled from a huge urn.

'What d'you call this cheese?' We were curious to identify it for future reference.

'Hvad hedder dette?'- Marianne turned to the rest of the group, holding up the mound on its plate.

'Gammel ost - old cheese!'

Laughter.

Somewhere amongst the group of thirty were a couple of teachers, but there was no way of telling by appearance.

Breakfast itself was a leisurely affair, but once finished, everyone threw themselves energetically into clearing it away and cleaning up. Again no one seemed to be directing the operation: some internal mechanism was programming everyone. Washing up, Hoovering, storing of unfinished food, stacking of chairs and tables was soon accomplished and they gathered in a group to discuss the day's plans. Marianne stood beside us.

'I must explain that you want to see round, so I will not be with them this morning but we will join them this afternoon.'

Which she did and received nods of approval from the group. We left them debating the re-decoration of the room – something they'd decided to do before their parents arrived at the weekend.

Looking round the whole site that morning it was clear that what we'd read whilst in England had only conveyed a very superficial impression of the scale and depth of the school: the print room where groups of people were working on magazine and poster productions for distribution throughout the whole country; the mechanics workshop – a hanger-sized building, with space and equipment to cater for the servicing of their fleet of vehicles consisting mostly of old buses used to carry whole groups across the country; the windmill and the solar system, both products of a self-sufficient attitude to energy production; the central kitchen where lunch and dinner for the whole school was prepared; the information house – the nerve centre of the complex, where all phone calls and letters were handled by a group of kids; the complex of buildings that formed the base for the high school, where several of the houses were being re-roofed.

'It's because the flat roofs they put on originally are now leaking, like our huts in the after-school,' explained Marianne, 'so we're changing them to sloping roofs. It is warmer too, because we can put in insulation.'

'And you do it yourselves?'

'Naturally – who else?'

Several times tractors with trailers trundled past us, carrying sacks of rubbish for building materials or crates of food – and always driven by one of the pupils.

'That's the builders group,' explained Marianne. 'They must maintain the whole site, and this week particularly, since we shan't be here for a while, it is important to clear out the rubbish.'

We'd noticed already, in the separate kitchens attached
to each of the four blocks, rows of individually labelled
plastic buckets:for food (to go to the pigs); for paper and
cardboard; for metal cans and foil; and for plastic to be re-
cycled or burnt where appropriate. Recycling and self-
sufficiency were more than just academic exercises.

Only the farm itself seemed out of character with the general atmosphere of attentiveness to the practice of their prescribed philosophy. Though the chickens and pigs were
clearly well fed and well managed, a lot of the arable land
was under-used and poorly tended. The large greenhouse,
which would have been the envy of any market gardener in
England, was empty. Not even a tomato plant – the mainstay
of an English garden greenhouse. It seemed very strange,
but maybe Annie's subsequent explanation of technical ignorance amongst teachers was reason enough (see Appendix 3).

What was strikingly obvious throughout the tour was that
the kids were doing all this, often unaided by any grown-up
direction.

Returning to the circle of huts that comprised the after-
school, the whole place was a hive of activity. In one
corner a pot of pitch was boiling over a small brazier,
whilst a group with buckets and ladders were engaged in
spreading the molten bitumen on the flat shingle roofs. The
re-roofing with cross-ties would wait till next year.

Across the yard, tables, chairs, guitars and carpets lay in
a jumbled heap. The rooms had been emptied of everything
ready for wallpapering. Rolls of hessian were neatly
stacked to one side and groups of boys and girls were busy
cutting and measuring and pasting, then disappearing inside,
struggling in twos and threes with sticky strips of fabric, to
the sound of 'The Who' at maximum decibels from an outside
speaker strung through the window.

'The teachers have all gone to a meeting,' explained Marianne, 'and we will try to finish most of the rooms before our
parents come tomorrow.'

In her own room she prepared coffee and her friends –
Lotte and Mona and Leila – joined us.

We plied them with questions.

Lotte, like Marianne a drop-out from folk school, had been
at Tvind a year. She was one of five to have failed the
exam, but was still determined in her choice of going to work
in a factory when she left that month.

Mona, a beautiful slender girl with a strong American
accent and professed love of everything about that country,

had been expelled from school. With another year to go before the real exam, she was intending to be a journalist like
Leila. What was really interesting in their attitude to work
was that all of them expected to spend some time in a factory
before pursuing their stated ambitions, and there was a
strangely positive attitude amongst them towards manual
work - quite different from our own experience with English
youngsters.

We talked about the academic work and what happened if
someone couldn't cope.

'Out of the people here this year, there is only one who
can't cope,' explained Mona. 'That's Lisbet - she's really
dumb, but all the others can manage.'

'So how does Lisbet fit in - does she accept the label
easily?'

'Oh yes, and it doesn't matter. We all know Lisbet can't
do mathematics or write so good and Lisbet knows it, but she
can do other things. I have tried to teach Lisbet mathematics for hours but at the end she never understands; it is a
waste of time for her.'

'What happens though if someone won't join in - doesn't
want to be with a group?'

'You remember Allan who made us tea last night in the information house? - When he came, he wouldn't fit in; he was
always arguing and wanting fights and wouldn't join us. So
we said "all right, perhaps if you won't join us, you would
help show visitors round, you can do that on your own."
And he did and he enjoyed it and now he mixes in with everything.'

What came across very strongly just talking with these kids
and the others we met in the three days was their commitment
to Tvind and their acceptance of its ethos of participation and
involvement. Yet they were still individuals, with very
clear individual ideas.

That evening we helped Marianne's group with the wallpapering. At 10.30, when we walked across to the information house to make a phone call, Lotte passed us, clutching
an armful of loaves and a bag of oats.

'Tomorrow we're going to Copenhagen to perform a play -
thirty of us in that bus. We must leave at 5.00.'

In the information house Allan connected us through to
England and brewed more tea. The four pupils manning the
building were balancing some figures in what looked like an
accounts book.

By midnight 'The Who' were silent and grey shapes flitted

across the gravel yard to their rooms in the four mixed
blocks. The rooms are all double ones, but they have a
rule about no sex inside to avoid all the problems of excluding other people. It makes sense in the atmosphere of
Tvind. If they want to make love they do so in the woods....
    Next day we were able to spend all the morning with
Annie. The recording of that conversation gives a lucid and
powerful impression of the school. We sat on the grass in
the sun behind the quadrangle of huts. The backdrop of
sounds were the shouts of kids papering walls and cleaning
rooms ready for the arrival of parents that night – and the
birdsong from the wooded surrounds. That morning Annie
looked much younger than her years. Wearing a loose red
jumper and grey slacks she rubbed her toes through the
grass as she talked.
    Annie's infectious laughter and the image of her slight,
energetic figure lying back to soak up the Danish sunshine,
can only be hinted at through the written word. But the ver-
batim transcript of this interview, reproduced at the end of
this book (Appendix 3) presents a moving and flowing picture
of the real Tvind. (6)
    It crystallised our certainty about the wisdom of their
approach and philosophy.
    Before we left Tvind, we had a long discussion on the last
evening with Marianne about our problems – how we could
develop our school to incorporate the principles we believed
in and could see working at Tvind. She was endearingly
interested and helpful.
    'You must tell the pupils what it is you want to do, so that
they feel involved in your school. You must let them decide
with you. Then surely it will work.... It must work.'
    Next morning, before leaving, we spoke with Disse – ano-
ther girl who'd been to Bristol on that February visit. What
did she feel was different about our kids?
    'They seemed younger in many ways,' she offered after
much thought.
    'Why do you think that is?'
    Again a thoughtful silence. 'Maybe it is because they are
treated so young by the teachers. The school I visited,
three of us in the group arrived at 8.15 and no one was
there, so we walked in to wait. When the teachers arrived
some of them looked at us very strangely as they came in.
All the other pupils in the school were waiting outside. We
learnt that no pupil was allowed in the school until after
half past eight. It seemed crazy, but that was the system.

They will not let them grow up if they treat them in that
way.'

We said our farewells – to Annie, who hugged us, and to
all the students, particularly Marianne, who'd hosted us so
welcomingly. From the road to Ulfborg we glanced back
occasionally to see the windmill blades gently rotating above
the pine trees that hid the rest of the school from view.

Chapter 2

Alternative provision in Britain

The school described in the previous chapter is in Denmark subject to a different set of government regulations and a product of very particular social and historical circumstances that are quite unique to Denmark. But in Denmark the Tvind school is not unique. To date there are 120 after-schools – residential provision that parallels the folk school provision. Of these a handful like Tvind cater predominantly for the working-class rejects of the ordinary state school.

In addition there are about 40 small independent schools of the sort described by John Holt in 'Instead of Education'. (1) The Ny Lilleskole in Bagsvaerd, a suburb of Copenhagen, is an example of an informal school which operates an alternative curriculum approach to the state schools, and yet is supported by the local government school inspectors. The Danish law that says 'if a certain number of parents can start a school and run it on their own for a year, the government will from then on pay 85 per cent of the operating expenses' is the enabling legislation for the development of such Lille schools – as well as the after-school network of the Tvind kind.

In England similar schools are non-existent. Our educational structure just doesn't provide an easily accessible route by which alternative schools, on the scale of Tvind, can be funded from statutory sources, whatever the extent of community support.

There are four recognizable and acceptable ways of educating school-age children in this country and none of them offer much hope for those who wish to initiate a LEA-supported large-scale alternative. Children between the ages of 5 and 16 must go to either a state school, a direct-grant school, a registered/recognised independent school, or be

educated 'otherwise'.   These are the only four categories
accepted by the DES.

For alternative provision on any scale the most obvious
categories would be 'independent' or 'otherwise'.

The White Lion Free School in London exemplifies the
former alternative approach.   Its annual economic crisis
typifies the financial constriction imposed on an independent
school that caters predominantly for working-class kids who
can't pay and is consequently dependent on charitable donations or a benevolent LEA - or both.

Their handbook, 'How to Set Up a Free School', (2) illustrates the complexity of the law that surrounds alternative
educational experiments.   What is clear amidst all the
vagueness of legality about what constitutes 'education' is
that a school in this country has no automatic right to financial support from the LEA whatever the strength of parental
feeling.

It is under this same category of 'independent' that
schools like Gordonstoun and Dartington and other progressive 'public' schools have been registered, but they cater
predominantly for sons and daughters of wealthy upper-class
Englishmen (or Americans, or Arabs) and all charge fees
(Gordonstoun £2,250 per annum, Winchester £2,160 per
annum, Eton £2,070 per annum). (3)

In an analysis of the progressive school movement since
the eighteenth century, W. Stewart describes efforts of various educational innovators to provide cheaper alternatives.(4)   Robert Owen's Lanark Schools, Richard Dawes's
School at Kings Sombourne, Maria Montessori's Methods, and
Homer Lane's Little Commonwealth are all examples of
efforts to provide an exciting and stimulating educational
atmosphere.   Certainly their work inspired other progressive educators like Neill at Summerhill - and perhaps
Duane's attempts to create a workable comprehensive in an
area that 'had some of the worst slums, brothels and clubs
in North London' (5) owed much to the influence of these
early innovators.

The late 1960s and early 1970s saw a mushrooming of
'free schools' in England (encouraged by the ideas of
Illich (6) and Freire (7) and other prophets of de-schooling)
where emphasis was on provision for working-class kids.
The Scotland Road Free School in Liverpool opened in a
blaze of publicity in 1971, creating the atmosphere for a
multitude of others to follow suit - generally in large urban
areas like Birmingham, Bristol, Manchester, Glasgow,

Edinburgh, Sheffield, Leeds and, of course, London. For
a while these enjoyed sufficient support, from charitable
organisations and educationalists, to maintain a workable
alternative.

In their criticism of the 'establishment' the de-schoolers
performed a useful task, by highlighting the deficiencies
within the existing system. Their arguments were many and
forceful: schools indoctrinate the ethos of profit motives;
they discriminate between rich and poor, widening the gulf
that already exists between the haves and the have-nots;
they consistently punish half the children, who are trying to
learn what society is trying to teach them, so making quite
sure that this failed half is bound to resist all future efforts
to induce them to learn; they legitimate the concept of childhood and subjugate individuals who would prefer to be adults;
they are institutional props, supporting the consumer-orien-
ted life-styles dictated by huge bureaucratic institutions;
they are mechanisms by which social hierarchies of class
system are preserved ... and so on.

However, the original protagonists of de-schooling like
Illich and Freire were speaking about a different educational system to Britain. They were particularly critical of
the South American school system, which was so rigid that
you couldn't effect change in it. But the reality in this
country is somewhat different. Schools aren't so rigid or
inhumane that they should just be swept away. In fact, what
is really encouraging is the vast number of teachers who are
trying very hard to improve the quality of the educational
structure, motivated by a belief that there really can be improvement from within - a belief for which they are prepared
to expend considerable effort, much of it in unpaid overtime.

Unfortunately, the de-schoolers in this country accepted
the theoretical analysis as universally applicable to Britain
and tried to implement it in practice. One consequence was
an aggressive stance towards LEAs and other statutory
bodies (from which they were at the same time making requests for funding) which weakened their foundation of support and eventually their 'independent' stance. In 1978,
for instance, three of the original 'Free Schools' (the
Durdham Park School in Bristol, the Delta Free School in
Southampton and the Barrowfield Community School in Glasgow) were forced to close down because of cash difficulties.
Of the five London free schools that existed in the early
1970s, only two are still functioning. 'Freightliners', in
York Way near Kings Cross station, lost its grant in 1976,

the 'Bermondsey Lamp Post Free School' was demolished in 1977 and deleted from the register, and the Community School in north Kensington de-registered in 1978 to be incorporated as one of the LEA's centres for disruptive pupils.

The two remaining in London, the White Lion School and Kirkdale School in Sydenham, are desperate to avoid such a takeover. The former regards such a move as a betrayal of the basic principles of free schooling, believing sincerely that LEAs should grant aid to independent schools who have clear parental support to the extent that White Lion enjoys, without imposing extraneous conditions.

Whatever the validity of their argument, the truth is that the £52 a week which paid the workers at the school out of a budget of £19,000 per annum for 1977, (8) is only guaranteed as long as trust funds' contributions and other private donations match the spiralling running costs of the school.

The acceptance by those like the north Kensington school of status within the 'Disruptive Pupils Scheme' has at least ensured their survival, even if it has meant compromising on some of their principles. Indeed it is this aspect of alternative (or quasi-alternative) educational provision that has mushroomed, in contrast to the demise of the free schools.

In the 'otherwise' category (the second of the two possibilities for alternative provision), LEAs are empowered to establish 'special units' under Section 56 of the 1944 Act which says 'if a local education authority are satisfied that by any reason of any extra-ordinary circumstances, a child or young person is unable to attend a suitable school for the purpose of receiving primary or secondary education, they shall have power, with the approval of the Minister, to make special arrangements for him to receive such education otherwise than at school'.

It is this word 'otherwise' which LEAs have been able to interpret to set up their 'special units' or 'sin-bins' or 'truancy centres', as well as enabling them to accept the legality of educational provision at home (as provided by home tuition) or in intermediate treatment centres or adventure playgrounds.

These special units are designed to cater for the educational needs of young people - predominantly adolescents - who for a variety of reasons find it difficult to accept the normal school framework. With the benefit of small groups and good teacher/pupil ratios it is hoped that such units can accommodate these 'school phobic' or 'truanting' children, and offer them a meaningful educational programme for the remaining years of their statutory schooling.

During the 1970s the amount of money spent by LEAs on
such provision has risen exponentially. Until 1967 there
were only six such units in the country. Ten years later
there were estimated to be 239 such units.
In 1979 the DES made available its first survey of special
units of this kind. In a booklet entitled 'Behavioural Units'
they summarised the national extent of this 'off-site' provision. (9)
The survey was conducted in 1977 of the 239 units known
to exist in English LEAs. HMIs visited about half of the
units, with the intention of examining the organisation,
staffing and programme of the units. Their report confirmed that such provision was a relatively recent phenomenon,
with the bulk of units being established since 1973. The
total number of pupils involved was 1,890 at the time of the
survey (compared to the 4 million plus in statutory secondary
provision and the 132,000 catered for in special schools)
and of these a significant majority were in the 14-16 age
bracket. (A more recent estimate in July 1979 for ILEA
put the figures at 1,200 pupils out of 400,000 in 'special'
units.) (10)
Generally the group size within the unit was less than
twenty pupils, though there was one unit with 146 pupils on
role (admittedly not all full timers!)
The DES survey presents an interesting analysis of the
national approach to such provision for 'disruptive' or
'truant' children. Though accommodation was generally
reckoned to be pretty poor (characterized by dilapidated
buildings, poor decoration, inadequate sanitary facilities
and lack of cleaning facilities), the staffing ratios in most
units were very favourable compared to normal provision
(ratios of 5:1 and 6:1 being the norm) which no doubt partly
explain the success rate as measured by attendance statistics. Average attendance figures were 85 per cent which
compared very favourably to previous attendance patterns
that often bordered on zero. Though authorities were
skimpy on provision of premises, their selection of staff reflected the necessity for well qualified and experienced
teachers. A good half of the teachers in fact possessed a
further educational qualification like MA, MEd or PhD, and
scale III and IV posts were the norm for those running such
units.
Clearly then, despite the demise of the free schools there
is a very extensive development of alternative provision
within the LEA framework. Whether in fact they merely

represent a sop to harassed heads of secondary schools, as die-hard free schoolers would assert; or fundamentally contradict the collectivist principle of comprehensive education as socialist teachers might assert; or are necessary containment establishments for bloody-minded pupils who need 'instruction', or whether in fact there is a real potential for change within their framework using the existing model, is an issue to come back to later.

Suffice it to say at this stage that there is considerable expertise (as measured by teachers' length of service, experience and responsibility) and enthusiasm (as measured by high attendance patterns of pupils and staff) within such units. Perhaps this mixture of enthusiasm and dedication presents a valuable opportunity for experimentation, at a time when 'cutbacks' and 'retrenchment' are keywords in educational planners' language.

During 1977-8 I was fortunate enough to have time to visit thirteen projects working on the periphery of education in similar ways to our own, with similar youngsters, in different parts of the country. Pressures of time restricted the length of my visits to half-days or days, but even such brief personal observation - in Oxford, Birmingham, Reading, Newcastle, Liverpool, Manchester and London - would confirm much of the DES inspectorate findings. The following is a brief report of some of the projects visited.

OXFORD

In Beauchamp Lane, Oxford, the Cowley St James Tutorial Group operated a weekly programme with non-compulsory afternoon sessions. Various rooms of an old primary school, three paid staff and twelve kids constituted the 'educational' oasis. I arrived on a very cold January day. The group had just come back from helping with a 'meals on wheels' delivery to local old people and were busily ladling out their own lunch from the contained offering that was provided. 'Are you the guy from Bristol, that Richard told us about?' asked a tall blond lad with the then statutory punk crucifix pinned through his ear lobe.

I nodded. 'Support Bristol City, do you? Real wankers aren't they? Did you see the thrashing they got at Southampton last week?' He laughed and thumped his fist down on the table so that the stew slopped over the container.

'Never mind, I'll clear it up after dinner. Have you had any yet? 'Ere Jim, give my friend some lunch. He's a Bristol City supporter who needs sympathy.'

The friendly, unstructured atmosphere was apparent in the kids' attitude and in the staff's unwillingness to coerce decisions about activities for the afternoon. No one wanted to 'go out' – and given the snow flakes outside the window I wasn't surprised. After a tour of the site, which mostly consisted of empty classrooms echoing the banging desk lids and ink-wells of a previous era, I joined their Monopoly game. With a Scotty dog who became the Rackman of the Bond Street set, I finally lost the battle for London to a combined rate and rent levy from the Trafalgar Square and Picadilly Circus set. Eric, the lad with the crucifixed ear, acted as banker with a dictatorial panache that would have impressed O'Brien of Threadneedle Street.

What impressed me, though, was their tolerance of my presence – and their interest in the educational implications of what they were involved in.

At three o'clock when I left to visit the LEA office before catching the train from Oxford station, Eric led me through the maze of new estate houses and concrete shopping precincts to the bus stop.

'Stick to Rovers,' he shouted and waved goodbye.

Funding for the Cowley St James Unit was provided almost exclusively by Oxfordshire County Council. The three staff were employed as teachers, and Richard – the nominal and executive head – was allocated a budget of £300 per annum to cover day-to-day running costs, apart from the necessary expenditure on heating and lighting and food. Equipment was inadequate and in short supply, with resourcefulness of the staff being the most plentiful commodity.

Subsequent conversations with an LEA adviser painted a rather gloomy picture of an authority with little enthusiasm for the centre, and a good deal of suspicion about the validity of such off-site provision. In answer to my question about similar provision within the county he merely shrugged and handed me a booklet outlining the extent of Oxfordshire's provision for the handicapped. My resulting depression waiting for the train back to Bristol had nothing to do with the snow flakes that drifted across the chilly platform.

BIRMINGHAM

In Birmingham the contrast between education 'otherwise'
and 'independent' was presented visually by a visit to the
Bridge Centre after a morning spent at the independent St
Pauls Community School (née Balsall Heath Free School).
In the latter Anita Halliday presided over a staff of five
teachers, all concerned with the full-time education of
twenty-five youngsters of secondary-school age. The
'school', a converted house, appeared relaxed and welcoming, and Anita and I sat and talked for an hour in her office
before touring the school. Her room reminded me very
much of my old grandmother's parlour with a kind of well-
used and welcoming feeling emanating from the frayed carpets and smudged walls. As I looked round the school,
what struck me most was the similarity in lesson content to
that of an ordinary comprehensive school. History that day
was the kings and queens of medieval England. Maths was
decimal fractions, and woodwork was the individual project
work that any youngster in a secondary school can expect to
enjoy. 'All the kids are sitting exams,' Anita pointed out
proudly, 'their choice of course,' and indeed there was an
air of co-operative application in the bowed heads, the exercise books and the rows of desks. The only obvious difference between Balsall Heath and statutory provision was the
atmosphere of informality in the relationship between staff
and pupils. It bears out what Rutter et al. have described
at length in 'Fifteen Thousand Hours'. (11) The important
thing is interested teachers who are professional in the
sense that they recognise and respond to the needs of their
pupils. Balsall Heath in fact was very much a recognisable
school - with emphasis on structured work, a 9.00-4.00
timetable, and lunch provided on a level with other schools.
It was interesting to compare it with the same school I'd
visited four years previously. Then the Balsall Heath Free
School was concerned with self-expression and personal
growth of the kids. In four years it had exchanged spon-
taneity and minimal structure for an atmosphere of progressive application. Some of the original warmth and vitality
had gone, but the achievements of the pupils were significantly greater in measureable and acceptable academic
terms.
The collusion with the LEA, by which they received grant
aid in return for the authority's representation on the governing body, had meant a significant shift from their early

days of financial uncertainty. They were quite 'respectable' by establishment standards, yet had retained enough of the Free School's original atmosphere to attract and keep kids who'd rejected ordinary provision.

At the Bridge Centre Andrew McLauchlin with a team of three full-time staff was struggling in the confines of an old primary school to provide an alternative patching-up exercise for kids of 14 and over who had rejected, or been rejected by, ordinary school. To the kids the centre was an oasis - quite removed from their own community, some considerable distance away. The Bridge operated pretty much independently of parental involvement, though the teaching staff were still concerned more with the social skill aspect of education than with examination attainment.

Andrew showed me around himself. The emphasis was clearly on pastoral care rather than academic advancement. In various corners of the shambling building staff and pupils were huddled in groups, engaged in intimate conversation. We entered the woodwork room to find one lad working on his own, trying to cut out a jigsaw. 'Is that for your brother, Alec?' asked Andrew.

'Yes it's his birthday tomorrow, but I don't think I'm going to get the bleeder finished,' Alec grumbled in broad dialect. At that moment the blade snapped. 'Jesus Christ! Shitting saw!' He flung the metal fretsaw on the floor.

'Steady on, Alec,' Andrew's protective arm gripped the lad's shoulder. 'We've got plenty more blades. I'll help you fit it - and sand the edges of the bits you've sawn ... yes?' Andrew picked up the saw and drew a box of blades from a corner cupboard.

The Bridge Centre was 'education otherwise', with the kids technically remaining on the register of their previous schools - a purely administrative device, since the schools invariably didn't want to accept the pupils back. They were kids who had rejected or been rejected by normal school and for them, as for all pupils under 16, the LEA in Birmingham has a responsibility to provide some form of education. The 'capitation' grant for the dozen kids was £1,050 per annum.

READING

The 149 Centre in Reading had a very different history. The stimulus for this 'truancy' unit had come from the Young Volunteer Force, who had agreed to fund a pilot experimental scheme in the hope that the statutory organisations would take it over if and when it had proved its worth.

When I arrived towards the end of the day, Poppy and Clare – two of the three full-time staff – were cleaning up the workshop with the help of a couple of kids. Joining in gave me a chance to sound out their attitudes. There was no doubt of the kids' enthusiasm – their only regret was that it was only open three days a week.

'But Poppy and Clare need time to talk with our Mums and Dads and the people in Social Services,' explained Darren – a 15-year-old boy who had been away from school for two years before social services had linked him with the 149 centre.

Over a few beers in the pub that night, Poppy and Clare filled me in on the background to the school. With three staff and ten kids, a minibus and a grant of £18,000 a year from YVF, they were assured of support for another year. The building was an old primary annexe that had been a craft and metalwork room they'd converted themselves. Two years before when I'd fist visited their 'school' they'd been renting a whole house in the seamier side of town, and catering for a whole cross-section of ages. In the transition to the primary school annexe they'd lost something of the homely atmosphere. Whereas before they'd enjoyed a multitude of small rooms, now they had to rely on creating an impression of delineation with colour and furniture. To their credit it worked very well. With skilful use of colours they had split two large rooms into definite areas. There was a general air of purposeful activity about the room, within an overall atmosphere of relaxed friendliness.

In describing their links with schools it was clear to Poppy that many teachers regarded it an easy dumping ground, so since most referrals came via social services, their useful contact with parent schools was pretty minimal. In their terms, they preferred to work with kids near, but not at, the bottom of the spiral – those who were either on the verge of truanting a lot, or on the point of conflict with the law or at home. Both of them were ambivalent about their effectiveness with proven delinquents.

A real problem for the two women running the school was that the predominance of females often required one of them to play a male role – which they felt only confused the kids. This difficulty was further compounded by a referral system weighted heavily in favour of boys. Like all other units I visited they found it easier to attract and work with boys.

Their general experience was that girls tended to have ties at home, like over-dependent mothers and younger siblings, which made regular attendance difficult even at an informal welcoming place like the 149 Centre.

Though their links with schools were tenuous, both Poppy and Clare were aware of the need to be active on the school front. But despite a helpful advisory group drawn from special schools, remedial advisers and teachers, they were still hesitant and uncertain about how to tackle the task. With their recognition that what was required was not so much a structural change in the institution as an attitudinal change amongst staff, they had focused on the single most obvious obstacle to change quite accurately. But from their vantage point of comparative and insecure isolation they were almost powerless to proceed.

'After four years I feel we should have made some inroads. Though we're now tolerated by schools, there's a general feeling that they're just happy to pass us on problems and forget them.' Poppy drained her glass and stared thought-fully at the beer mat. 'Perhaps I should just be content that we've got a base and we can work how we want with the kids who come - but somehow, for me, it's not enough.'

In all these visits to the dozen or so centres that hosted me so welcomingly, including those just described, what came across very strongly was the enthusiasm and commitment of the staff involved. A summary of the general characteris-tics about structure, staffing, intake, curriculum and fund-ing bears out many of the findings of the report and is worth elaborating.

First, the physical structure: all the units were based in old primary school buildings, church halls or crypts or old houses, and furnished with second- or third-hand equipment. that had been discarded from other schools or scrounged from offices and homes nearby. Nearly all the centres res-tricted their numbers to about a dozen pupils (St Pauls Com-munity School and White Lion School, to their credit, being notable exceptions with 25 and 50 on the register respective-ly).

Second, the staffing: the average staff/pupil ratio was at least one to four. In several cases the use of paid non-teaching staff and voluntary help, particularly students, meant an almost 1:1 ratio at times. Staff tended to be in their late 20s or early 30s and though most had relevant ex-

perience working with difficult adolescents in ordinary
schools, it was unusual to find any with specialist training.
Indeed, it is questionable that such training exists! Nearly
all the centres were in charge of a scale III or scale IV
teacher – though at one extreme there was one being run by
a man on the senior teacher scale.

There was no in-service training of staff and little contact
with others working in similar situations, though some
centres had regular meetings with management committees
comprised of educational psychologists, LEA advisers,
social workers and others with relevant experience. Regular staff meetings were a common feature: often the whole
day or part of a day was set aside, with the pupils either
absent from the centre at those times or engaged in a pre-
arranged activity like a visit.

Third, the pupils: intake was generally restricted to
fourth- and fifth-year pupils, with a minimum stay of at least
a year. Attendance averaged 90 per cent, which was the
most obvious hallmark of success in outsiders' eyes since
the previous non-attendance of the kids was the original
cause for concern. All centres had evolved some degree of
admission procedure and, though it was exceptional for the
staff to have the deciding vote in principle, in practice their
opinion would prove decisive, since they would obviously
work best with those pupils they felt most positive towards.
As in all therapeutic communities, the centres that were most
aware of their admissions criteria and selected carefully
were those that appeared to be the most positive. Interestingly, all units felt uneasy at coping with violent behaviour
problems or very 'maladjusted' or ESN children. The clear
preference was for the 'withdrawn' truants.

Fourth, the curriculum: in describing the aims of their
centres, staff pointed to a philosophy of approach that was
common to all. Emphasis was less on specific subjects and
more on approaches and skills: increasing self-confidence,
careers guidance and work experience, social skills and
relationships, developing expressiveness, basic literacy
and numeracy work.

With this broad framework the actual structure of the
weekly timetable varied considerably. Some units had a
highly organised programme, with areas like English and
maths pinpointed and restricted to certain sessions, whereas
other units had an almost 'free' structure, where the day was
developed with little preplanning. Most centres operated a
work experience programme and there were significant

attempts to involve the youngsters in outside activities like
camping expeditions and visits, though the finance available
restricted the possibilities. Since all centres tried to
operate as full a weekly programme as possible, midday
meals were provided for staff and pupils – usually from the
LEA subsidised meals service. Facilities for preparing
food on site were limited generally, and staff were inclined
to discount this activity as too time–consuming, although
aware of its educational advantages.

Last, finances: annual budgets varied tremendously and
this represented the area of most disparity between units.
Some had as little as £200 per annum for expenditure on all
items other than salaries, rent and electricity, whilst for
other centres, £200 represented the annual capitation per
pupil. All centres felt the need to attempt their own fund-
raising to supplement their capitation. The single most
common problem was the necessity for ready petty cash
sums. For many, the bureaucratic obstacles to this proved
insurmountable, thus undermining their flexibility quite considerably.

The one thing that did vary considerably between units was
the political awareness of the staff involved. Though an insight into the socio–economic factors causing truancy may
actually have very little influence on the effectiveness of the
teacher/pupil contact, it certainly makes a difference to
staff attitudes. At one extreme there was the acceptance of
the youngsters essentially as transgressors, where adverse
experience at school was regarded as <u>their</u> failure. At the
other was the perception of the youngers' predicament as an
inevitable consequence of a societal attempt to use schools
as agents for social control – the youngsters in this case
being regarded as those with the native wit and courage to
see through the 'con' and vote with their feet against the in-
dignity of the system.

Awareness of the socio–economic context within which
these units are operating is important if the area of concern
is wider than the immediate intake of pupils.

Though such centres can be adventurous and challenging
for the children who attend it is arguable how much more
they do than simply prop up the secondary school system.
If the interpretation by staff involved is that basically the
children themselves are at fault, then such an unquestioning
acceptance of the status quo will do little to alter the structure of the larger schools. However, if the staff involved
reject the notion that the youngsters are inherently malad-

justed, and instead regard them as merely symptomatic of a
disturbing malaise within some comprehensive schools, and
if those in the LEAs begin to recognise the growing force of
such arguments, then it may be possible to influence mainstream provision.

In their book 'Born to be Invisible' (12) Rob and Angie
Grunsell describe three years in the life of one of the early
London truancy centres. Their account highlights the pit-
falls of parochialism that can so easily afflict those working
in such centres, where caring for the kids can become such
a preoccupation of the staff that they tend to appear dismis-
sive of school or community.

Though the book is an interesting and evocative description of one attempt at alternative education within the system,
it barely refers to the socio-economic context within which
it was operating. Consequently, it does little to dispel the
establishment view that such units are the panacea for growing adolescent disenchantment with school.

Many 'special' units are merely regarded as containment
exercises, and their book could support the prevailing
attitude that failure at school reflects on the individual child,
rather than being read as symptomatic of something more
complex, that may actually have as much to do with inadequate schooling as with inadequate personality.

The extent to which such centres can influence mainstream
education depends of course on many factors, like how
'schooling' is regarded by those in authority; the heads and
senior advisers and education committee members who dictate policy and curriculum philosophy within the school; and
like how committed those working in the centre are to attempting to influence mainstream provision. It is a hard climb
with many false peaks. Winning acceptance for the validity
of the shop-floor work itself with the kids concerned is difficult enough.

The image of long-haired radicals knocking 'the system' is
deeply ingrained in the minds of those who handle the purse
strings. It takes time and patience and a certain degree of
tongue-biting at moments of acute frustration. Once established, though, and 'successful' in ways that overlap with
the prevailing view of success as seen through establishment
eyes, the next step is to attempt extrapolations for other
kids and other teaching styles.

There are excellent theoretical sociological critiques
which testify to the inequality of the existing school structure
and point out ways of practical change. The message impli-

cit in the writings of some of these is discussed at the end of
the book. At this stage, though, the work of actual practi-
tioners in the field is worth studying in depth to see whether
their experience holds any clues and <u>practical</u> suggestions
for shifting the emphasis with statutory schooling.

A significant example of the schools operating outside the
system is the White Lion Free School in London, and in its
various bulletins (1-4) (13) and its handbook on 'How to Set
Up a Free School', considerable space is given to 'curriculum' and 'structure'.

The White Lion development is indicative of the evolution of
the free-school philosophy generally, moving as it has from
a completely open situation that characterised it, early
beginning, to the comparatively highly structured situation
within which it operates at present:

We are obsessed with structure, though not of a compulsory sort. The whole significance of the school lies in
its pioneering of new structures - both in relation to the
community and in terms of curriculum ... the role of
parents, teachers and students, and of day to day organisation. (14)

They argue that statutory school structure is out-dated,
and the problem for education is not just a question of up-
dating existing curricula, but more a question of asking what
new structures might be appropriate, given the conditions
appertaining to Britain in 1979.

Their 'curriculum' incorporates a belief that certain
skills like reading, writing, some number work, talking, and
the ability to research, digest and evaluate information from
a range of sources are essential, but they question the value
of much of the information commonly taught in school.

What is more important though is not the content, but the
way in which teaching and learning are structured.   Pupils
and parents are drawn into the running of the school and in
assessing the value of what is included in the curriculum.
They present their 'curriculum' not as a list of English,
maths, history, French, etc., but as a series of strategies,
which include such things as how they organise a 'card index
- of adult volunteers with particular skills to offer, of sympathetic, local employers, and of all the out of school learning
experiences and learning resources we can find'.   In their
terms it is more revealing to describe how they structure
their week than to ask what they do in a week.

Significant features of the school are:
(a) A lack of the hierarchical authority characteristic of

schools, where teachers are invested with status because of academic qualifications.

(b) The number of pupils is small (50) and the ratio of
adults to pupils is high (8 full-time workers and a
whole host of voluntary helpers – especially parents).

(c) Regular weekly meetings with all parents, teachers
and children, and daily meetings involving all adult
workers.

(d) An emphasis on 'basic skill work' as a regular part
of morning activity.

(e) Tremendous local support and interest from teachers,
colleges of education, institutes of education – but
piecemeal support from the LEA (Inner London in
their case).

(f) Low rate of truancy, with 90 per cent attendance being
the norm.

(g) Discipline is enforced by a process of talking through
confrontational situations – (which some would describe as nagging!)

(h) A multitude of rotas – for cooking, for cleaning, for
washing up, answering mail, handling the petty cash,
organising the maintenance of the building.

(i) Use of old premises that no one else really wants.

Reference to the literature, and the personal observations
of some of the state-supported 'special units', like those
described already, shows considerable overlap of 'curricula' and 'structure' with those of the White Lion School.   It
all suggests that it may be possible to incorporate alternative curricular ideas into the statutory umbrella – albeit on
a small scale initially.   Certainly at present the smallness
of these 'units' and schools is one characteristic they all
share and is probably a determining feature of their acceptability to LEAs.

Despite the argument that all these 'sin-bins' or special
units succeed in doing is supporting the existing weaknesses
in schools and are actually an obstacle to change (which may
well be true in some cases), they do at least provide a framework for experimentation 'within the system'.   With their
relative financial security compared to the free schools, they
can concentrate on developing curricula and structures appropriate to the individuals with whom they work, unfettered
by distracting anxieties about their mere survival.

The remainder of this book is a study of one such 'unit' –
the Bayswater Centre in Bristol – which has been experimenting with curriculum structures and content, predominantly

for working-class youngsters, since 1975. The school
itself provides full-time education for 'phobic', 'disruptive'
and 'maladjusted' 15-year-old adolescents who have stopped
attending ordinary school and for whom the only alternative
is residential provision in homes or assessment centres.
By describing what actually happened in a documented year
with a whole intake of youngsters two years after its open-
ing, at a time when it was in its transition between independence and state support, the book will probe beneath the
labels of failure/phobic/maladjusted to show that a meaningful full-time educational programme can be offered and accepted, despite disastrous home backgrounds or a previous history of complete failure at school.
By comparing the curriculum and structure then with the
current curriculum and structure two years later, the book
will exemplify the evolutionary process through which such
units need to develop, and will give some insight into the
administrative complexities of such a transition.
Like many similar units the Bayswater Centre began life in
dingy premises, with no equipment, very little statutory support, and only the strength of committed (and poorly paid!)
staff to carry the work through. Four years on it now occu-
pies suitable premises and has really begun to run an education programme that takes account of individual needs.
As well as the description of the year, the interviews with
the youngsters after they had left school, the comments of the
parents and staff, and the perceptions of the students who
have helped at the school all give valuable insight into what
really are appropriate curricular models and structure for
adolescents. By pointing to the success of an ethos that
gives working-class adolescents responsibility and participation in planning their own education, and by reference to
the other educational alternatives mentioned, particularly the
Tvind school in Denmark, the book discusses the implications
for state provision.
One thing that stands out quite clearly, for instance, from
interviews with the youngsters themselves, is the frequent
references to the 'adult' atmosphere, and the 'trust' situation, where they were given and expected to cope with responsibility. This highlights the point made earlier about
the White Lion School, that it is the 'how and why' that is
really significant about the curriculum, not so much the
'what'. Specific references to curriculum content include a
predictably enthusiastic response to 'practical learning situations', like work experience placements, visits, speakers

and camps. In 'State School', (15) Mackenzie writes very
lucidly about the educational advantages of taking school
children from urban environments into rural situations,
where the realism of the living situation itself was relevant
education.

Like the White Lion School, Bayswater Centre has evolved
from an open situation to one with a fair degree of structure.
The emphasis is on responsibility, trust, co-operation, par-
ental/pupil involvement, and experiential education. Our
Three Rs would be listed as Responsibility, aRticulation and
Relevant education (slightly more grammatical than Reading,
'Riting and 'Rithmetic!) As an example of the former,
pupils share the responsibility of running the building – handling post, answering the telephone, ordering milk, cooking
meals, writing letters, keeping petty cash accounts in order,
and so on. The high attendance (92 per cent on average)
suggests that it really is possible to provide meaningful education for working-class adolescents.

Again, like the White Lion School, it is more revealing to
look at our structure than our content. When people ask
'What do we do' our reply must be that it isn't 'What we do'
that's really significant since much of it parallels the curriculum content of mainstream education. What is really significant is the way we go about doing it.

At this period in time we are organising one of our occasional Open Days. The most important part of this is the
process by which the Open Day is arranged. The identification of tasks, the allocation of areas of responsibility, the
acceptance of individual preferences and the debate about its
actual value are all crucial areas for preliminary discussion.
By the time the Open Day arrives, much of the real education
has taken place already. The doing of the Open Day represents a process of approach that is more significant than the
activity itself.

In describing our processes this book will describe what
actually happened at the school in one year, and is intended
to be more than just a polemic about theoretical approaches.
Though it describes the school at a time when it was housed
in inadequate and ill-equipped premises – two rooms of an
old abandoned primary school – and at a time when our evolution of ideas and practice was at a fairly rudimentary
stage, it is an accurate portrayal of the possibilities and the
limitation of alternative provision. It certainly shows how
meaningless are labels like 'school-phobic' and 'maladjusted', and that these labels merely conceal a whole host of

causal problems, which must be taken into account, at an individual level, in educating children. It highlights some of the problems that these kids have to cope with, and shows that school failures can actually succeed (even at academic subjects) if the educational provision is relevant in their terms, and offered on an adult basis.

Criticism of 'special units' like Bayswater Centre, often concentrates on the expense of running them and the impossibility of replicating the provision on a larger scale for more youngsters, either inside or outside the schools.

Part of their function, therefore, must be to show schools how their ideas could actually be incorporated into the statutory framework - or how the statutory framework could be amended accordingly.

In a recent article for 'Socialism and Education', Mike Golby outlined a few practical suggestions as to how the experience of those working in 'special units' could be made available to a wider audience. Ideas like the investing of staff in units with adviser/counsellor status, in relation to a comprehensive school curriculum design committee or governing body, would mean a permeation of their professional experience through to the mainstream. He concludes his article by saying

> The creation of new educational institutions (special units) presents a very great opportunity to test out experimental ideas in both method and content and to see their promotion through to all pupils when they prove their worth.... Too much of education is timorous and time-serving. The energy and dedication of teachers in units, properly directed, has much to offer us all. (16)

This would, of course, need a radical reappraisal of the hierarchical structure of schools, and serious evaluation as to whether exam-dominated curricula are appropriate for all but an academic minority. It could be done though, and the model espoused by the Tvind school involving 120 youngsters and ten adults shows that increase in size is not necessarily synonymous with lack of teacher/pupil co-operation and participation - and does not have to signal a retreat behind the apparently safe barriers of credential acquisition.

In arguing for educational reform to redress the balance in favour of real education for working-class youngsters (as well as their middle-class colleagues), as schools like Tvind and the various alternative projects in the UK are demonstrating can be done, it is important to be clear about how much we are arguing for institutional reform, and how much for the abolition of institutions.

In Britain there is a general acceptance that much is all right with most primary schools, and it is the secondary school structure that has been the focus of criticism. It is to this part of the institution of schooling that this book is addressed, in the hope that it may contribute towards reform of existing schools, in contrast to the outlook presented by socio-economists like Bowles and Gintis, who are quite gloomy about the possibilities of teachers and schools actually being able to pioneer social reform. (17) Bowles and Gintis may be right, and it may be that the few alternative school projects currently operating will continue to do so under a kind of symbiotic patronage of LEAs, who can afford to accommodate one or two such units within their provision, but who have not the serious intention of developing further models, or of using the ideas on a wider scale.

Perhaps, though the raising of the school leaving age, the rise of youth unemployment, the lack of satisfying rewards from a materialistic society, will all create the kind of confusion and bewilderment amongst educational administrators where the signposts already erected by the existing alternative schools could point the way to imaginative reforms in education which utilise the full potential of the educational system for contributing to social prosperity.

Chapter 3

A tale of two classrooms: the Rs that count

'I arrived at school at ten o'clock and had a cup of tea. Then I made a smart ring with a red J on it. For dinner we had curry. It was all right I suppose.'

So wrote Jim as his contribution to the communal diary on the first day of the new school year. The five others who started with him that term wrote equally brief comments. But they wrote the diary daily and from their comments and those of the rest of the ten who joined them later, and our own journal extracts and memories, it is possible to represent that year in an honest attempt to reconstruct what happened and maybe give some clues as to why the apparent anomaly of a school for school refusers is a credible proposition.

Six arrived that first day: Jim, Martin, Clive, Alec, Debbie and Joy. We greeted them with a steaming kettle whose contents were soon transformed into mugs of sugary tea. All of them had met several times before in the summer term at 'introductory' sessions. Indeed four of them, the boys, had been away for a night's camp together – the sole purpose of which had been to 'break the ice', so we expected any shyness to be fairly short-lived. They greeted each other warily, though; six individuals dressed differently, behaving differently, but sharing the common ground of being school rejects. Initially the girls were much more forthcoming than the boys and in making decisions it was always they who took the lead.

'Well, what are we going to then? Did you get the message from my Mum? I've got to go to doctor this afternoon' – Joy addressed us, and then without waiting for an answer, turned to Debbie. 'Didn't see you at the Bamboo last night. Heard you had an argument. Errol wouldn't take me home

until two o'clock. I'm tired.' Joy lay back on the sofa and
closed her eyes.

To begin with we just sat and talked. The room we were
in had been the old staff room. High ceilings and long, tall
windows, with a tiny gas heater in the corner promised a
cold winter ahead. For the time being, though, in September, it was still warm. Most of the space was taken up by
'easy' chairs in various stages of disrepair that had been
scrounged, or 'collected' from nearby skips. Along one
wall was a sink, next to which we had sited our domestic
science equipment (one Baby Belling stove) on which we
would attempt to cook a meal for a dozen people each day
throughout the year. The whole enormous building had been
empty for many months before our occupation of two adjacent
ground-floor rooms, so the impression of what had once been
a comfortable staff room had vanished completely under several layers of accumulated dust. But it didn't seem to
matter; we sat, almost oblivious to the grey-cream walls
and the cracked, white light shades on their long flexes that
reminded us all of our own primary school days.

Joy and Debbie dominated the conversation: the former,
an attractive West Indian girl, with characteristic 'afro'
hair, was easily the most articulate member of the group,
and in poise and maturity of looks and expression only
Debbie, who could herself have passed for a woman ten years
older, was in any way Joy's intellectual equal. Debbie had
in fact been employed in the local authority's education office
as an evening cleaner for several months before she joined
us - her real age being well concealed beneath a 'saucy' exterior. The irony of sweeping out the administrative offices
of the system that had failed her was quite lost on Debbie who
just 'needed the cash'.

Jim, with an amazing similarity in looks and temperament
to Alan Bates's characterisation of the ousted Mayor of Cas-
terbridge, was the eldest of the boys and had been with us
longer than the other three, which fact gave him an edge
over them in confidence and leadership. His warm smile
and infectious chuckle under a mop of curly blond hair topped
a frame that was already showing signs of bulging at the
seams. The influence of Pernod and beer, consumed under
the watchful eye of a Dad who 'preferred 'im to drink with me
where I can keep an eye on him' was assisting Jim in developing a healthy paunch.

Clive was almost his physical opposite: long and thin with
straight, lanky hair, he looked so morose and cheerless that

he could easily have swapped his load with Atlas, so great
was the burden he was obviously carrying. He sat quietly,
listening and watching. His Mum had been very critical of
the school he went to 'because they let the other boys gang
up on 'im and didn't try to stop anything – and he's so thin,
he needs to stop at 'ome often, but the doctor won't give 'im
a certificate. "Lazy," he says, that's all; well what help
is that, when I know Clive would go if he was well enough.'

Alec, on the other hand, was demonstrably restless. At
his birth someone must have slipped a liberal dose of itching
powder in his bloodstream; it was almost impossible for him
to sit still. Of the four boys, he was the sex-symbol.
However scruffily he dressed, Alec's gentle, handsome face
always seemed to exert a magnetic influence over girls –
apart from Debbie and Joy, who never succumbed to his
errant charm. His matching, casual Levi-combination had
obviously been carefully chosen for the day.

The fourth boy, Martin, reflected his nickname of Match.
Thin and wiry, with a schoolboy's manner, he was physically
much less mature than the others and was the only one whose
voice had yet to break. His genuine eagerness and willingness to participate showed through right from the start. He
had clearly already decided to make something of us. With
creased trousers and well polished shoes he was the nearest
any of them came to appearing like a school pupil and, initially, was the only one who sat without a lit cigarette.

All six of them reflected their personalities in manner and
dress: a testament to the liberating effect of lack of uniform.
It is sad that large comprehensive schools, which militate
against individuality by their very size, destroy it still further by insisting on impersonalised school uniform. There
are, of course, good reasons for retaining the idea of recognisable dress, but it does reduce the possibilities of children
being able to demonstrate their individuality quietly. (Con-
tinental schools have managed for centuries without uniform.)

There was a lot of business to sort through: timetables to
discuss, bus passes to explain and distribute, a possible
camp to Wales to talk about, a cooking rota for dinner which
we drew up with everyone's agreement. This last was a
real achievement. The previous year the group had baulked
at cooking lunch, and had opted for the much simpler preparation of bread and cheese. Every lunch time they'd shared
exactly the same meal, with no variations in the kind of
cheese; it had to be Cheddar! On the one day we'd tried to
broaden horizons with a lump of Double Gloucester there was

open revolt. So this year we broached the cooking suggestion with some trepidation. Apart from the inevitable com-
plaints about who wouldn't eat this and who couldn't cook
anyway, we managed to draw up a skeleton rota. Everyone
would take it in turns.

This idea of cooking lunches was something we'd agreed
before the kids came. It would have been much easier to
concur with outside suggestions that we should accept 'meals
on wheels', but we felt strongly that preparation of lunch was
a valuable exercise in itself (responsibility being the key).
The arrangement was to have ingredients collected from the
nearest school every day, and we would make what we could
from these - possibly supplementing it from the local shop.

That first day it was Alec's attempt. With Alec and his
proverbial 'ants in his pants' it was easy to see one reason
why he'd never fitted into an ordinary school. Since he
couldn't sit still for more than a few minutes, it would have
been inconceivable to succeed in containing him easily in a
class of thirty others for a double period of working at
desks. He was a vibrating collection of tensed muscles.
His birthday had been three days after the statutory leaving
date and he resented having to stay on when he'd already
got a job lined up - and a motorbike to race around on. But
the judicial system saw fit to compel him to remain at
'school' - which meant us, since he'd given up ordinary
school a year before.

Alec had never cooked before, not even a boiled egg or a
piece of toast, but he was prepared to have a go - with
assistance. His interest was mixed with a certain amount
of trepidation, probably because of the critical audience.
But his curry and potatoes completely disappeared down
appreciative throats - and even merited the comment 'it was
all right I suppose'.

In fact the cooking worked well throughout the year: there
was never any real dissent, because the group could see that
if they didn't share the job then lunch wouldn't just happen,
and since almost all of them arrived straight from home with
no breakfast there was strong motivation. None the less
for some - perhaps all - the responsibility was a strain. 'I
didn't like knowing that if you mucked it up the others
wouldn't have anything to eat. You wanted other people to
like what you'd done and sometimes people like Joy would
call it a load of muck. That really annoyed me,' was
Match's comment, reflecting on his time with us one evening
after he'd started work.

We had decided to try and use lunchtimes for discussion.
The captive audience and the intense concentration over a
shared activity seemed the right sort of medium. Before
term started we'd drawn up a list of topics that we'd try to
'feed in' as well as the meal.
That first day it was unnecessary. Spontaneous discussion erupted about colour prejudice, initiated by Joy, herself a half-caste product of a mixed liaison. The line-up
was strictly girls vs boys, black vs white. A lot was said,
but in fact it wasn't really a discussion since no one was
really listening to what the others had to say. They all
wanted to be listened to. 'They ought to go back home'
probably reflected a deeply ingrained parental attitude which
nevertheless was now equally ingrained in the kids themselves. 'They take our jobs and houses - it's not right.
When everyone in this country has a job and a home, then
you can let 'em in - but not before.' Clive's Dad had been
unemployed for four years.
Pointing out that Joy had been born here made little impression. 'Shouldn't be allowed,' retorted Clive, with a
cynical smile. 'It's too cold for darkies here anyway.'
As a change of subject, we introduced our preprepared
idea of discussing smoking by reading a small newspaper extract. It was at least received in silence.
''Ang black lungs from every corner lamp post.' was
Debbie's suggestion as to how to stop smoking.
'Don't make no difference,' was Alec's retort. 'I've seen
all 'em films as well, and it don't stop me.'
In fact out of that group there was only one who didn't
smoke and there were a good number who smoked a packet a
day. Apart from the sheer addictive aspect of their smoking, it fulfilled the very important function of socialising
them into a group. The 'give and take' of sharing out cigarettes and the equability of distribution so that no one went
without was an interesting exercise in communal living. So
though smoking is physically destructive and a habit we dis-
courage by personal demonstration, it does have beneficial
spin-offs. The glib disclaimer that it's merely affectation
- an adolescent mimicry of adult behaviour - is quite erron-
eous. It may be that some of them started for those reasons;
but for those that join us, it is a very ingrained necessity
already - as we found to our cost on a four-day stay in Wales,
when shortage of money caused a cigarette crisis on the last
night and a consequent, and almost disastrous, rise in irri-
tability. Anyway many adults use cigarettes as a social prop

- how much is the proffering of cigarettes to others in a
group a plea for acceptance? Sadly the kids who come are
already addicted and it is rare for youngsters in our groups
not to smoke, though there have been encouraging signs recently of an increase in numbers of non-smokers - and we've
progressed to delineating no-smoking areas.

The honeymoon of that first meeting carried over into the
clearing up, and we walked to the market in two separate
groups - the boys eager to appear as an intimate group apart
from the girls, who were anyway miles behind on their platform heels. To encourage their sense of identity we'd
deliberately not bought crockery for the school, thinking it
better that we were all included in the choosing and purchas-
ing. So the suggestion was put that we go to the market
that afternoon and look at what was on offer. At the market
we chose our crockery - individual mugs for everyone - Jim
insisting on one with a car and Clive wanting one with a
pigeon.

At three o'clock we split up - they to their various corners
of Bristol - the two of us to the school for another coffee and
post mortem.

We were pleased, but aware that the 'harmony' was probably more a result of it being the first day than any particular feeling of group cohesiveness amongst the youngsters.
This six and the six who joined later would be with us till
May, except for the one or two who would leave at Easter,
and in the months between it would be our sole responsibility to provide the final phase of their statutory education.

What had happened to bring them to the point where they'd
rejected school and were prepared to risk going away from
home into residential care? Forcibly they'd voted with their
feet - but why?

And what was it that attracted them to these two abandoned
rooms in an old primary school miles from where they lived?

And what would we do in the next nine months that was
appropriate to their needs - given their vast range of abilities and interests?

And what were the implications for state education generally - if these twelve youngsters were representative of a
much larger group? In fact the number of referrals was
well in excess of the places available, and those actually referred were still only a small percentage of the 15-year-olds
in Bristol truanting from school on a fairly permanent basis.

There are 72,000 secondary school age pupils in the
county of Avon. If the figure for hard-core truancy is even

5 per cent (well below the figure resulting from a recent survey in Scotland, which found poor schools reporting a 10 per cent group of persistent truants) the number of truanting pupils is in the order of 3,600.

For us at that moment in early September, the immediate problem was to establish a direction for the individuals coming. The five times they'd met during the summer had been largely social occasions – where we'd gone out, or sat and talked, or played games in an attempt to break down some of the barriers.

We'd begun a little numeracy and literacy work, as much to give us an idea of their ability as to give them practice at maths and English. The four boys had gone to Wales for an overnight camp and come back friends – bearing out what we have always experienced about the camaraderie engendered by 'roughing it' away from home. For those five meetings we had deliberately not recruited the whole group. The intention had been to form a working nucleus into which we could introduce other youngsters.

We felt that if we had begun immediately with a larger group, we could very well have chosen ten youngsters with such separate interests that common activities would be difficult to establish. Whether this is actually so in practice remains uncertain, and since 15-year-old adolescents can be counted on to be interested in sex and clothes, food and drink, and having fun, our hesitancy may seem rather ridiculous. However, in a management sense, it is much easier to begin by only needing to relate to a small number and establish a rapport with them individually first. The problem is one of ethos. If a positive attitude can be established amongst a small group of youngsters, then their enthusiasm and willingness to participate will communicate to the rest without us needing to spell out everything to every new entrant.

It's really a question of group dynamics.

Our elation over that first meeting was soon rudely shattered: the second day, Debbie and Joy failed to turn up. Subsequent home visiting elicited the fact that one was 'ill' and the other had stayed away in sympathy. This pattern of one being away when the other was off for some reason continued for months, and their explanations ranged from the ridiculous like being run over by a car, to the mundane like oversleeping. What was consistent was their surprise and annoyance if their explanations were not immediately accepted.

Equally consistent, though, was our persistence in not ignoring lateness or days off. We'd tackle them the next day prepared for the inevitable argument and outburst of temper. Where had they been? Why hadn't they rung in? Did they really want to come to us?

The last was a crucial point. Though at their initial interviews we had presented coming to the school as a mutual choice, the reality was often that their choice was limited between us or residential care – which is hardly choice! But we used it in maintaining our expectations that they would attend every day – having chosen to come. For youngsters who had been truanting from ordinary school for many years, this pressure to attend regularly must have been hard to cope with initially. But we were determined and, after all, as we pointed out occasionally, there were plenty of others who would jump at the chance to join the group. Interestingly, though, the group as a whole were united in a belief that anyone who didn't regularly come should be 'chucked out', and at our first meeting we'd agreed with them that anyone who couldn't make it in for any reason would always phone up. To this end it is important to have the parents as allies. Without doubt one of the reasons for their poor previous school attendance is that the parents themselves weren't that supportive. Many sociological papers have analysed this problem – and of course, very simply, for parents whose own experience of school was bad, it is likely that this attitude will communicate to their children. Schools find that parents' evenings only draw in a percentage of parents – often less than half the possible – and usually and characteristically the 'middle-class' parents. It isn't surprising. A formally typed, duplicated message, relying on pupil delivery is unlikely to reach all parents – either in body or spirit.

But it is possible to draw parents in to schools, and given their crucial effect on attendance it is something schools can't afford to ignore. At our school we always see the parents before admitting a pupil and we always stress that their support is essential and we always let them know what is happening and make a point of visiting frequently – not in a 'well intentioned, do-gooding sense', but because it is important they are in contact, and it pays dividends later.

The 'TES' described a successful experiment in parental involvement in one comprehensive school, where the standard accepted pattern for a parents' evening just meant a whole year group's team of teachers being 'available' for

discussion with parents who came along and took pot-luck on
their being available and not over-booked.   The normal
attendance was about 35 per cent and predictably the cross-
section of parents who came were those whose own educational attainment corresponded mostly with the professed
exam-oriented syllabus of their children's school.   However, one form teacher took the trouble to write to all the
parents of the children in his class – thirty-two in all.
Though for most the <u>letter</u> was duplicated, the envelopes and
the heading to the letters were all hand-written and the
letter itself was both personally written and informative.   It
gave a choice of evenings and asked parents to state their
time preference – allowing fifteen minutes for each parent.
To five parents – those least likely to come – the letter was
hand-written completely.   The replies came back via the
youngsters (with whom the whole idea had been discussed already) and a timetable was arranged so that all parents knew
what time the teacher could see them.   Coffee and biscuits
were offered as they arrived, with some of the youngsters in
the group doing the serving.   Twenty-nine parents came and
the remaining three sent apologies.   The evening took four
hours each of the two nights – inevitably an additional unpaid
commitment for the teacher concerned – but all the parents
did at least visit the school and knew something of what was
going on, which must have helped the pupil attendance.
    One of the key factors in this was the involvement of the
pupils in the discussions about the evening.   The original
idea was the teacher's but it was not presented to the pupils
as an imposition, where their only involvement was as cheap
bearers of the notifying letters.   The purpose of the evening was explained to them first;   they were asked what they
thought, their positive support was encouraged.   There was
never any suggestion that the occasion was something that
didn't really concern them – being only the children under
debate by higher mortals.   Without being soppily sentimental
it makes sense to involve kids in their own education.
    We ended that first week by drawing up a skeleton time-
table for the weeks ahead.
    'Don't make it like school with everything decided and
changing over every hour.'
    'Can't we have project sessions – whole mornings or
afternoons.'
    'I'd like to learn typing.'
    'I'd like to do some climbing or caving.'
    'Could we do anything like helping other people, you know,
community work – like with little kids?'

Our expressed expectation was that some time should be set aside for reading and writing and maths. They concurred quite willingly and we agreed on two mornings a week – Tuesday and Wednesday. Monday would be a 'group' day with us all doing something together, perhaps going out on a visit, perhaps just staying in talking. With Thursday given over to 'art' work and Tuesday and Wednesday afternoons set aside for 'individual projects', there was at least some sort of structure to work to initially. Fridays were loosely defined as a day to 'get to know Bristol'.

By lunchtime on Monday they were all at 'school', joined by a new girl Liz – predictably quiet and withdrawn amongst a group of people who clearly knew each other and us very well. Everyone drew up their individual timetables for the week – eagerly writing in English and maths and very bothered by empty spaces where it hadn't been decided what they – or we – were doing.

This desire for 'structure' from kids who had rejected the constricting structure of schools is an ingrained feeling; though it both surprised and amused us then, we have recognised it as a recurring pattern in their expectations of what will be provided. Perhaps the simple explanation that domestic insecurity required a reciprocal security at school is accurate. Certainly, we find ourselves urged into constructing a framework for them, within which they can operate freely.

It is as true for the students who came to us at 21 on the verge of their teaching career as it is for the kids. The students, with all their savoir-faire and social skills, flounder equally in the sea of uncertainty prescribed by 'doing your own thing'.

After lunch we drove to the nearby Dogs' Home – our first 'group' outing made memorable by their unified clamour, which drowned that of the canine captives, to adopt a school dog which 'Hil could 'ave during the holidays'.

Already obvious personality traits were appearing naturally, encouraged by the uninhibiting atmosphere of the small group. Alec's bouts of near hysteria fluctuated with periods of intense concentration; Clive, already adopting the mantle of leader of the group, appeared very level and perceptive.

We were agreed to try and establish some degree of routine that week – hence English and maths periods on the timetable were adhered to firmly. Interestingly, though this was the one part of the timetable that corresponded most

closely with ordinary school, it was something they nearly
always settled to readily.

Of the two subjects, they responded to maths more easily,
probably because of its more obvious structure, with immediate sense of reward and achievement. Tea, brought in
once they'd settled down, became the pattern. Aided by
cigarettes and liquid refreshment the atmosphere resembled
a building-site lunch break with everyone studiously studying form.

Each of them had an individual approach to the subject and
we encouraged them to work in whatever way they chose
(grateful for their acquiescence in actually doing it!) Liz
and Joy were particularly interested in exam work – which
meant studying CSE syllabus and questions and answers.
In Joy's case this was a perfect opportunity to get individual
attention. Any problem that she found difficult was immediately brought to our attention, and it always took three or
four explanations and reiterations before she acknowledged
an understanding. Perhaps it was our lack of expertise in
tutoring the subject, but the smile that flickered at the
corner of Joy's lips suggested that there was more to her
misunderstanding than simply ignorance. Whatever the
truth, she was rewarded enough by her efforts to persevere
throughout the year and consider a college course at the end
of it all. Debbie valiantly tried to copy Joy's approach but,
lacking her aptitude, was soon floundering in a sea of meaningless concepts. Clive wanted straight addition and sub-
traction exercises from books – something he knew he could
cope with. By the end of the first term we'd weaned him
onto multiplication, but he never broached the problem of
division! Martin, Jim and Alec (whose ability in this direction was almost rock bottom) began by using our tutor packs
– a sort of programmed learning with staged indications of
success built in. Rather than use the apparatus available,
Jim would always write the answers in his notebook. In all
cases – except Joy – they very soon wanted to know how
many exercises they needed to do before they'd start. It
worked best by arranging individual contracts, estimated on
what we knew of their abilities. The minimum agreed
period was always an hour – by which time we were all
ready for more tea!

After lunch those two days the plan was to develop individual 'projects'. Once the university term started we could
rely on PGCE students (see Chapter 10 on student involvement), but till that time we would have to divide ourselves as

best we could between individuals. Fortunately Howard
from New Careers joined us at this point.

New Careers is a Home Office funded project aimed at
'rehabilitation' of offenders through placement in social and
community work situations. For several years we had used
people from there as a staffing resource, in addition to the
regular placement of students from the university and polytechnic. In the case of students from New Careers we had
anticipated the likelihood of their being able to establish a
good rapport with the youngsters we'd accepted – since
they'd often shared similar experiences. It seemed more
probable that, with regard to delinquent behaviour and an
appreciation of the consequences, our group would be influenced more by the real presence of New Careerists than by
any moralising or counselling from us, however sensible or
appropriate – particularly with reference to TDA. Taking
and Driving Away is a rampant disease amongst the boys
(and some girls), partly because of the element of danger and
risk which is denied them by their passive role as adolescents. (1) It afflicted Clive most seriously, as will be seen
later in Chapter 7.

With all students including New Careerists, we hoped
their presence would widen the degree of choice available to
the youngsters over their 'individual project'. The problem
with choice, though, is that it's often unfair – because
whereas choice between this and that is fairly easy, choice
to do 'what you're interested in' is much more threatening.
In retrospect it was unrealistic to leave the choice wide
open, and we have amended our choice quite dramatically
since. But our intention then was to use as a starting
point their interest in something. For Jim and Alec this
was easy – car mechanics; for Martin it was fishing; for
Clive it became the building of a disco unit. The girls were
more of a problem to get going – partly because in Debbie
and Joy's case attendance was so sporadic initially that it
was difficult to maintain impetus with ongoing projects.
Typing and making clothes elicited some interest and enthusiasm. Mostly though they just wanted to talk. Debbie (with
a black boyfriend) and Joy (with her West Indian Dad) would
chat for hours about their respective problems. From their
conversation and the seeming intensity of their out-of-school
social activities, it surprised us that they ever came! Both
would often be up until the small hours of the morning –
which explained their recurrent lateness most days. There
was a certain sort of oneupmanship they fell into the habit of

using, which involved discussing their sexual exploits and
consequences by innuendo and hint, usually in undertones
loud enough to distract the rest of the group. Though both
had fairly 'stable' relationships, they found it difficult to
relate to the boys in the group except in an aggressive way
- which in Joy's case resulted in deliberately bigoted retorts
about 'niggers', mostly from Clive. A certain mature arro-
gance emanated from the two of them, which set them apart
from the rest of the group and was something they probably
wanted anyway!

Thursday was set aside for 'art work'. Initially emphasis was on fairly instant craft work - like enamelling or
leather making. These kinds of activities always went down
well and produced personally satisfying results. Rings and
wrist bands were often in evidence for some time afterwards.

To youngsters who have 'failed' at subjects dominated by a
prerequisite for fluency in the written word, such creative
activities can offer a taste of success. This is important.
Those of us who may have experienced frequent success find
it hard to imagine a state of mind where people would prefer
to do nothing rather than have a go at something new that
they know won't work.

Friday was the end of our first full week and we'd set time
aside for planning the Wales trip.

Lester, a new boy, joined us that day. Small and wiry,
his friendly attitude and easy-going manner soon attracted
him to others in the group. Alec surprised us all by greeting him as a long-lost friend, and it transpired that they'd
met already through the city supporters club and shared the
Tote-end camaraderie on many occasions. Though Lester
said little that morning, he was clearly wanting to be involved.

The underlying aim of the Wales trip planned for the next
week, especially to include Lester, was a hope of bringing
them together as a cohesive group. If we succeeded in
taking them away, we felt sure that the mere fact of sharing
a complete living situation for several days would bind us
more closely together. The 'residential' effect of these
camps is their supreme value. In such a situation, responsibility - taking note of other people's existence and wishes
and reacting appropriately - becomes a meaningful necessity. Experience with other groups suggests this to be true
as long as the expedition isn't planned so early that the initial ice still hasn't thawed before going away. It's a difficult balance.

As a round-off to the week and to set a pattern for the
Friday idea of visiting different areas of Bristol, we took
off to Liz's 'stomping ground' in the minibus and accepted
her invitation for coffee.   There was something slightly in-
congruous about nine of us squashed into her parents' sitting
room, waiting for the kettle to boil and not quite knowing how
to react in such comparatively palatial surroundings!   Fortunately the sun came out in time for us all to decamp to the
grass outside and share out the sandwiches we'd brought,
before returning to drop everyone off at the city centre and
give the two of us an afternoon alone to review the week.

Looking back through the diary entries for that first few
days it was interesting to see how often food was mentioned
– usually favourably.   Perhaps this had more to do with the
fact that the diary was nearly always written at lunchtime
with the food itself very much in evidence!

Our intention to use the overnight visit to Wales as a focus
for group cohesion was sadly torpedoed at the last minute.
Debbie and Joy both opted out – despite a signed promise
from the former the day before, stating she definitely would
go! – which left Liz as the only girl.   Of the boys Alec –
anxious about something he wouldn't elaborate on – had cate-
gorically and excitedly refused to come.   On the day itself
Jim, who'd spent the morning making a model and intending
to come, changed his mind – mumbling something about his
father needing him at home.   It is too easy when arranging
these camps to forget that for youngsters who've got problems at home (where parental security is certainly not guaranteed, and where return from a few days away may find an
empty house or an embittered home), staying away can be a
terrifying experience.

With a 'group' of four we left at lunchtime before anyone
else could change their minds.   Match and Clive had been
before, so knew what to expect.   Liz and Lester came willingly.   For a night and a day they turned the old cold farmhouse in Wales into a friendly home.   They had fun fishing
in the river, throwing stones into the sea, baking spuds
over a log fire, talking till past midnight, helping at the
milking and blackberrying....   It was only thirty-six
hours, though, and they all wanted to come again for longer
before Christmas.   We hoped their enthusiasm would seed
itself into the others.

The value of such 'camps' both in themselves and in the
opportunities for self-development that they offer is discussed at length in 'In and Out of School'. (2)   Almost without

exception, such time away from home is worth all the headache and problems of arranging them.

Between returning from camp and half term, which was
five weeks away, we stuck very much to the timetable we'd
planned that first week. The slots for English and maths
were rigidly adhered to and the afternoon sessions broadened
greatly in scope once the students from the polytechnic and
university had arrived (see Chapter 10).

The importance of routine should not be lightly disregarded
in favour of an 'open unstructured situation'. Most young
people, particularly these who are referred to us, need to
feel secure before they can begin to experiment, to take
risks or to try anything new. A 'free' situation with no
structure to the weekly programme, where everything is
decided according to the mood of the moment, may be fine for
upper-class children who have the guarantee of financial
security and an elitist future ahead of them, but for youngsters who lack security at home and for whom even the immediate future presents a mire of uncertain complications, such
'freedom' is a disservice. They do not in fact want, or know
how to use, freedom in the radical tradition.

The mistake that teachers make is to confuse structure
with imposed discipline. It is quite possible to incorporate
a structured timetable into a framework of corporate self-
determinism with a minimal authoritative imposition of regulations from above.

Two more youngsters joined the group before half-term.
First was Dirk, whose surly exterior concealed a warm and
generous nature which revealed itself at vulnerable moments.
Mostly though he hid his feelings behind a gruff abruptness.
The second, Maggie, appeared at first meeting a very quiet
and interested girl who seemed to present possibilities as a
good match for Liz. This was important given the continued
erratic behaviour of Joy and Debbie. By the time these two
newcomers arrived we had a fairly solid group to refer to –
and though we'd initially interviewed them ourselves, we suggested that the group have the final say. They voted over-
whelmingly in favour of both of them coming.

On the last day before half term we spent the time talking
with them and reviewing the previous seven weeks. From
their diary entries and our own journals it was possible to
see what had been achieved – mostly a lot of little gains. In
terms of personal projects, one or two had done a great deal.
Clive, for instance, had begun to build a disco unit (a wooden
frame for two turntables and a control deck) with help from

Howard and anyone else who could offer more than just advice. His persistence was remarkable, though inevitably there were days when he didn't want anything to do with it and threatened to destroy the whole thing. We weathered those tantrums and it grew in size and shape. In fact by Christmas he'd finished it and we delivered it to his house. Proudly he carried it into the front room and was obviously pleased at Mum and Dad's reaction. Building this unit gave Clive an obvious status which he very much needed. He wanted to be seen as the leader of the group - and his diary entries were liberally sprinkled with signatures of 'Clive - the Fonz' and crucifixes emblazened with his initials. But the group never really wanted a leader, since it was too much a collection of individuals. At points of crisis when it did need directing it was usually Jim, in fact, who stepped in. For instance, it was noticeable that when I was absent for almost a week, Jim took up the reins and assisted Hilary with the organising. At one point, on the maths morning, when everyone else threatened open revolt and persisted in lounging in their easy chairs drinking tea, he calmly disappeared into the work room and reappeared after a quarter of an hour's absence to say how easy it was, which broke the barriers very effectively!

Of course in any group there are bound to be individuals from whom the others take a lead, however unconsciously. In situations where such leadership is apparent it is quite crucial in any teacher/learner situation to have the support of the perceived leader. As Hargreaves testifies so lucidly in his book 'Social Relations in a Secondary School, (3) the problem facing a teacher working with bottom-stream classes is that his values and those of the individuals in the group with most peer-group esteem are almost diametrically opposed. He has no chance of achieving much progress since there will be an overwhelming rejection of his values in favour of the acknowledged leader.

In our situation, we can only proceed if our values and our ideas are explained to the group clearly, so that the leaders at least accept our direction. It means a continual exposure to a process of analysing content for relevance and applicability.

Jim's own project, which he'd worked on mostly with Alec, had been to try and renovate the old car in the playground A mechanic friend had offered to help them with the dismantling and stripping down of the engine. This arrangement had worked well to begin with but both boys became increas-

ingly impatient at their having to watch rather than do, and
enthusiasm waned – though sporadically Jim would tackle
something on his own, like changing tyres or replacing a
window. His inventiveness at such jobs was amazing, and
was a good indication of the perceptual ability that lay hidden
behind his deficiency in literacy skills.

Both boys whenever they did work on the car proudly
donned overalls which they would wear for the rest of the
day. However this symbol of real work was no guide to
their willingness actually to consider what job they might
eventually do. Bitter experience the previous year, when
we'd started talking about job prospects early in the year,
immediately producing all sorts of adverse reaction, warned
us off from discussing the subject. In fact the only time it
rose was spontaneously from visits by past group members
and even then the reactions were disturbing enough! This
attitude to jobs is not just symptomatic of anxiety over going
to work – though inevitably that must play a big part. For
these youngsters, away from the props of institutional life,
the thought of knuckling down to a mundane routine was probably quite frightening, and for many of them who doubted
their own ability to even get a job (though no one ever admitted it openly) this was a double hurdle to cross. This made
us resolved to introduce work experience for all of them if
we could in the term before they left – in the hope that practice at work, whilst still being supported by us, might help
in the transition. (4)

Their antipathy to discussing job prospects was no measure of their hesitation to enter the world of work. To a man
and a woman they wanted to leave and start work as soon as
possible. Again, referring to Hargreaves's study, (5) it
is quite clear why. They think that the work situation will
give them the status denied them by schools. They will
become adults – and smoking fags, and drinking and swearing are all preparatory props for this adult role. So in
their eyes, 'work', whatever it is, will rectify their low-
status position. Understandably they are anxious to leave
school and, equally understandably, they are anxious not to
have their fantasies about the actual job exposed to the light
of a reality which may require a reappraisal of status.

So they want jobs but don't want to discuss how they'll get
them.

The importance of work experience is that it is just practice work – and is a situation where they can fail without it
being a complete disaster; so that they will put themselves

at risk, with the possible gain of real practical experience
and developed confidence.

Debbie, in fact, was the only one with any kind of part-
time job at the beginning of the year and she'd already appreciated the economic benefit and social-life gain of paid employment. For the rest it was virgin territory.

However some of them did make positive efforts to find
part-time jobs. Lester, interested in stable work, was
lucky enough to be given an address to which he wrote off
asking about possible vacancies. Alec, who'd professed an
interest in building-site work, finally got round to writing a
letter to Wimpeys - which he did at home and proudly produced the next day. The envelope took an hour to write with
a great deal of grumbling! Liz was the only one with immediate success - a part-time typing job for a mail-order firm.
She was greatly exploited - typing addresses for envelopes -
and didn't stay long, but at least it was a start and, more
importantly for the rest of the group, it encouraged them to
feel that job-getting was possible.

In terms of writing practice, part-time job applications
were a useful carrot. For some of them anything that encouraged the putting of pen to paper was a valuable exercise.
Only Liz, Joy and Clive had any real command of the written
word, and in the case of Alec and Jim their written vocabulary was almost non-existent, which is one reason why we
persevered with the diary. Interestingly, Alec's entries,
though laboriously written with a great deal of assistance,
were usually the longest. In fact Alec was the one most
prepared to practice his reading - aloud to one of us - which
none of the rest ever did. His jumpiness, though, was often
too much to contain, and his concentration quickly evaporated
if success didn't come easily.

In behavioural and attitudinal terms what had happened?
And what was the group interaction after two months together? At base level, attendance compared to previous
school attendance was amazing (see Appendix 5). Apart
from Joy, Debbie and Lester we could count on regular attendance from all the rest - and in Clive's case he'd only missed
one day. The pattern of ringing in if late was constantly referred to - a kind of social training exercise - but only Joy,
Liz and Martin ever did this. Jim, Alec and Lester could
just be absent without trace and, usually, without parental
knowledge!

In terms of sharing and group cohesion there were positive gains. Liz, particularly, was generous and helpful and

had gone so far (as mentioned already) to invite the whole
group to her house one morning for coffee. But though it
was possible to initiate discussions with the whole group,
it required considerable effort on our part and, since
Debbie and Joy were the most articulate, they tended to
dominate any discussion. Generally the nine of them didn't
want to behave as a group, and though there were indications
of a sharing approach in cooking lunches or decorating the
rooms (which started on their initiative one afternoon in the
fourth week), most of the interaction was at small group or
individual level. In this respect Match (né Martin) was
the most noticeable 'loner', having been rejected by Clive,
who'd turned in preference to first Jim or Alec, and subsequently Lester.

Martin was often unsure of his place within the group and
very conscious of his looking younger in appearance than the
other boys. Any indication that we might think so too was
revealed with hostility, like the day I ruffled his hair in
jest at a shared joke, when he bristled with 'Fuck Off' and
left the room. Being noticeably less mature in physical
appearance, he tried to make up for it by developing 'adult'
habits, like smoking and swearing, and indeed was often
more at ease with the students than with his peers in the
group. Encouraged by Clive's successful start on the disco
unit, Martin began to work on two small speakers for himself. This project, intermingled with regular fishing trips,
accompanied by a student, at least gave him a sense of
achievement.

Swearing was one behavioural trait that developed marked-
ly for the worst that term. On the whole we ignored it,
though occasionally would point out how often they used
abusive language. From experience with other groups,
though, it seems there is natural development towards a peak
use of abusive language – and once that point is reached it
is possible to do something about it. They at least did know
when they were swearing, because in the presence of visitors it generally became insignificant, which indicated to us
that for them it was a conscious play with language: perhaps,
as with Martin, to demonstrate their maturity. Again, like
the smoking, it could have had something to do with status:
swearing is something that adults do. Alternatively, ling-
uists might suggest that paucity of vocabulary choice was the
explanation, like the soldier on leave from abroad who came
back 'after three fucking years in fucking Africa and what do
I fucking well find? – my fucking wife in fucking bed, engaged

in illicit cohabitation with a fucking nig-nog!' It's a universal adjective to describe anything but the act itself. The
bold ones even wrote it in the diary. If it got it out of their
system it seemed worth the earache. Certainly it shocked
the students! Swearing apart, their reaction to strangers
was interesting.

This introduction of 'visitors' was something we regarded
as very important, though we always approached it with
trepidation because of 'unfortunate' experiences the previous
year. Then, a new face had generally had a disturbing
effect on the group and their 'acting out' often degenerated to
an infantile level, with the visitor completely ignored or at
best an accepted spectator.

One mistake we had made in the previous year was not always to enlist the kids' concurrence beforehand. We should
have secured their agreement to the visit before making
arrangements. The problem here is that, like good medi-
cine, some of the visitors may appear very undesirable - yet
may actually be quite beneficial for the kids to meet. To
obtain their assent in some cases is very difficult and their
unwillingness to welcome new faces is understandable. For
youngsters who have found security at a school for perhaps
the first time in ten years, and who feel safe amongst the
recognisable faces of those others in the group, it is not
easy to widen the circle and admit the unknown. Like hermit
crabs they need to take that risk if they are to grow and
develop.

So we approached introducing visitors very carefully -
usually mentioning the possibility of this over lunchtimes
when an even-tempered response was more predictable. We
had a number of ideas for visitors up our sleeves. Some,
like the woman from the Brook Clinic to talk about contracep-
tion, were a guaranteed hit - though often at the time unsettled the group, particularly the boys. Some, like the
police, were a guaranteed problem - producing instant and
unanimous rejection of the idea, most vociferously from those
with a 'record'.

'No bloody pigs coming here while I'm around,' is a fair
representation of a general feeling. It is mainly because of
that antipathy that we persevered with such a visit and made
arrangements for the Chief Inspector concerned with public
relations to join the group one morning before lunch. En-
listing their support was a difficult game.

'If he comes, I won't be here.'

'Why not?'

'I hates 'em.'

'Well perhaps you ought to tell him that.'

'What?'

'Look, the only way he can know your side of it is if you tell him.'

'You mean tell him the police are pigs - to his face?'

'Or tell him how you think police handle things badly - where they're in the wrong.'

'Yeah - my mate got picked up and taken in last night - and all he was doing was walking home minding his own business.'

'Well there you are - tell him about that.'

'All right, I will.'

And so, doggedly, we obtained their concurrence. In our terms such a visit was quite a catch. Usually he addressed school groups of hundreds - mostly clustered in rows in the spacious impersonality of a school hall.

'How large is your group?' he asked.

'About ten.'

'Ten! That's rather a small number.'

He explained about the hundreds and we pointed out that instead of addressing a hundred youngsters, many of whom wouldn't listen, he'd at least be talking to the ten in that hundred who really needed it!

He accepted the argument.

For the visit itself eight were present and what had threatened to become either a slanging match or a complete flop because of total non-attendance became instead a very useful dialogue.

The Inspector was well aware of their animosity and he played the meeting very skilfully (after all his job was Public Relations!) But in audience terms this was certainly one of his most testing.

He played down his 'authority'; he talked about football, about motorbikes, about discos - about anything they'd talk with him about - and after a time he swung the conversation round to discussing the police and the group's own attitude and hostilities. And the kids responded; they recounted umpteen tales of unfair treatment; he listened with an air of acceptance and even admitted that some police were pigs (but then so were some adolescents, and so were some teachers and so were some employers!) Yet he followed through to the point where there were some grudging admissions that sometimes kids did ask for it and it wasn't always the police in the wrong. At least he presented a human face

to the police force and for our kids that was worth every
penny of his salary for that morning's work.

The attitude of these youngsters to police is very interesting and should at least serve as a warning message to
those responsible for administering such police authority.
They are always anti-police - particularly the West Indian
youngsters - and often aggressively so. No doubt this attitude is in part inculcated from parents and forms an unwit-
ting heritage, but in most cases antipathy has a component
of personal experience. Relationships between West Indian
youth and police are certainly bad and, to a lesser extent,
working-class/police relationships are poor. The fault
may not necessarily be with the police. Indeed in many
cases the provocation stems from the youngsters themselves,
but what is dishonest of the police is an attitude that relationships aren't really that bad, and anyway if they are it
doesn't matter.

It does matter and they are bad and someone, somewhere,
somehow should be doing something to improve it.

In this instance the point of the Inspector's visit was
clear. By bringing the two sides together at least they and
he could listen to another point of view. If he took away a
perception of the youngsters as something less hairy and unmanageable than his preconceptions, that was a beginning.
If they came away feeling that at least one copper wasn't an
out and out pig, it's a beginning.

'He's alright isn't he?' was a comment that summed up
their approval - culminating in a joint letter of thanks that
they all signed.

Apart from information-giving, visitors offer an opportunity for the youngsters to talk with another adult apart from
us. This is important for adolescents who lack reliable
adult models with whom to identify. In a home where Mum
or Dad are absent or at best an intermittent presence, the
search for identification during adolescence is bound to be
confusing. The more adults they can meet in our situation
the better. The question of identification and its implications for the staff's behaviour and responses is dealt with in
more detail in Chapter 8. (6)

One source of visitors arises inevitably from the unique-
ness of the unit; those people (educationalists, administrators, teachers and the curious) who have heard of the work
and are interested in seeing for themselves what happens.
Believing as we do in the importance of 'spreading the
gospel', we regard such visits as important, but there is a

real danger of allowing them to be too frequent and of a zoo-
like nature, where the visitors watch the kids as if from the
other side of a cage.

With such visitors we stress the importance of them giving
something when they arrive; like coming prepared with an
activity or an interest that gives a reason for their presence
– apart from that of mere curiosity. Nowadays we always
discuss it with the group first and point out to them the
responsibility of explaining to such visitors their thoughts
and perceptions of education and schooling. It usually
works well, though some visitors are intimidated by the
adult assertiveness of the youngsters and withdraw into
silent and embarrassed observation!

This exercise of involving the youngsters in decision-
making was something we persevered with throughout that
first half term. It must be hard for them to be required to
take that kind of responsibility, when their experience of
decision-making has usually been that of a receiver to other
people's dictates. Success was limited, because though
they would manage to reach group decisions, the expectation
was nearly always that we would implement the decision.
For instance, they may all agree that giving a party on
someone's birthday was a good idea, but they would be very
loath to follow words with action. However there were instances where they acted as a group, and not always con-
structively.

One example was the television. In our pre-term planning we had reviewed the whole series of HTV and BBC programmes for schools and decided that three of them might
well be worth watching with the group, recognising that
since the telly would have to be housed in a room above our
office in a building a hundred yards away for safe-keeping,
it would need to be seen as an attractive proposition to draw
the group away from morning tea and the warmth of the gas
fire. We opted for a large colour set, knowing full well
that anything else would be seen as very second-rate by
comparison with their own home situations (out of ten in the
group, seven had colour television at home, and two of them
had their own set in their bedrooms! Little wonder that one
mum complained she could never get her son up in the morning 'cos he watches telly till it finishes at night'). The
first programme was watched by the whole group but the intended discussion we hoped it would spark off fizzled out
after a few minutes. They were much more interested in
the reality and the fantasy of their own situations.

Next week the six who arrived in time grudgingly walked
the hundred yards up the hill to the room above the office
and sat in resentful silence.

The third week the same happened. The fourth week two
of them refused to go.

'I'll do me maths instead,' offered Joy, who in all honesty
probably had no intention of doing anything, but understood
the psychological force of such a statement.

'Don't you like the programmes?'

'Load of rubbish. Stupid bitches.' This referred to the
incident the previous week, involving a fracas between
mother and daughter about who should look after daughter's
illegitimate baby.

'But don't you think they're useful in getting you to look
at situations and problems you might come across?'

'I wouldn't be that daft – fancy getting yourself in the
club.'

(The irony of the last statement is that Joy was pregnant
within three months of leaving us and had to abandon the
college course she'd struggled so hard to get into with our
help.)

'Look – if you really all think it's a waste of time we'll
stop – but Hil and I reckon they're worth watching.'

The vote they called was unanimously negative. We sent
back the telly – determined to try again next year!

We were tempted to insist that they should spend the time
instead doing extra English or maths. But we didn't. It's
important to present these subjects as something less than a
burden. It is sad that English and maths are often used in
schools as punishment tools. Writing lines or essays or
doing problems in detention for misbehaviour can only reinforce a dislike for subjects so linked with punishment.

A more positive example of group responsibility (in our
terms) happened the day before half term. We were discussing the possibilities of another trip to Wales before Christmas with all the boys – except Martin who had left to go fishing with a student.

They were adamant they'd all be able to find the £4 it
would cost, but I mentioned that Martin would probably have
difficulty because his Dad was out of work.

'Can't we all chip in 50p?' suggested Jim. 'But don't
make a big thing of it – don't show him up – I wouldn't go if
you did that.'

The other four agreed – and in fact did just that when it
came to it five weeks later. Martin never knew.

The last day of that half term when we reviewed the previous seven weeks with them, the main issue under discussion was their reliability, which had been a cause of several
arguments earlier that week.

Communally they agreed that in future any commitment from
them would be held to be binding.   If they arranged to do
something we could hold them to it.   The test of their intent
came within half an hour.

We had arranged for four of them, Liz, Clive, Martin and
Jim to go to the zoo, having been offered complementary
tickets by an ex-pupil who now worked there as a zoo
keeper.

'I don't want to go,' said Liz.

'You're bloody well going,' replied Lester.   'If you said
you'd do it you fucking well do it, you divvy git.'   He
laughed.   'But I'll go instead if you don't want to go.'

Liz smiled back.

Over lunch, Alec suggested we have sandwiches next
term - 'Bring our own.'   Fortunately for our scheme of
things he received no support.

'All right, I'll bring in sausages and chips on me own.'

'For 15p,' scoffs Clive.   'You won't even get a bloody
potato.'   (This was at the time of the 1976 potato shortage.)

'And don't bloody well ask me for any grub when we're
'aving our lunch,' adds Lester.

The zoo visit was an interesting reflection of their
attachment to each other.   At the entrance gate, once we'd
shown our tickets, I suggested they met me back there an
hour later, thinking they'd probably prefer to go round on
their own.

'S'all right,' said Lester.   'You can stay with us - you
don't show us up that badly.'

This issue of being 'shown up' is in fact quite important
and indicates the underlying urge for conformity amongst the
youngsters - perhaps particularly important since they'd
been labelled as oddities by schools and society.   None of
them liked going out with us if we were dressed at all oddly
in their terms.   This was particularly noticeable if our
clothes suggested any ambivalence about femininity or masculinity.   Hilary with her Wellington boots or myself with
shoulder bag was a guaranteed deterrent to their venturing
outside the school accompanied by one of us.   No doubt it
throws into doubt their own apparent identity, and should
friends or neighbours or parents or acquaintances notice
them...?

Fortunately I was dressed as usual in well-faded denims.

We wandered round together, almost the only people in the whole zoo apart from the keepers. Their very real fascination and enthusiasm showed through so strongly, despite initial attempts by Jim at a sang-froid that was meant to indicate the millions of times he'd seen it all before.

Bristol Zoo, as zoos go, is a beautiful zoo, and on a sunny day, empty of people, it has a strange magic of its own. That afternoon we all imbibed it, and the Mars bars and coffee in the cafe were a suitable culmination of a satisfying visit.

'See you next Monday,' shouted Lester when I dropped them back at the Centre, and then, remembering it was half term added, 'if you can't bear to be on holiday either!'

As a general statement: for youngsters who had been written off as non-school attenders there was much that seemed positive; but the fluctuations in mood and co-operation in most of them were still wild and often unpredictable. We'd have been kidding ourselves to think we were having much influence in many cases. The reality of home situations for some was too overwhelming to let them unwind enough at school to be open to influence. For Debbie, who was sharing her Mum's traumas about which of her several boyfriends she should marry, and who worked every morning with older women (for whom the job that Debbie regarded as part-time was their full-time job), what we were offering was, bluntly, fairly trivial. All we could do was be there and welcoming whenever she chose to turn up – and hope that the security of the group atmosphere might draw her in too. Yet although there were instances when she demonstrated a real caring for others in the group, like 'Can't we do something for Martin – he's only moody 'cos things aren't working out at home', her involvement never became a commitment and Debbie proved to be that year's drop-out, with personally unfortunate consequences. The other three girls had difficulties of their own at home to contend with – Maggie and Liz with parents threatening to split up, and Joy with a father in Southampton 'in trouble with the law' and a mother who'd 'adopted' their lodger.

With the boys it was a similar sort of story. Parents either split up, or Dad on the dole – and in most cases little real support given to their continued attendance with us.

It would be wrong to lay the blame for their abandonment of normal educational institutions completely at the parental door, but without doubt their background left them poorly

equipped in terms of the personal resources necessary to
cope with performance demands and behavioural expectations
of the ordinary school that sends these children on to the
road to rejection. If Leach and Raybould (7) are listened
to it is crucial to apply compensatory features at an early
age to minimise the frustrations caused by personal inadequacies. Certainly by the time they reach 15 their low tolerance limit is well ingrained. And yet they can joke about
their situation. Two days before half term I dropped Jim
outside the cinema near his house.
   'Do you ever go in there?' I asked.
   'What me? Don't be daft - bloody Pakki place ain't it?
I've got enough trouble understanding you, let alone them!'
He smiled and waved goodbye and walked towards his home -
a three-room flat at the top of a decaying Georgian house,
where a leaky roof served as a shelter for his Mum, Dad and
a fluctuating number of brothers and sisters, depending on
who was 'doing time', or out of work, or separated from
their spouses.
   Jim was lucky compared to some of the others in that his
Mum and Dad were actually interested in what he did when
he came to us - but to compare his stableblock to the apart-
ments of his middle-class peers in Clifton is to begin to
understand why school had much less chance of working for
Jim, and what we were up against.

Chapter 4

School phobias:
the myth of labelling

What had happened to bring these kids to the point of rejecting school so forcibly?   Many youngsters register a dislike
of school but few are prepared to risk the wrath of officialdom.

The road along it is no easy path.   'Dropping out' of
school is not the idealistic gesture suggested by the college
students who've coined the phrase.   It means visits from
the Educational Welfare Officer – still the 'Board Man' to
many families.   It means a succession of visits, initially
helpful and encouraging, but becoming progressively sterner
and more forceful as nothing seems to change, and culminating in a report to the Chief Education Officer bringing the
case to his notice.   The parents are notified officially that
action will be taken to enforce attendance, with perhaps a
summons to the Education Office to 'discuss the matter'.

When that fails and all hope of achieving attendance is
abandoned, the case is brought to court, where the full
weight of society's authority is invested in three magistrates
who consider the evidence and direct appropriate action.
Usually the court appearance is preceeded by a spell in the
'Assessment Centre' where the behaviour, attitudes, ability
and performance level of the kids are closely monitored.

Dropping out from school – truanting – inevitably leads to
close scrutiny by officialdom, and often means enforced separation from home for a while, before a court appearance
which is at best sternly paternalistic and at worst plainly
hostile.   The first appearance usually ends with a supervision order and an official direction to attend school, though
the actual institution itself may be changed to accommodate
anti-feelings from parents and pupil as well as the staff of
the original school.   If the supervision order fails (and

that means regular contact with a Probation Officer), then
it's into 'care' – that of local authority – which means in
most cases residential placement well away from Mum and
Dad.

Whatever the reasons for their rejections, they must be
pretty deep-rooted to sustain the youngster through the bar-
rage of official interference which is the inevitable consequence of persistent truancy. If the measure of their feeling is their resolute action then it must be seen as more than
just a passing whim – and perhaps it's a gauge of something
wrong which affects many more pupils than those who actually take the drastic step of voting with their feet. And
perhaps schools aren't necessarily the root of evil; perhaps the reaction to school is a symptom of a feeling which
has its roots in something quite unconnected to the educational framework.

Take Colin from the year before, for instance: the
middle one of five brothers living in a small council house in
one of the 'new' estates, built on the city's periphery to re-
house the bombed-out and expanding population. The house,
though not gerry-built, was cheaply and quickly erected –
the council's alternative to prefabs. Three bedrooms and
a garden. When we first met Colin, all five brothers were
living at home still and his sister had recently moved out to
'get married'.

It doesn't need much imagination to picture the scene
during Colin's formative years. With Mum and Dad in one
bedroom, the six of them had to sort themselves out in the
remaining rooms for sleeping. Once his sister reached
adolescence it was considered reasonable that she had a
room of her own, which left the five boys to arrange themselves through the rest of the house. In fact Colin and his
youngest brother Clive spent most of their nights on the
couch in the living room – once telly had finished and everyone else had gone to bed. Staying up till the invisible voice
announced 'Don't forget to switch off your set' was a frequent event – particularly since Dad, who was a 'regular'
drinker, never came home before eleven and always wanted
to watch telly before going to bed. Since Dad was often on
the dole, late evenings were no problem for him, as he could
lie in till late morning, leaving Mum to prepare breakfast and
usher the kids off to their respective schools.

Privacy was a foreign word in that house. In no sense
could Colin – or indeed any of his brothers – regard any
room as their own. In the dormitories of most public

schools they allow the pupils personal bedside lockers.
In Colin's house there was the kitchen drawer, or the table
beside the telly – if there was any room apart from the
'Radio' and 'TV Times' and back copies of 'Sporting Life'.

At a personal level for Colin, it meant no opportunity to
be alone at home for any reason, and to engage in hobbies or
homework would have meant constructing organised space
from the chaos and defending it against the inevitable and
irresistible encroaching of the other eight humans – not to
mention the boundless energy of the Irish Wolfhound Shawn,
who was treated with as much reverence as anyone else in
the family.

Mum worked very hard to keep the family fed and together
and prepared for the outside world. The problem for her
was that all the boys were large and growing – Colin, like
all his brothers, was over six feet tall before leaving
school. Just feeding the family was an organisational headache – both in preparation and quantity. It was not uncommon for eight loaves of bread to disappear in a day and the
milkman frequently collected a crate of empties from the
back door. In such situations, a national bread strike or a
milk shortage precipitated real family crises. Exhortations
by TV announcers and 'personalities' to 'bake your own and
enjoy the therapeutic effort of kneading your own dough and
watching it rise in your own home' may well have been received with sympathy and interest by housewives with time
and energy to spare for 'creative' labour; but for Colin's
Mum, those eight loaves a day represented a lot of instant
stomach filler that gave her time to concentrate on other
matters, like the cleaning job she had taken to supplement
the income from Social Security. Not that Dad was always
out of work. Indeed, there were many occasions when he'd
be employed for long stretches – mostly as a labourer and
often 'on the lump'. But such cash made little impression on
cash available to keep the house together, since the kind of
work was the thirst-creating variety that required beer at
midday and in the evenings to satisfy.

So Colin grew up in a home situation such as this, and in
many ways – because his Mum and Dad were at least still
together and there was a strong family bond that held the
'Tibbles' together – he was much more fortunate than many of
his peers, where drunkenness and violence and divorce were
the rule of thumb.

But to compare that domestic situation to the 'normal'
family with Mum, Dad, 2.2 children, cage of gerbils and a

semi with garage and landscaped garden, where holidays to
the kids mean more time for hobbies and reading and visiting,
or other leisure activities with friends, is to realise the gap
in life-style and attitude that exists side-by-side in every
city in this country. Which, of course, is no more than
many sociologists like Jackson and Marsden with their erudite studies about 'working-class' life, have testified. (1)
But it does explain why working-class children tend to do
less well at school and why, thirty-six years after the 1944
Education Act,the percentage of working-class children who
enter university is still only 4 per cent - a figure unchanged
for forty years. (2)

Consider Colin and school. How is it possible for school
- with its emphasis on 'brain power' and orderliness and
social graces, to appear as anything but a foreign world -
albeit a world shared with many of his mates. If his parents, like most middle-class parents, really accepted and
believed in and supported the stated aims of the school, instead of vaguely assenting to the notion that it would be good
for Colin to take exams, then at least Colin would have been
motivated to try and accommodate himself within this foreign
world. In their book Jackson and Marsden pinpointed the
difference it made to a working-class boy if his parents as-
pired to the middle-class values that predominate in school,
and David Hargreaves, analysing the factors that cause delinquent behaviour in schools, (3) concluded quite definitely
that parental attitude to the school was a determining factor.

But in Colin's case his Dad saw school as something to be
endured for the legal requirements and useful only in the
sense that perhaps it taught 'em how to read and write:
'Look Rog, where did school get me? I hated the teachers
and they hated me. I wasn't any good at anything except
woodwork and that wasn't considered at all important - so I
left as soon as I could at 14. What I've learnt, I've learnt
outside of school anyway; it didn't help me get a job, and I
can see it's the same for Colin. He's like me, he's not interested in all this bookwork stuff - he wants to get out and
do something, not be stuck to a desk all day.'

His Mum was more sympathetic - knowing from conversation with other Mums that it did make a difference what your
school record was like when it came to looking for jobs, and
though she hadn't been academically brilliant herself she'd
mostly enjoyed her own schooling. 'I got on well with most
of the teachers and you see we did some useful things - like
cooking, and sewing and child care. I'd like to see Colin

do better at school, but honestly you know, I don't understand the things he's doing and whenever he'd ask me to help
him I could never help him or be of any use. He doesn't
bring homework back now.'

So it's small wonder that Colin didn't 'do very well' at
school. Primary school was more fun than secondary, but
even there the lesson content had little relevance for a boy
whose family were preoccupied with food and finance, and
where books were foreign objects and reading was restricted to the racing form section of the 'Sun'.

Till he started school at the age of 5 Colin had never
fingered a book, never counted in any rational sense, and
though he could distinguish 3 from 2 or from 1, a collection
of four or more objects found him without a vocabulary to
describe them. So he started behind in the scholastic three
Rs, and in the equally important skills of expressiveness and
response-ability he'd had little practice, living as he did in
a front room with eight others and a dog. Gentleness and
consideration would be allowed little space in such a menag-
erie.

So though in no way could you describe Colin's background
as deprived by comparison with many children brought up
amidst the poverty and shortage of the third world, it was
certainly not a background conducive to good school attainment, where the emphasis was on book-oriented learning and
information acquisition. Colin's early school reports described him as 'drifting along aimlessly through school' and
later school reports as 'unco-operative and uninterested'.
Finally, of course, he 'dropped out'. Soon after his fourteenth birthday he was in court for non-school attendance.
Though his only 'crime' was a silent reaction to a system
that had never seemed related to his own situation, he did in
fact spend some time in an Assessment Centre, rubbing
shoulders with other lads up for more socially destructive
acts, like vandalism or assault or theft.

A hundred years ago, Colin would have been employed
within the family in some role. Childhood as we experience
it – a long period of 'growing up', lacking role definition
and a productive purpose – was short. By 6 or 7 most children were helping with something at home – perhaps with the
responsibility of a part-time job to supplement the family
income. And in most homes children were getting practical
experience through everyday tasks, from food preparation to
repairing furniture to making clothes. Schooling that presented factual acquisition and academic learning would have

been balanced by the child against the reality of his practical experience. At least he could compare the school with
the reality of his own home situation – where he had a role
and responsibility.

Today, twentieth-century living has removed the opportunities for practical experience at home. Many things come
pre-packed, pre-cooked, pre-assembled, and, after use,
are easily disposable and replaceable. Food isn't cooked
but merely warmed, clothes aren't repaired, just replaced,
broken gadgets aren't mended, just discarded.

And at school the emphasis is still on factual acquisition
and academic learning. For the child, until he is 16, practical experience and responsibility for productive effort is
limited to the fortunate few who are able to secure a badly
paid paper round or a grossly exploited Saturday morning
job in a shop.

Perhaps, this has drifted some way from the initial question of 'why these youngsters reject school', but it is important to probe beneath the glib assertion that 'school is an
irrelevancy', or the equally glib assertion that there is
something necessarily wrong with a child who won't go to
school.

Maybe we need to look at the problem differently, by
starting with a consideration of what education is really
appropriate and necessary for youngsters in a situation like
Colin's. In Erich Fromm's words,

A Sane Society is that which corresponds to the needs of
man – to what his needs are objectively as they can be
ascertained by a study of man. Our task is to ascertain
what is his nature, and what are the needs that stem from
this nature. (4)

Often our immediate response to a problem is to search
for a label to categorise it. Once physical illness can be
identified and labelled it becomes less frightening to both
patient and doctor. The mystery of an indefined sickness
holds a hidden terror. The same is true of mental illness,
and since the labels are longer and more scientific the
relief is tinged with a certain lay incomprehension that sets
the sick person apart from the rest of the 'normal' world.
Flu we can all understand. Schizophrenia we can understand as a word that means 'split personality', but in terms
of actually understanding the symptoms and treatment the
disease is shrouded in mystery.

Because we all know how to treat flu it holds no fear, and
though the terror of a person who exhibits split personality

traits is lessened by our being able to label it as schizophrenia, our fear of it as something mysterious still remains. However, being able to label it somehow renders it
someone else's problem: responsibility is devolved onto
someone else (onto a doctor in the case of physical illness).

Similarly with school phobia: the problem is categorised,
its claws of intangibility blunted by description. A 'school
phobic' becomes the responsibility of Education Welfare or
Child Guidance. Though maybe still interested and involved, parents and teachers become outsiders - and so to a
certain extent does the child.

It is interesting that to describe a boy as 'someone who
won't go to school' invites the question 'Why?' as an inevitable response. An explanation is anticipated and expected.
To describe a boy as 'school-phobic' is to pre-empt further
discussion. The label itself contains the reason: phobias
are fears and everyone knows that to ask why someone is
claustrophobic is meaningless. It is unlikely they can give
a rational explanation, though psychoanalysis may hint at
childhood terrors of being shut inside cupboards and being
unable to escape. But generally we accept claustrophobia
as a description. Likewise school-phobic is becoming an
accepted adjective - as a shorthand description for some of
those children who won't go to school.

The danger of such labelling is in its disguising of causal
factors or the real situation. In short the phrase is meaningless - except as a shorthand. Used professionally that
is fine, but its general use tends to blur the issue. Inher-
ent in the label of phobia is an implication of deficiency in
the person referred to. Some phobias like vertigo or
claustrophobia we may well be sympathetic with (though cat-
lovers have little sympathy for felixphobia sufferers).
However, in spite of the sympathy, there is a general feeling that to be phobic is to be an incomplete person - something is missing and it's the sufferer's fault. But we know
with 'school phobics' that the fault is not necessarily theirs,
and equally school phobia isn't necessarily an attitude influenced by the school. That is neither new nor profound.

Explanations for 'school phobia' may derive from incidents
at home, at school, or with friends - where the fault was not
that of the youngster concerned. Perhaps it results from a
traumatic first day in infants school, or being intimidated by
a gang of bullies, or intuiting the parents' own dislike of
school and absorbing it.

Take Match, the lad described in the previous chapter,

for instance. Primary school reports indicated an above-average boy with a good sense of humour, well liked by his friends. With attendance and motivation both good, he promised to do well at secondary school: and yet within a year his attendance slumped; his sense of humour oscillated with bouts of moody depression; he became abusive at home. Finally he gave up attending school altogether.

School-phobic? Certainly - but why? Was it his lack of physical maturity, which contrasted strikingly with his more developed pubescent peers? Was it domestic tension created by a 'sick' mother who was often away for months at a time in a mental home? Was it the model of his father who had been off work for several years because of 'back injury', and who quite clearly had no intention of working again? Did the contradicting parental attitudes to school and the value of education destroy Match's initial enthusiasm?

Or take Royston, for whom at 13, because of his inability to attend ordinary school, the suggestion of residential provision was put to his mother. She agreed and drove Royston to the school on the appointed day. Dropping him off, she told him she would collect him later that day. It was three months before Royston went home at the end of term and he never went back to that school. When he came to us for interview he wouldn't let his mother out of his sight and wouldn't stay after she'd gone. Another school phobic - but the reason why is very different from Match. The more detailed story presents a very depressing picture.

Royston had been placed in the 'special' unit at school before his seventh birthday - against the wishes of his mother who herself was well satisfied with the standard of his work. From the day he entered the unit till the day he was referred to us, he never attended school regularly. Throughout his junior school period he became progressively more difficult - troublesome at home, problematic at school. His mother's dependance on him and her jealousy of his relationship with any other adult militated against him becoming involved with teachers. Though she could exhibit anger about his non-school attendance, she would collude with him about his reasons for not going.

As he grew older and started secondary school, his mother's anxiety increased with his own school 'phobia'. The residential school was a culmination of her inability to cope with him at home and the Education Welfare Service's concern at his urgent need for remedial provision. He did in fact do well at the school initially but his parents were

unsuccessful in returning him for the new term. Finally
he was removed from the roll, and subsequent non-school
attendance brought him before the juvenile court.

Referral to us was the last possible hope. We interviewed him, with his parents, agreed to take him and
crossed our fingers that he might come. The arrangement
was for him to cycle over the first day and the suggestion
seemed to appeal to him. By lunchtime there was still no
sign of Royston.

His mother apparently had refused to let him ride his
bike, considering it too dangerous.

Royston in fact never came to us.

Fortunately, through an elaborate home-tuition programme, which involved initially coaxing Royston from his
bed on the visited mornings, we were able to provide some
sort of ongoing link. The tutor concerned managed to use
Royston's interest in motorbikes to forge a relationship of
sorts – which at least meant the boy had to make some responses. He survived the year – just (see Chapter 10).

Percy was a different 'case' altogether. His attendance
at the local school was generally good until his fourth year.
Large and affable, he wasn't considered particularly bright,
but he certainly wasn't a problem. Though some of his
teachers were concerned at his lack of friends in his own
age group – he always seemed to mix in with boys several
years his senior – this was understandable enough, given
his obvious physical maturity. He was out of place in his
own year and Percy was always to be seen at break times or
after school with his older mates.

Towards the end of his fourth year his attendance slumped
and before the end of that year he was up before the juvenile
court for various offences committed whilst he should have
been at school. But Percy was determined not to return to
his school, and would have gone away if it hadn't been decided to offer him a trial period with us.

We were sceptical from the beginning. He lived well outside Bristol and the journey in would take at least an hour,
with a mile to walk from the nearest bus stop. Compared to
the fifteen-minute bus ride from his house to school, getting
to us would be a veritable marathon. Within a week we expected Percy to stop coming.

A year later Percy was still arriving before ten o'clock
each day and on the day of the heaviest snow that Bristol
had seen for a decade he was one of the four to turn up,
whilst two within walking distance rang in to complain that
the cold necessitated them staying in at home.

Why Percy's school phobia?

Perhaps it wasn't the school's fault, or his parent's fault – or anyone's fault. But once his friends had left, what was the motivation to stay at school? That at least was Percy's explanation in retrospect.

The truth may be more complicated. Percy's parents were divorced. His Dad had been in the army and Percy's childhood memories were linked with the foreign places where his father had been posted – Germany, Cyprus, Singapore: all rather a difference from the hamlet of six houses in rural Gloucestershire that he now lived in with just his mother and his memories for company. Perhaps his unwillingness to go to school stemmed from a deep-rooted fear that maybe his mother too would leave him, and one day he might return to a completely empty house.

Perhaps, as one of his teachers sympathetically said, 'the pressures of a hustling, busy school are too great for him. He needs a small group situation, where his shy introversion can be handled carefully.'

Perhaps it was his size. How many adolescents are so embarrassed by their own physical oddities that it drives them to extreme measures? The girls obsessed with the fear of being overweight who diet themselves into a state of anorexia are not uncommon. Embarrassment is a singularly difficult state to come to terms with – however honestly recognised and warmly supported. A strong personal fear is of having to sing. I am too embarrassed to even join in an informal group chorus. Though I love music and listening to singing, the thought of going to something like a carol-singing evening fills me with dread if I think I may have to participate. It may stem from junior school experience of being ridiculed for being 'out of key' – certainly I have a vivid memory of being made to sing in front of a class and having my faltering efforts scorned by the teacher in charge. Whatever the cause I am embarrassed to sing now – though in many situations I would very much like to. Even the support and encouragement of friends doesn't help. I either clam up or deliberately sing coarsely and out of tune in a mockery of self-ridicule. So I can understand that Percy may just have been too embarrassed by his physical appearance to go out of the house and meet his friends. It could have been that simple – and that difficult.

The myth of labelling these kids 'school-phobic' is exposed by their attendance with us – in some cases almost 100 per cent. The contradiction and injustice of describing such a

person as school-phobic is clear.   Likewise with the mis-
nomer of 'maladjusted'.

Nick, who'd been avoiding school for two years, was finally referred to us.   In the interim, amongst other placements,
he'd spent some months at one of the Child Guidance units.
His mood there had oscillated between gentle co-operation
and physical and verbal aggression.   His label was maladjusted.

The day he came to us I was struck by his smile.   That is
almost all I can remember of that first meeting – a shy, quiet
boy with a smile that said, 'Try me.'

We did.   In the year Nick was with us we saw no sign of
the tantrums that had characterised his stay at Child Guidance.   After he'd been with us three months we had cause
to visit Child Guidance.   The room we sat in was a mess:
paint had seemingly been splattered on walls and ceiling
from the centre of the room in liberal wallops.   The plasterboard notice boards had gouges several feet long and inches
thick.   New putty in the windows hinted at several dozen
broken panes.

'What holocaust hit this?'

'Oh Nick in one of his moods.'

'Why?'

'Maladjusted?'

Nick's explanation shortly before he left us was more
straightforward.   'If they thought I was all right they'd have
sent me back to normal school, wouldn't they?'   Perhaps it
was a rationalisation, but there is a disconcerting element of
possible truth.   Certainly it was a rational act in the light
of his expectations.

It would be unfair to put Child Guidance clinics in the dock
as the bogeymen here.   Staffed by caring, sensitive, perceptive people they achieve miracles with many kids – but
there are some youngsters who recognise that a function of
Child Guidance clinics is to enable them to adjust to ordinary
school.   They react accordingly.

The label 'maladjusted' may be a true immediate analytical
description, but does it mean more than just not manageable
under a normal school regime?   The label does nothing to
suggest a solution, and in many cases the aura of the label
itself hinders the application of palliative measures – or a
questioning into causal factors.   Labelling often takes no
account of the range of problems behind the symptoms.

Raymond 'freaked out' at 15.   Though a nervous, shy boy
he had never given any indication of a serious underlying

problem. But one day he went off to school still in his pyj-
amas, unnoticed by his mother, and rambling incoherently.
He was picked up before reaching school and within hours
was under the 'qualified' supervision of a nurse in a mental
hospital. His label was 'a very disturbed boy'. Since his
early childhood Raymond's mother had impressed upon him
how hopeless he was compared to his elder brother. Nothing he attempted was expected to succeed; if it did, luck
was the cause not ability. Raymond had grown up in an atmosphere calculated to smother any sprouting self-esteem.
Not surprisingly he had none: his self-confidence was neg-
ligible and it took many months of skilful nursing to convince
him that he did have some value and ability. He now spends
weekends skydiving and parachuting to the envy of his
friends and adulation of his girlfriend.

The lengths that some youngsters go to to avoid school is
alarming. Those First World War soldiers who shot off
their feet in a desperate bid for repatriation away from the
front line have their counterparts in some of our youngsters.

Kev had not been to school for two years when he was referred to us. The example of his elder brother who had
himself been a habitual truant – and whom both parents had
failed to relate to – was there in the background. Kevin's
truanting led to several occasions when he 'ran away' from
home at night and his Dad called in the police. To prevent
such escapades his mother slept in his room and his father
wired down the window, but his school attendance never improved, though he maintained close friendships with former
school friends. For two years he escaped the clutches of
the welfare service and the law.

What had he done with the time? 'I spent a lot of days in
the front room sitting to watch for the Education Welfare
Officer or my social worker coming round so I could slip
out the back before they knocked at the door.'

Two years spent waiting for the 'school board' instead of
facing school! For Kev, like most of the others referred,
the road to us is not easy. The kids are not being rewarded
for bad behaviour; their single-minded, apparently self-
destructive, opting out negates such a glib retort. In many
cases it is easy and tempting to just blame the school for
creating 'school phobia' – since it is the school that the
youngsters are apparently reacting against. Even if it is
the school's fault it is unrealistic to expect one school to be
'right' for all the children in its catchment area. In the
same way that a packed beach at Bognor or Skegness is

heaven for some and hell for those who prefer the isolation
of the Scottish Highlands (away from points accessible to
the motor car!) we should recognise that one school will not
suit all pupils. Perhaps we should be amazed that so many
youngsters actually attend school at all! The truth is of
course that most youngsters want to go to school. Suspen-
sion from school is an effective weapon, as those teachers
working in disruptive units for suspended pupils can well
testify.

In searching for causal factors it is easy to end by apportioning blame. The fault is somebody's. But apportioning
blame only has validity if it changes something. Identifying
the causal factors is fine if something happens as a result.
Blaming parents, or school, or friends, or society is a
fruitless off-shouldering of responsibility, if the exercise
ends there. It is only helpful if blame is supported by practical suggestions for preventive action.

The fact that a child withdraws from school means that
there is something about the experience that he finds painful. Now it may be true that the causes of this pain were
rooted in experiences at home, quite unconnected to the
school, but if the school is unable to alleviate the pain so as
to make being there actually rewarding, it is unrealistic to
expect the pupil to keep attending.

C.M. Fleming, writing in 'Adolescence: its Social Psychology', (5) outlines what she feels are four basic human
needs, the need for Acceptance, the need for Expression,
the need to Contribute Usefully and Responsibly and the
need to Discover and Enquire and Explore. Consider the
four in relation to the child. Acceptance should be met
within the family from birth onwards. Expression is tradi-
tionally met through communal and recreational activities
where affection, frustration, pleasure and creativity can be
explored and developed through friendship and relationships.
The need to contribute socially has become the function of
work and sadly, increasingly, society has no use for children, except as an investment in their future worth as par-
ticipatory adults. Indeed, it is only the twentieth century
that has recognised the twilight world of adolescence as an
acceptable state between childhood and adult responsibilities. If the other three needs are met, then school can
attempt to meet the fourth. With their resources of man-
power and equipment they have the facility to surpass the
home and family in terms of potential learning experiences
offered to the adolescent. Sadly the other three needs are
not often met.

Take the need to contribute. In pre-twentieth-century western society children had a role to play in the social order of things. From an early age they were expected to take a part in the productive work of the family unit; in rural homes this could mean helping on the land, in urban homes it may mean factory work or some other task where they were actually contributing to the family. Of course, in Victorian England exploitation of children reached its peak and the reality for many kids was menial, repetitive and exhausting enforced labour - where any question of their contributing socially and responsibly in response to their personal needs was quite irrelevant. No one would wish to put back the clock, but the pendulum has swung the other way; now children do very little that's socially useful and there are few real demands to take on responsibility. They are rarely put in a situation where someone needs their help, or where there is any expectation that they have a contribution of value to make in a social sense.

The need can be sublimated by a parental emphasis on deferred adulthood through long apprenticeship in the twilight world of studentship, where the emphasis is on studied application and not necessarily on responsibility. But for families where academic achievement is not a substitute for initiation into adulthood, it is no surprise that many adolescents, feeling under-valued and superfluous, react accordingly.

On the need for expression, there is no doubt of the universal human desire to communicate feelings and moods and experience to others. To deny human beings opportunities for such expression is to deny their humanity. We have all experienced a frustration of not being able to communicate what we feel at certain times - be it love to a boyfriend or girlfriend, or anger in response to hurt. The extreme examples where physical disability bars outlet for expression are only too well known. The story of Helen Keller, (6) where frustration and determination finally broke through the barriers of darkness and silence, and, more recently, the very moving book by Joey Deacon (7) are descriptions of two people who experienced very severe denial of outlets for self-expression. In the latter case it took years before Joey, so badly affected by spasticism from birth that his speech was completely incomprehensible to any other human being, met another inmate of the mental institution to which he'd been confined who could actually understand what he was saying. Between them they wrote a book. It took three painful and laborious years to write, and stands as a sad indictment to society's disregard for the severely handicapped.

There are many people with less obvious handicaps. The 2 million functionally illiterate people in Great Britain must experience continued frustration at living in a world where the printed word lies with the spoken word as a medium of communication and supercedes it as a medium for information transmission and storage. At an immediate level concerning the illiterate adolescent pupil, schools may almost certainly not be solely to blame, but their emphasis on reading and writing as the chief form of self-expression merely compounds the frustration. This is not to suggest that schools should necessarily shift their whole emphasis to other expressive mediums. That would be somewhat naive. But they need to be sensitive to the vulnerability of a semi-literate adolescent and not compound the sense of frustration by criticism and blame. Human beings will avoid pain like any other animal. If learning is made painful through criticism and failure, rather than made rewarding through praise and achievement, it is not surprising if so many children withdraw from it. Which is exactly the experience of many adolescents.

Though the above-mentioned needs are obviously important, it is the first that Fleming mentions – the need for acceptance – which subsumes the rest. Any child, any adult, any person needs to be accepted. Our basic gregarious instinct is rooted in this need for acceptance. The most painful punishment is solitary confinement. The withdrawal of human contact, the rejection by others of your kind,is more painful than physical hurt, being a denial of your very self. The 'sending to Coventry' that features as a form of peer-group ostracism in public schools is a very effective weapon that can produce a frightening imbalance in the victim.

For a small child the need for acceptance must first be met within the family. It is there that the foundation of personal security is laid. It can only be the family to begin with, since it is to mother, and subsequently father and siblings, that the young child looks for human contact. For a child to start school without this inner sense of acceptance must be a frightening experience – especially if, for whatever reason, the school compounds the feeling of insecurity by criticism or rejection. Though not the school's fault, it can almost unwittingly destroy any enthusiasm for engagement in activities within its walls.

Lacking a sense of acceptance, the child is hardly likely
to risk the discovering and exploring that would satisfy one
need; or take the very exposing course of open expression
of feeling and moods that would satisfy another; or be prepared to regard school as an agency for offering opportunities for useful and responsible social contribution.

The result at the adolescent phase, when problems of
identity and acceptance become painfully acute, may then
well be a complete withdrawal. The label of school phobia
is merely a convenient tag to compartmentalise the problem.
The underlying symptoms which, as we have seen, may have
nothing to do at all with the school, can be overlooked in
society's overwhelming concern that the child's educational
needs are not being met.

It is disturbing to note, when looking through the social
enquiry reports of the youngsters, that they were often
known to 'officialdom' as problems long before leaving primary school. Somehow there must be an intensifying of
remedial and preventive work at an early age if first efforts
fail to bear fruit. Maybe the action needs to be quite un-
traditional and maybe local authorities need to assume more
control more quickly in cases where parents are clearly inadequate. There is no doubt that ambivalent parental love
can only be counteracted by unambivalent secure affection
from another adult – and this may only be possible away from
home. That is a harsh truth and harsher for the parents
than the child, but it must be faced up to.

Chapter 5

Autumn term

The honeymoon feeling of the last parting was shattered
abruptly on the first morning back. In typical school-
teaching tradition we'd decided on a 'structured' beginning.
'Start off firm and then loosen up' is the maxim offered to
student teachers. It has its attractions – enabling order to
disguise a host of under-the-surface confusions. We intended to follow a straight discussion with some English work –
the normal expectation for Tuesday morning.

But they hid behind sheets of newspapers and refused to
talk – or work. Fortunately we abandoned the attempt to
produce 'work' and concentrated instead on making lunch
and refilling coffee mugs. They began to unwind and talk
to us and each other. Our mistake was to assume that the
intimacy and camaraderie of the last day of the half term
could carry over. But ten days had passed since then and
home situations had inevitably intervened to cloud their
allegianceṡ.

It is too easy to forget that, though the half-term holiday
may be a 'break' to us, for many youngsters it represents
increased exposure to stress and tensions – perhaps from
home or from peers – or just the old enemy of boredom.
Though there was no way of probing beneath the surface immediately to discover what had happened in that time away,
it was clear from the odd remark that two of them at least
had had a far from 'relaxing' holiday. Clive's brother had
been brought to court and sent down for two years for lar-
ceny and Debbie had been acting as mediator in a violent
dispute between her mother and her mother's boyfriend,
with the latter threatening to abandon her to the poverty of
Social Security and the former threatening to bring a maintenance order for the care of her unborn baby. And maybe

some of the others had had an equally rough ride. Is it possible that some of them could even have felt abandoned by us?

Lunch brought them together – even Alec, who had either forgotten his original promise to buy fish and chips, or was just more impressed by the quantity and quality of food set before him. We reintroduced the idea of going to Wales and their eagerness was surprising – Joy actually offered a quid on the spot, 'Because I'm sure to have spent it by tomorrow,' she said, peeling it away from a roll of notes. That day she had £21.00 on her and it all went on a dress.

Before half term, Lester, who'd often complained at our lack of football facilities, had arranged a match at a nearby youth club with a small, fenced-in court marked out for football. We all went, but only two of the opposing team arrived. Then it started to rain. Puddles of wet tarmac glistened through the window as we hovered round the football table, half hoping the rest of the opposition wouldn't turn up. They didn't and it carried on raining – and yet at Clive's suggestion the boys formed two teams between them and engaged in a ten-minute-each-way battle which Liz recorded on tape with a running commentary, assisted by the other dripping spectators.

In the nearby cafe, drinking our coffee at 10p a cup, thinking how much cheaper and better and more plentiful it would have been at the school, we listened to the recording and laughed at our dampness. We were a group again.

Perhaps this concern about 'group feelings' merely reflects our own paranoia at any apparent disintegration. It certainly makes it easier for the staff if the kids do coalesce as a group, but more importantly our experience suggests that group harmony and feeling leads to a much more enhanced willingness for individuals to risk themselves and explore new situations. The kids draw a lot of support and strength from the 'group', and peer-group pressure, as the magistrate courts know so well, is very forceful. One of Rutter's consistent findings was that 'shared activities towards a common goal, which requires people to work together, are a most effective means of reducing inter-group conflict'. (1)

Apart from the immediate benefit of the identity it offers the youngsters, our hope is that the group themselves will pass on this 'ethos' of the school – through their identification with its tenets and principles. If the group participate in devising and maintaining the structure, they will auto–

matically take responsibility for its transmission to new kids (see Chapter 11 for a further discussion of this issue.)

The next day they were all prepared to work at their maths, with the unease of the previous morning just a distant memory. At lunch we discussed a topic dear to their hearts: Taking and Driving Away. Sparked off by the recent knowledge that one of last year's group had just been sent down for his fourteenth offence, it wasn't difficult to kindle their interest.

Our moralising about the dangers and inconsiderate risk to innocent people fell on deaf ears. 'You just don't understand,' explained Jim. Our suggestion that maybe if they had both vehicles and a place to drive it would satisfy the impulse and quell their urge to joyride at night met with a mixed response, ranging from Clive's scornful laugh to Alec's 'Good idea'.

This tendency to joyride is an endemic disease amongst the youngsters who come to us. That year, though none were actually in trouble for TDA, a goodly number were in the habit of 'borrowing' cars at night. Arguably the illegality is all part of the thrill, so any attempts to provide a 'safe' place where they could race around with only their own necks to break, would be doomed to rejection!

In a discussion of contemporary issues affecting young people Erikson says:

The motor engine, of course, is the very heart and symbol of our technology, and its mastery the aim and aspiration of much of modern youth. In connection with immature youth, however, it must be understood that both motor car and motion pictures offer to those so inclined, passive locomotion with an intoxicating delusion of being intensely active. The prevalence of car thefts and motor accidents among juveniles is much decried (although it is taking the public a long time to understand that a theft is an appropriation for the sake of gainful possession, while automobiles, more often than not, are stolen by the young in search of a kind of automotive intoxication, which may literally run away with car and youngster). Yet while vastly inflating a sense of motor omnipotence the need for active locomotion often remains unfulfilled. (2)

It is a problem we haven't resolved. Our approach that year was to try and actually teach them how to drive – using the resource of a student who had a car and was willing to 'have a go' and allowed them to manoeuvre the car in the playground before trying it out on a disused airfield. This

activity soon developed its own pecking order and gave
some of them – particularly Jim – enhanced status in the
eyes of the group.

Though we were worried that such a brief experience in
the yard would be just an appetite whetter, we felt we had
to do something, and making sure that they had some ability
at least seemed the most sensible course, since we were
unsure how effective our 'counselling' would be in influencing their attitude to TDA. Subsequent events showed how
disastrously mistaken we were (Chapter 7). For the while,
though, 'car driving' as an activity became a regular feature
of the timetable: a prized slot which we used mercilessly as
a motivation for other work, particularly reading. Learning the Highway Code was a precursor to any driving, and
though we toyed with the idea of using it as a spur to attendance by imposing sanctions for irregular or unreliable behaviour, we never actually organised ourselves, or them, to
accept it.

A recent newspaper article described an attempt by one
senior probation officer in a local authority to 'cure' stealing teenagers of the habit. In a converted garage groups
of teenagers on probation worked in teams at 'doing up' sal-
vaged wrecks from the council's dumps. In their spare
time they repaired the cars up to a standard where they
could be 'raced' on a nearby circuit. The status of actually competing in a race, having 'customised' their own car
was carrot enough to wean them off joyriding – especially
since one of the self-imposed rules was that any misdemean-
our by a member of the group would disqualify the whole
team from racing. Out of 100 boys who participated in the
scheme, only 2 were subsequently convicted for motoring
offences. (3)

Subsuming our plans for the second half of the Christmas
term were intentions to concentrate on more activities that
would bring them together in working groups. To this end
we hoped the students, who by now had developed a workable relationship with the youngsters, would initiate such
small group activities on the sessions they were with us.

The car driving was one such example. Another was
their involvement at 'the field'. In 'In and Out of
School' (4) we discussed the rationale for taking city kids
into the country, and we had negotiated the use of a couple
of acres of hillside in the Mendips for the purpose. For
adolescents born and bred in an urban environment it can be
a completely novel experience just being somewhere where

the only sound that breaks the silence is a bird song, or
grass sighing or a lamb bleating in the distance. It sounds
trite and corny and smacks of romanticism, but those who
scoff are those who perhaps take such things for granted.

In one sense it doesn't matter what we do at the field;
just being there is often experience enough, especially if
the adults present are at least alert enough to give something - I wonder how old that hedge is? How would you
know this is a badger sett? Is that an oak tree?

That may sound a patronising level at which to operate,
but those who would ridicule that perhaps don't understand
the informational ignorance of many 15-year-olds. Trees
to many youngsters are just trees and to suggest that there
are in fact varieties of trees - that one kind can be differen-
tiated from another, or that this knowledge has application
in terms of what you use the tree for - is to unveil a new
perspective of the countryside. It is impossible to know
which of these unveiling attempts actually succeeds and,
rather like Rutherford with his fusion experiments, you
bombard with ideas in the hope that some at least will hit
the target and implant themselves. Perhaps the seed then
doesn't actually germinate for some years. It's rather
like the situation where you're at the theatre watching a
play, and a word or a line rings a connecting chord to something someone may have said many years ago. Perhaps it
was funny and you laugh, and in explanation to the curious
glances from your friends next to you, you say, 'Now I
understand the joke about the strawberry,' and they of
course forgive you for being mad'.

Such is the value of experience and the rationale for VSO
and D of E schemes, and other activities, which 'broaden
the horizons' of our young people by offering a range of experiences, some of which will be remembered and used.
So on one level the visit to the field is good just because
it's a new experience.

We did have a plan though. The aim was to build a log
hut - the sort of cabin that is commonly associated with Boy
Scouts or the Canadian Rockies. The first day out - the
Thursday of the second half of term - the gods were with us
in providing fine weather. Blue skies and crystal clear air
above, as Lester, Clive, Jim and Dirk piled into the minibus.

On the way we produced photographs of other log huts,
and discussed the possibilities of our building a similar one.
Their interest was high as we bounced up the barely navig-

able track to park the van by a water board reservoir.
'Which way?' shouted Jim, leaping gleefully from the
front seat. We pointed to the right, down a muddy lane.
'Along there? You're kidding – in that mud.'
'That's what the wellies are for.'
Wellington boots: what every countryman possesses and
understands as a necessity, and what city children ridicule
as symbols of rustic stupidity. Lester refused to put them
on, not wanting to be 'shown up'. However as the first
flecks of mud spattered his new drogues and threatened to
destroy the pristine purity of his Oxford bags he changed
his mind. 'But one of them new pairs,' he insisted. 'Not
a muddy set.'
There was almost a holiday atmosphere that day. Clive
and Lester (with his whippet pup, Brandy) stomped down the
hill with a water container to collect water for coffee to be
brewed later over a gas stove (or fire if the wood could be
gathered). Jim and Dirk made a start on clearing an area
of ground, having decided where the best site would be.
We'd already arranged for enough tools to go round: an
important factor in preplanning anything like this. Everyone needs to be able to be involved without having to wait
their turn to use the instrument of their fancy. Within ten
minutes Jim had bent a scythe and broken a billhook by trying to chop down the stump of a small holly bush. The axe
we handed him did the job in seconds, and at least we had
the satisfaction of knowing that next time he might reach for
the right tool before he started.
Dirk had brought along his tape recorder and was picking
up the mixture of chatter and obscenity that filled the air.
'How about a song then? Rog chooses one beginning with
the letter A and then I'll choose one beginning with B.'
Silence! My strained brain clicked away.
'I can't think of any lines beginning with A.'
Jim chuckled. 'Ay Mr Tambourine Man, play a song for
me,' he began to sing and we joined in, managing to finish
the first line before collapsing in laughter.
That first day we managed to clear a sizeable area of
ground from brambles and weeds and level it off. The sun
was low in the sky as we splashed back along the track with
a very bedraggled whippet sniffing his way between pairs of
Wellington boots. Lester's were no longer quite so immac-
ulate, but at least his drogues were still in good repair.
The following Thursday we collected the basic support
posts from a forestry firm on the way. The mounds of cut

logs of varying thicknesses and lengths sparked off conversations about which wood was best and the most suitable
ways of preserving it from rotting.

The seven-foot uprights needed humping along the track to
the field: a coolie labour exercise which tested everyone's
strength and endurance.   Finally though, we dragged the
wood to the chosen site and surveyed the barren area of
ground.

'Now what do we do?'

'Stick 'em in the ground.'

'How?'

How indeed?   Suggestions ranged from using a sledge-
hammer to using a pneumatic drill.   We offered pick axes
and shovels and - given the rocky nature of the ground -
threw in a couple of post-holers for good measure.   These
solid bars of steel, tapered at each end, proved the most
useful implement, but it was still hard work.   They soon realised that a six-inch deep hole would be quite inadequate to
hold the post upright, and that a job that everyone had
thought would take a few minutes was likely to occupy many
man-hours of labour.

The enormity of the coolie labour exercise began to dawn
on some of them and enthusiasm was flagging before the first
hour was up.

'Whose horses are those?' asked Clive, pointing to the
next field.

'The bloke who owns the riding stable down the hill.'

'Oh.'   Clive surveyed the two mares critically.   'I
wouldn't mind a horse like that.   Can we ride 'em?'

'Well, he usually charges about £1.50 an hour, but we
could arrange it.'

At that moment my attention was distracted by an argument
between Jim and Lester about whose turn it was to use the
post-holer, so I didn't notice Clive slip away.

A few minutes later came a shout from the other side of
the fence: Clive grinned proudly down from the back of a
fifteen-hand chestnut mare, clutching some makeshift reins
in his left fist.

For most of them that was the end of digging holes for the
day'. The other horse was soon rounded up and 'bridled'
with odd bits of rope the boys had found.   Seeing them gal-
loping bareback across the field with the November sun setting in the clear blue sky above, we were reminded of
'Equus'.

'That boy has known a passion more ferocious than I have

felt in any second of my life.... I envy it,' says the psychiatrist referring to his 'patient''s midnight escapade on horseback. (5)

The competence of all the boys surprised us: no one fell off, no one lost control, and nor did we fortunately when it came to our turn. Only Jim demurred to try, being quite noticeably scared of the horses. He made up for it by sinking the deepest hole!

The group co-operation amongst the five boys was tremendous: each helping the other on and off and apportioning fair riding shares all round.

The atmosphere in the bus going back was electric, and there was no doubt about enthusiasm for a return visit next week: which was just as well, since the weather changed dramatically. A biting north-easterly wind whipped the dry leaves through the streets of Bristol but the kids were still undeterred.

Suitably equipped with cagoules and gloves and our ever-present Wellington boots we stomped along the lane to the field.

'Today we'll finish that hut,' said Jim.

'Bloody well better 'ad,' retorted Clive, 'before we freeze to death.'

They set to with characteristic fervour, encouraged by the need to keep warm through physical effort.

Within an hour of communal effort the four corner posts were in place - sunk two feet into the rocky soil and very solidly upright. Liz, who'd joined us that day, produced mugs of coffee at that point, having been hunched over the little camping gaz cooker for half an hour. We warmed our hands on the hot china and discussed how to fill in the walls. Ideas ranged from mud and sticks to plasterboard and weatherproof paint, 'Except if you do it that posh,' said Jim, 'you'll need to put bloody rugs on the floor to match.'

The horses arrived almost on cue, and Clive and Lester re-captured and reined them. Again they cantered and galloped and raced bareback around the field. Liz, though too scared to go on her own, accepted Clive's offer of riding two-up. 'Are you sure it won't hurt the horse though?' she asked as Lester bunked her up behind Clive. Like Sir Lancelot of old, he cantered off into the distance with his rescued damsel.

Martin, who'd also joined us for the first time, though fascinated by the spectacle of the others cantering round the field, was unwilling to try himself.

'I'd rather do it properly,' he said, 'with a saddle and things - I wouldn't feel safe like that - can we go one day?'

That afternoon was memorable because of the complete lack of the usual squabbling and bickering and complaining. There was only good-humoured playfulness. Jim and Clive led the singing going back in the bus.

The last time we visited the field before Christmas, Clive opted out and it remained for Lester and Jim to make a start on the walls. Their dexterity at weaving the fresh stripped branches between the uprights to resemble a makeshift wattle lattice reassured one that human resourcefulness hadn't entirely disappeared with the arrival of television and the 'consumer' age! Lester's whippet interrupted their work by dragging a bleeding rabbit from a corner of the field. 'Got a knife?' Lester turned to Jim, who handed over his switchblade. Neatly Lester nicked the fur and in minutes had peeled it away from the steaming red flesh underneath. Martin was nearly sick, but Lester's matter-of-fact attitude defused the initial brutishness of the situation. 'What else should we do with the little sod?' he asked. 'Let him rot for the crows? He was well dead, so we might as well make use of him. I'll cook him tomorrow.'

Clutching the skin in one hand, and holding the carcase by the legs in the other, he presented an evocative spectacle as he strode down the lane, crackling through the thin ice that had formed on the muddy surface.

For five Thursdays we'd bussed out to the field and though Lester and Jim were the only two who had not missed a trip, all the others had spent some time out there. What they had learnt is impossible to define or measure at all accurately. Just to experience the countryside and its moods was a novelty for some; to appreciate its silence, and not to see it as just something to be merely traversed or passed through in a journey between cities, was a valuable exten-sion of awareness.

Certainly for all those who had come each afternoon had been an opportunity to share as a group, which was what we'd hoped would happen that term. This emphasis on the 'group' is not simply bred from a pedagogic urge for order-liness; almost all the youngsters' social enquiry reports before admission stressed their lack of ability and experi-ence in forming stable relationships - both with peers and adults. There is, generally, a character trait of depres-sing introversion. So doing things together and not indi-vidually is important.

It was interesting that term to see how friendships blos-
somed, fluctuated and died.

Clive, who wanted to see himself as leader, allied in turn
with most of the boys, although he clearly regarded Martin as
his inferior, physically at least, and Dirk and Jim he was
suspicious of at times because of their 'threat' to his authority. Though building his speaker was the main preoccupation of the term, he was quite ready to join in with the
others. His mood ranged from gentle co-operativeness,
like the time he spent a whole afternoon helping Lester mend
the gas fire (our only means of heating, in a draughty room
that would have tested the strength of a central heating
system five times as powerful), to sullen non-communication,
like the various times he would draw Alec and Martin into a
huddle round the same gas fire, where they'd sit, silently
brooding and demonstrating their 'group' disapproval.

Dirk, who'd joined us at the beginning of November, was
probably the most 'sociable' of the boys, being prepared to
do anything with anyone, provided it caught his interest - a
cross-country race against Lester through the streets of
Bristol, a toy-making session with Maggie producing soft
toys for a playgroup, an afternoon with Clive forming mosaic
patterns on hardboard, a project with Martin to help him
renovate old bikes, and a day painting white-lined boxes with
Jim for reserved spaces in the nearby car park. At the end
of that day's work, they proudly showed off the results of
their labours: their paint-spattered overalls, a testimony to
the 'real' nature of the work. They were blissfully unaware
that RESREVED was an original spelling, and we didn't
bother to point it out. What's in a letter or two after all,
when the message is clear?

Lester (who, in discussion with us just before he left in
the summer term, described his initial perception as one of
seeing us as a 'couple of head-bangers') found it difficult to
settle in to the group at first. He would often arrive late,
or not at all, and leave early to hang around his old school
where his mates still went. It was more difficult for him
than the others, since he'd arrived after they'd already
formed a group. He had the added problem of integrating
himself into existing friendships, so it wasn't surprising
that he still turned to his old mates, though he'd long ago rejected the school institution they went to.

It took him at least a month to realise that even if we were
head-bangers, it wasn't a bad set-up for nutters, and his
attendance improved. When present he was nearly always

the most co-operative, a complete contrast to his behaviour at home, where his mother could never get him to help with even the smallest household chores. Even 'masculine' tasks like decorating or chopping wood left him quite cold at home, and yet during that second half of term the sight of Lester standing by the sink or stove with an apron tied round his waist was quite common.

With Maggie, one of the students who came on Fridays and whom he referred to as 'Mum', he was always ready to join in a cooking activity: making sweets, or baking bread or, as was the case that last day at the field with his dog, making roast rabbit sandwiches. There was a general air of unselfishness about his attitude to the others. He tended to be considerate - making tea for everyone, not just himself; leaving the room when arguing, rather than continue to irritate other people with temper tantrums like Alec; waiting his turn at lunch rather than grabbing the nearest saucepan and emptying the contents. Like Martin, he was often more at home with the students than with the other boys, but that may have been more to do with his willingness to participate - his lack of apathy - than a declared preference for their company. Lester had a very definite circle of friends in his neighbourhood, so, unlike Clive or Dirk or Martin, he was no 'loner', which also explained his apparent air of independence. A devout City fan, it was not unusual for him to arrive some mornings, hungover and tired, after a sleepless night celebrating on a coach from an away match at Liverpool or Leeds. On such occasions he would simply curl up on the sofa and ask to be left alone.

Lester was a good catalyst though, when awake and alert. His general air of enthusiasm was infectious to anyone he was paired up with and his presence in a small group or as one of a pair made serious conversation and concentrated thought much more likely. He was also the only boy who seemed to mix easily with the girls, whom he treated with varying degrees of condescension. Perhaps he was perceptive enough not to be confused by their demonstrative sexual flaunting, like Joy's habit of very obviously crossing and uncrossing her legs beneath a hitched-up skirt. Such provocation he would defuse with a comment like 'Knock a nail in, that'll hold em' or 'You nig-nogs are all the same, never still for a minute, must be our climate'. Such derisory comments were somehow acceptable from Lester, who could be honestly blunt to anyone in the group without their taking offence. It was something about the way he said it that

defused the potential tension of his personal remarks.
Lester could be direct in a language that would have drawn
instant abuse if we'd used it. If Jim was the group philo-
sopher and chairman, Lester was the Jiminy Cricket.

Two weeks after half term, and encouraged by the
friendly support of Colin who ran the local corner shop,
Lester's declared interest in horses had led him into contact with a racing stable near Wantage. From his weekly
order of 'Hare and Hounds' to conversations with Colin, who
had given him the address of the stable, he followed a connecting thread of 'luck' and coincidence that reached the
point of an arranged interview in the middle of November.
We travelled up with him in the train. With a bravado tinged
by understandable apprehension, he left us at Didcot to make
his own way to the stable.

That night he phoned to say he'd been offered the chance
of a trial placement for a fortnight in the spring.

This 'success' had a very positive effect on the group's
attitudes to jobs. Given the unemployment situation there
is a general air of despondency and apathy amongst our
youngsters towards 'work' - especially when most of them
know that the reality is a choice between a boring, repetitive factory machine or the comparative poverty and empti-
ness of the dole queue. Contrary to the popular myth expressed by such factions of the conservative press as the
'Daily Telegraph', not all young people who leave school
without qualifications are feckless by nature. It takes a
lot of determination to persevere beyond the tenth consecu-
tive rejection letter, especially when every application form
is an agonising exercise of grammatical complexity.

Lester's success prompted several of the others to make a
positive effort in the direction of job-finding - either as temporary work experience, or as part-time evening and weekend work, or with a view to a full-time job. Alec, for instance, who'd all along expressed a keen interest in 'building', had within a week of Lester's visit written and negotiated a visit to Wimpey's local head office. Predictably on
the actual morning of the visit he got 'cold feet' and didn't
want to go - 'I don't want a building job anyway' summed up
his attitude. But Lester, still riding high on the laurels of
his stable success, had agreed with us to go with Alec - because he could also see that Alec certainly wouldn't go on
his own with one of us. They went, and though the site
manager bored the pants off the kids by a schoolteacher
address for half an hour in a conference room equipped with

blackboards and chalk, at least Alec sat and listened – a
feat in itself. Unfortunately Alec's flightiness was growing
with his confidence and even in our situation the label 'disturbed' actually seemed appropriate. He was the most uneasy at meal times, which may well be the explanation for
his recurrent suggestion to 'bring in fish and chips' or just
''ave sandwiches'. It is commonplace for some youngsters
to express a violent antipathy to eating lunch as a group
around the table. It's not just that for many it's an unusual
habit because meals at home are often haphazard affairs,
with no effort or intention to create a family occasion.
That may well be true, but more significant is that many,
like Alec, react against being watched as they eat. It is
particularly noticeable whenever strangers join us for
lunch. Behaviour and conversation can alter dramatically
at such times.

Yet cooking lunch and eating together is one of the activities we are insistent about, and is one of the things the kids
always remember subsequently as being of value. To sit
and talk and consider other people for half an hour, or an
hour, in a day that will otherwise be spent selfishly alone
or in small groups, is very good 'social training', middle
class or not! And the fact that they are responsible for
the preparation and clearing away of the meal adds to its
importance.

Although Alec reacted so strongly against cooking meals,
he was never unwilling to take his turn in the kitchen and
indeed like all the others, especially the boys, he took
pride in preparing the food.

Covered pies with 'Eat me' emblazoned across them in
artistic pastry curves were Jim's speciality, and Lester
was always called on to 'do the custard' since 'no other
bugger can make it without lumps'. When it came to
'roasters' the job was always Liz's and since, without an
appropriate pan, this was the nearest we could come to the
revered chip, she was often on call more than once a week.
But it still wasn't without problems.

'I didn't like the responsibility of knowing that if you
mucked it up, the others wouldn't have anything to eat. You
wanted other people to like what you'd done and sometimes
someone would call it a load of muck – which really upset
me,' was a comment from Martin reflecting on his year at
the school.

Apart from lunchtime, Alec was generally 'high' and unpredictable in mood and behaviour. His flashpoint was

always much lower than the others and memory and concentration were both very weak.   The others accommodated his fickleness surprisingly well and were used to Alec flaring up or making a decision only to change his mind a few minutes later.   In one sense confrontation with Alec was inevitably frequent, because the decision agreed by the group that a commitment made by them must be honoured put him in an awkward position, given his tendency to change his mind at whim.   But with Alec like the others we tried to be consistent.   From the point of view of the students, who only joined us once a week and planned the following week's session before parting, this consistency was essential to honour commitments.   The following incident illustrates the point.

One Thursday Alec had arranged to go climbing with Lester and Matthew, a student.

Matthew had promised to collect the gear and meet them at school at 10.30.

At 9.30 Alec was in early and found Hilary on her own.

'I ain't going climbing – I'm going to play snooker.'

'But you arranged it with Matt – he'll be here with the ropes and stuff soon.'

'Bugger that – I don't want to go.'

'But you've agreed – Matt's gone to a lot of trouble to collect the stuff.'

'I ain't going.'

At that moment I arrived.

'Rog, I ain't going climbing – I want to do snooker instead.'

'Hadn't you arranged it all with Matt?   I thought he'd promised to collect the stuff?'

'Yeah, but I don't want to go.'

'You did arrange it then?'

'Yeah, but that was last week – I don't feel interested now.'

'But you've agreed – Matt's gone to a lot of trouble to collect the stuff.'

This apparent collusion was all too much for Alec who stormed out of the room banging the door.

Lester came in at that moment.

'What's up with Alec? – he just shouted "fuck off" at me as he walked past.'

We explained why Lester would be climbing on his own that day, so he made himself a cup of coffee and sat waiting for Matthew.

At 10.30 Matt arrived, with ropes and hooks hung professionally round his neck. Behind him followed Alec carrying
helmets and boots. We didn't say a word.

Matt told us later how they'd spent the whole day clinging
to the cliff face of the gorge. Alec had been the perfect
pupil, listening and watching and taking it in.

He very much needed instant success though, presumably
because any delay raised doubts in his mind about his possible achievement. Yet throughout that term he remained
friends with most of the boys – though the intensity of the
friendships fluctuated daily. It was quite common for him
to arrange to meet with some of the others in the evening –
Clive and Lester and Dirk all joined him at local disco night-
spots several times.

The one boy he never seemed to mix with was Jim, who on
more than one occasion referred to Alec as 'plain daft'.
Like the rest he tolerated Alec's moodiness – which was in
direct contrast to his own reliability. It was Jim whom
Clive regarded as a threat to leadership, though in fact Jim
never asserted himself like that aggressively. It was quite
remarkable how he could have a calming influence when
things got heated – without resorting to anything more than a
sharp word or humorous smile. Despite the continuous
drinking bouts under his Dad's 'watchful eye', Jim usually
arrived on time. When late, he resisted questioning, as if
such interrogation was an affront to his professed commitment to the school. 'If I'm not here, it's for a good
reason,' summed up his feeling. And there were many times
when he had good reason, since his Dad was often tempting
him away to 'help on a job' or one of his brothers needed
'help with a car' or 'his mate called round'. Despite all
this he missed only three days that Christmas term and was
an invaluable catalyst for many group activities, very willing to help the others with their own projects, like Clive
with his speakers, or Martin with his bikes, and quite prepared to try his hand at anything 'creative' from craft work
to art work, from metal work to mechanics, from woodwork
to glazing. His enthusiasm inspired the others. Once Jim
had begun a project, he would pursue it to its conclusion,
preferring to finish things rather than break for lunch or
postpone completion for another day. Coffee tables, rustic
benches, art work had to be finished the day he started, and
he'd only begin if that target seemed reasonably assured at
the outset. His assessment report had described him as 'of
low academic ability, but good with his hands'. The latter

was certainly true and the former a quite inaccurate assessment of frustrated potential. Jim was extremely bad at
maths and English – and clearly there was no way he could
have achieved anything in print–dominated subjects at
school. But, within his ability, the standard he set for
himself was very high, and in writing the diary he needed to
have someone close by to whom he could refer when uncertain of his spelling.

'I w... – come on. How do you spell it?'
'Went? Like it sounds E–N–T.'
'To T–O– right?'
'Yes.'
'The ... club.'
'Yes.'
'With ... H – hey, Howard, how do you spell your bleed-
ing name?'
'Two FFs you dozy git....'
Finally he'd completed his sentence.

Concern at presenting their written work neatly was unanimous. None of them were happy about sending a letter
which contained crossings out or spelling mistakes and all
were very critical of their own efforts. Sadly, though they
knew what standard they wanted to reach, few of them, apart
from Joy and Liz, would ever achieve something that satisfied themselves – which was yet one more reason for their
unwillingness to have a go.

But in discussion Jim was a master of the laconic word.
In the morning, before 'school' started (a deadline Jim made
by seconds, as Great George chimed ten down the hill) and
at lunchtime, spontaneous discussions would develop –
usually when drinking coffee after the food and before
starting the afternoon programme. This presented an excellent teaching opportunity and needed careful tuning between us. We'd abandoned our original idea of trying to
channel the conversation in predetermined directions and
instead just tried to alert to possibilities presented by the
general drift of conversation. Our aim wasn't necessarily
to feed in factual information, but more to act as catalysts
for reflective and discursive thinking.

In terms of preparation outside the work with the group,
there is little of the formal subject structuring and marking
that is a feature of the life of most secondary school
teachers. Our preparation is less obvious, and relies on
mental alertness and co-ordination between the staff. In
discussion apart from the kids, we chew over problems and

work out possible solutions or strategies: who will tackle so
and so over that issue? What will be our common approach
on this topic? How do we intend to introduce these plans?
And so on. At the level at which we operate, strategies
and co-ordination are of more value than factual preparation, since the fluidity of the learning situation may negate
such pre-planning. Our emphasis in educational terms is
on learning by doing and participating, which requires an
alertness of mind amongst the staff to enable them to capit-
alise on situations as they arise.

Our input to the general conversation might be just an odd
sentence here and there like 'Yes, OK, but what would
happen if ...?' 'Maybe Joy would feel differently, given
her own interest in....' 'How long could you go on doing
that before...?' And so on.

The following is just a recorded extract from one lunchtime conversation:

Liz: The other thing I don't think is important is school
uniform. As long as you go that's what matters.
Some mothers like mine, couldn't afford it.

Us: What are the arguments in favour of school uniform?

Liz: It's supposed to hide the fact that some people are
poor.

Lester: Did you hear about the girl in the paper whose
school uniform cost £84? She did jumble sales and
raised £40 and Prince Charles gave her the rest.

Liz: I think what's silly is having to do things like wear different shirts for hockey and tennis and PE. I think
that makes people like me more resentful.

Alec: I don't like rules about having to wear a tie.

Lester: Yeah, if you have to wear a tie, why can't you wear
one you'd wear out at night? I suppose one good
thing about uniform is that you'd get certain people
like Punk Rockers turning up in their gear and I
can't stand Punk Rock!

Clive: Pass your plate if you want a piece of pie.

Sometimes conversation grew fretful, like the endless
debate about whose turn it was to go driving. The system
was organised on a rotational basis, two or three in turn
each week, planned so that everyone interested would have
an equal share. But since people were ill or late or absent
for other reasons, the rota was often no more than a symbol-
ic gesture and it was not always very clear about whose turn
it really was. On one occasion Joy, who'd been away for
two days, turned up at lunchtime just before the lesson

started – intending to join in the activity. But in her ab-
sence that morning the boys had agreed their own nominees.
'Clive's going in your place today,' explained Lester.
'But it's my turn and Clive went last week,' Joy retorted.
'No I didn't I was down the docks, don't you remember.'
'Oh yes, but that's your fault – you didn't have to go did
you?' said Joy quite correctly.
'Well, you should have been earlier if you wanted to go –
you can't just come in when you feel like it you know. It's
not a bloody doss-house,' this from Clive.
'Hark at 'im'. Who was away on Monday with a hangover?'
'At least I phoned in – which is more than you ever do,'
retorted Clive.
Joy turned to us. 'Can't I go driving?'she pleaded.
'Well Joy, you haven't been here all week and Lester and
Match and Clive are all prepared to go now.'
'That's not fair – just because I've not been well, you're
taking it out on me.'
'Well, if you came more often, you wouldn't be left out
would you?' said Kevin.
'But it's MY turn,' Joy stamped her feet.
'No it's NOT.'
'It is.'
'You're fucking well not going.'
Jim banged on the table. 'LOOK 'ERE – THEM THREE'S
GOING TODAY. YOU CAN GO NEXT WEEK AND THAT'S
THAT.'
There was no more argument and Joy spent the afternoon
doing maths.
Driving was an activity that all of them wanted to have a
go at, and though a pecking order of proficiency was quickly established they did allow each other fair shares on the
afternoons they practised with the student. Occasionally
in the playground outside they would practise manoeuvring
the bus round obstacles. Martin, who'd never touched a
steering wheel before, was predictably the least confident
and tended to take the whole thing more seriously than the
rest, swatting up on his Highway Code to fulfil the agreed
prerequisite of going out driving. 'But I get scared driving the bus,' he volunteered once. 'I'd rather just stick to
the car, if you don't mind.' Though probably not the least
confident in other things, he appeared to be because he
would more readily admit his lack of expertise or knowledge.
For example, at the field when the others were riding, he
actually articulated his unwillingness to 'have a go', pre-

ferring to plan an organised ride under instruction. Being
noticeably smaller and less mature than the rest he tended
to be the outsider, and in the beginning had allied himself to
Clive as his sidekick. But whereas many youngsters in
that situation (being the odd one out of a small group) would
have become the butt for group teasing and ridicule, that
never happened in Martin's case. Perhaps it was a reflection on the group themselves, that they regarded Match as
part of it and accepted his immaturity. Or maybe they were
just impressed by his prowess in non-physical ways - like
his regularity of attendance, his commitment to improving
his academic standard, particularly in the numeracy and
literacy field, and his enthusiasm to try new activities -
under the right conditions of safety and supervision. In
some ways, he was more mature than his physical elders,
because he was less inclined to be distracted from his selected goals into the sort of aimless inactivity that characterised many afternoons for one or two. Nevertheless he
adopted smoking and swearing as regular habits and was
pleased to be accepted as 'grown-up' by the others and the
students. Getting into an X film shortly before term ended
was a milepost in developing his self-confidence. Apart
from that one occasion though, Martin never saw the others
away from school, and a lot of his activities were fairly
solitary, like going fishing, or doing up bicycles, or making
some speakers. Martin wanted to 'get on with things', and
though attracted to being 'one of the boys' he managed to
maintain a healthy balance between 'clowning around' and
pursuing his own interests. His perception of the value of
such schools as ours presented an interesting perspective:
'You know this place isn't suitable for disruptive kids.
The ones who really need it are those who aren't getting
on at school because of disruptive kids. I think schools
should be tougher on the big kids who set on little people
like me. You get fed up being picked on, so you stay
away from school and then the law picks on you. But it's
not really your fault; it's the fault of the people making
you stay away.'
Amongst the girls, though there was no obvious loner, the
friendships between them were more fragmentary - apart
from the tie between Joy and Debbie, which threatened to
distance them completely from the rest of the group. Their
attendance had been erratic since the start of term, so when
this pattern continued into November we felt we had to make
a decision about their continuing on the roll. Debbie was

the more flighty of the two and never seemed particularly
interested in much that we had to offer – except the warmth
and companionship. Her experiences outside the school –
at clubs and discos, and with boyfriends and work – were
so completely different and removed from the atmosphere of
the school, and bore so little relation to what we considered
important, that it was perhaps inevitable that she should
fall by the wayside. The boys, as a whole, were unanimous
in their censure of both Joy and Debbie's lateness.
'Kick 'em out.'
'If they wanted to get here they would.'
'Give the place to someone else.'
In an effort to pull them into the group, we leant heavily
down on them to join us in a proposed visit to London. For
the two of them it wasn't so much a choice as a final ultima-
tum. Either they came to us, joined in the group, and gave
something, or they may as well leave and we'd give their
place to someone who would actually use it.
This London visit, planned for the end of November, became a focal point for group interest. Mention of it had
been met with varying degrees of enthusiasm – depending
largely on the day of the week we brought it up. We found
that the beginning of the week was always a bad time for
planning or discussion. Any talk at those times was usually
directed to Hilary or me, not amongst themselves; which
nearly always made the idea of a group discussion quite unworkable. So our planning for the week devolved to Fridays – a time when people were generally more relaxed and
secure. It was then that they drew up their individual
timetables for the following week.
On several Fridays when we'd mentioned London the response was unanimously enthusiastic, with numerous suggestions about what we could do. But by Monday there would
always be one or two who had changed their minds.
'I can't come to London, because me Mum'll need me to
babysit that night....'
'Couldn't she get someone else in? Just for once? It'd
be a shame for you to miss the trip.'
'Well maybe ... what day is it we're going...?'
'I shan't be able to get the money for that trip' – this from
Debbie, who earned £9.00 doing her part-time cleaning and
who spent a third of it on cigarettes. 'My mum says if I
want some new shoes I'll have to buy 'em meself.'
'How about putting some money aside each week then – say
75 pence? Then in four weeks you'll have enough. If you
don't want to go that's different.'

'Oh, I want to go - but I need some new shoes you see -
and that'll cost £20.'

In truth, they all did want to go, and it's hard to understand and penetrate the barriers they often put up. But to
go to a strange city (for most a foreign city) by a strange
mode of transport (four had never been on a train) to meet
strange people (the idea was to visit another school similar
to our own) is asking a bit much from youngsters whose experience of anything 'new' is characteristically one of failure. 'I'll try anything once' may be an apt motto for our
public school breed of confident leaders, but is an ill-fit-
ting tag round the necks of many of our group.

This unwillingness to risk and explore is an endemic
attitude amongst our kids. How much of it is due to lack of
satisfaction of basic needs, as described by Fleming and
discussed in the previous chapter, is hard to say. Certainly they are more likely to come once they know and trust
us - which suggests a lack of security and need for acceptance. And of course, acceptance is the key to our
approach. We take them as they are - as the individuals
that arrive - with their deficiencies and failings and irritating habits. Criticism is a tool we never use with new arri-
vals. There is no point, until there is some feeling of
trust and acceptance.

The girl who came one year with a hare lip was a case in
point. Her experience at school and at home was of ridicule and mockery, with her family as well as her school-
mates taunting her for her scarred mouth. In point of fact
it was only a tiny hairline fracture of her upper lip, but to
Sandra it must have felt a mile wide. She had stopped
going to school, and would only go out very occasionally
with the few friends she trusted. Boyfriends for her were
mere fantasies of the imagination. She came to us very un-
willingly, aware that the alternative was residential placement away from home. We were probably the lesser of the
two evils. In conversation she would always cover her
mouth with her hand, a habitual gesture that persisted for
months. She refused point blank to eat with the rest. We
couldn't ignore the issue, though we had previously ignored
her disfigurement. It had to be talked through. Six
months later Sandra no longer covered her mouth when
speaking, always sat with us at lunch, and her tales of
nights out with boyfriends at least contained some elements
of truth. She left us determined to join the Navy - and
though she never realised her ambition, at least she had
gathered confidence enough to try.

For the group in the year described here there were many
Sandras, whose experience of new situations had been one
of the persistent failure or rejection, so that to 'go away'
was a risk they were basically unwilling to take.

But since the Wales trip had foundered for most of them
earlier that term, we were determined to try and repeat that
experience before term finished, and a visit to London to
bring them together as a group beforehand seemed a good
idea.

The difficulties of organising such a trip are always worth
the trouble. It's not necessarily the case that everyone is
starry-eyed about visiting London – the capital, where 'it
all happens'. The trouble is that the few who aren't interested tend to act as a damper to enthusiasm for the others.
The result is often a see-sawing of commitment, depending
on mood and inclination in the days before the visit. Two
things cement their determination to go: the first is when
they've paid something towards the fare, the second is when
they've done something towards the preparations, like
writing letters or finding out what's on, or making food for
the journey or spending a morning looking at maps of London
and thinking about possible places to go.

Of course, once on the train to the metropolis itself, they
are alone and isolated except for each other; and unsuppor-
ted by the recognisable props of their own city, they inevitably draw together as a group, which is a large point of the
trip.

We had arranged to visit a school near Whitechapel run
along similar lines to our own. The hope was that the
pupils there would host us round their area and then come
back with us to the centre of London for a sightseeing tour.

We went by train. Only Judy didn't come. It may have
been slightly cheaper by minibus or coach (though British
Rail school group concessions of £2.20 per head in 1979 for
a party ticket seem excellent value compared to the £8.00
plus for an ordinary day return) but no other form of transport offers quite the same style. Trains provide such a
relaxed and excellent opportunity for talking, playing games
and planning. The only drawback is that the buffet car is
often staffed by stewards who couldn't care less whether
their clients are under age or not. Predictably, within
minutes of leaving the station, Dirk and Clive had 'disappeared' towards the other end of the train. Five minutes
later they returned. Dirk looked rather irritated and came
straight up to me.

'He won't serve us,' he snapped.

'Really — well, you can't blame him, you are under age after all.'

'He would have — except that you'd told him not to as soon as we got on!'

I had to laugh. Dirk was quite right and I explained my reasons. Previous experience had shown me that not everyone could cope with the effect of a drink on the way up, and that for some it had completely ruined their day. It made people irritable or depressed or tired — none of which was beneficial to a day in London. Though maybe Dirk could 'take his drink' there were bound to be some in the group who coudln't.

He saw the point. 'Mean bugger' — but his smile belied the force of the words.

Actually, drinking is one of the most serious and difficult problems we have to contend with on visits or camps. There is a conflict between wanting to give kids responsibility and freedom, and knowing that in some cases that will be seen as licence to drink. It is important to adolescents to be able to drink; not surprisingly since the emphasis through media presentation is on the virility symbol of downing pints. But we know that for many drinking will create awkward, aggressive youngsters — who will consequently spoil the visit or camp for themselves and others. Quite honestly we would like to agree a rule not to drink — not from any puritan temperance, but because its effects are unpredictable and often uncomfortable. There is a contradiction though in saying to youngsters 'we are going to treat you as adults', and then, at the point where they want to engage in what they regard as the most adult of activities (apart from sex), applying sanctions to stop them. The only solution really would be to reach a situation where they agreed amongst themselves not to drink — and were prepared to police that decision. That requires a lot of trust and security.

At Whitechapel we arrived as lunch was being served. In the basement of a large Victorian mansion the school occupied three or four cellar-like rooms, one of which could be temporarily transferred into a dining room.

Hesitantly our group shuffled in from the staircase and took places at one end of the dining room — quite removed from the other group.

'Don't like this place ... rubbish, boring ... let's go home.' The mutters were barely audible. It was a good

quarter of an hour before there was any hint of possible integration – sparked off by a suggested visit to Petticoat
Lane. Jim, Clive and Liz remained behind – Clive to compare tattooes with an unsmiling boy of the same age. The
conversation soon broadened to a comparison of 'their
school and our school' and what they did and what we did.
    'What time do you start?'
    '9.30.'
    'Same as us.'
    'Do you do English and maths?'
    'Every morning.'
    'Oh, we only has it twice a week.'
    'Do you cook your own dinner?'
    'No – we get it on wheels – horrible.'
    'Oh, we does our own – it's good – except when Rog is
doing the pastry!'
    The similarities were quite surprising, but what was
noticeable was the greater cohesion of their group – due in
part no doubt to the community orientation and catchment of
the school.
    Later we joined the rest on a tube ride to Trafalgar
Square. By now the girls had already arranged to put up
some of the Londoners if they came to Bristol before
Christmas.
    As always the pigeons were a source of fascination.
Every city has its pigeons, but only those in London know
where there's free food any time any day.
    Squeals and cries of terror as Joy was buried beneath a
cloud of feathers. Pigeons fluttered and clung to her afro
hair.
    'Take a picture, Jim – go on,' the group urged. Jim,
who was carrying the camera, had earned himself the role
of official photographer.
    He captured the highlights of the day on celluloid – the
visit to Whitechapel, Trafalgar Square, the 'tourist trek'
down Whitehall, Downing Street, Houses of Parliament.
The names on the Monopoly board came to life, Picadilly,
Leicester Square, Oxford Street, Park Lane, The Strand.
    'Where's the Vine?'
    '– or Old Kent Road?'
    'We'll show you on the map on the train.'
    The day passed quickly – hamburgers and coffee, sand-
wiches and cans of coke and they just caught the 6.00 train
from Paddington.
    In the corridor, Clive was furtively hiding something
under his jacket.

'What's that - beer?' I asked, suspicious as always.

A smile, and he opened his jacket to display a bundle of ruffled feathers; it squeaked and fluttered to escape.

'Quiet, quiet.' Gently he stroked the nape of its neck and the pigeon relaxed in his hand.

He let it go before we were out of London. It headed straight back towards Trafalgar Square.

The mood at 'school' was noticeably lighter the rest of the week. Next day the talk centred around the events in London.

'Did you see me when....'

'Wasn't it funny that....'

'Good crack in Trafalgar Square.'

'What about that mile-long queue of taxis in Oxford Street?'

Our follow-up to this in structured terms was a quiz-type questionnaire about the city - using maps and timetables as resources. Only Debbie, who hadn't turned up since the trip itself, didn't join in. Even Judy, who had been subjected to embellished accounts of the day's events and must have felt quite envious of the others' good fortune, was keen to do it.

The point was not to find out how much they'd gleaned about London's history or geography - it was much more an attempt to pinpoint the visit in their memories by concrete reference to place names and areas that they'd visited, which were represented on the map sheets in front of them.

Their general ignorance was saddening. Of course ignorance is a subjective word, but in this case it meant ignorance of basic knowledbe about 'how to get around' and what aid a map can be; what schools would call geography. But their starting point was pitiful. What the hell can Scotland or holidaying abroad mean if you don't even know which way to go?

Perhaps it doesn't matter. We know that after the visit to Wales before term ended, when they'd spent four days in a 'foreign' country, there were still one or two who couldn't pinpoint it on a map or even describe which way we drove from Bristol. And it was the same with the London trip. Only half of them could remember which town the train had stopped at first after leaving Bristol.

The really worrying thing is that there must be many kids who go through school without teachers being aware of their fundamental knowledge gaps.

That day was Debbie's swan song. She appeared two

days after that and stayed for a brief chat with Hilary –
mostly to tell her that she wasn't pregnant after all as she'd
feared for the last three weeks – then disappeared. The
following Monday she rang to say she'd got a dental appointment. Four days later her friend Joy rang to tell us she'd
seen Debbie and thought she was now 'on the streets'.

That evening Hil and I talked about Debbie and Joy. With
Debbie the situation seemed hopeless, but maybe with Joy
there was still a chance. In both cases, though, our situation had not geared itself to their level of maturity.
School for either of them had very little relevance – much
less so than for the others, who were still partially imbued
with ideas about the usefulness of practising reading and
writing, for instance. Debbie, particularly, didn't care at
all. Living was her only concern and that meant preoccupation with boyfriends, discos, clothes and her Mum. For a
girl like Debbie, the childlike atmosphere of comprehensive
school – with uniforms and Miss this and Sir that and rules
about smoking and two lessons of PE a week in gymslip is
quite ridiculous. If childhood is a buried memory for whatever reason, such an approach can never work. Debbie
had adult aspirations, and, however ill-equipped, was eager
for them to be accepted as such. In her case the twilight
world of adolescence where decisions are made about you
and around you but without you – was quite irrelevant.

After much hard thinking we agreed to use Debbie as an
example – something we had never done before – but our
hope was that if we handled it right we could draw Joy back
into the group.

Next day, they were all at the school, except Debbie.
We explained our decision that if Debbie wasn't going to
make use of her place then we were going to offer it to
someone else. She would be given one last chance. Hil
was to go and see her and discuss our attitude and the ulti-
matum would be that either she came every day for the rest
of the term, or she'd be out. We couldn't work any other
way. There was general assent from the group, though Joy
was noticeably silent.

Hil visited the next morning, shortly before lunch. Persistent knocking aroused Debbie from her bed. The conversation was depressingly predictable – supplemented by
pointed comments from Mum. Yes, Debbie was staying in
bed all day and going out at night. Yes, she had lost her
cleaning job. But that didn't matter. She was all right
for money and she didn't care whether she came to us or
not. Nor did Mum it seemed.

We agreed to 'give up' with Debbie, but tried to do three things we thought might help her. One was to ensure that there would be no further prosecution for non-school atten- dance, which would just have been an unnecessary aggrava- tion; the second was to request her social worker to main- tain a regular involvement with the girl; and the third was to recommend formally that the care order on Debbie be in- voked to give her a place in a hostel away from home, where supervision may have been more beneficial for her. Unfor- tunately her care order had expired two weeks previously and there was nothing anyone could do.

Our first obvious failure.

But the effect on Joy of Debbie's 'expulsion' (which was nothing more than our acceptance of the status quo) was quite marked.

Both girls had come to London, but whereas it had been Debbie's swan song, for Joy it was a turning point in her involvement. We'd 'talked' to both girls explaining our feelings and the alternatives open to them. Debbie had taken no notice, but with Joy it had an opposite effect.

Between then and the end of term a month away she missed only three days, which for a girl who'd regularly absented herself two or three days a week beforehand was quite a turn round. More importantly perhaps, from her point of view, she arrived early enough in the morning to be part of the chat session. The rest of the group were positive in helping to draw her back in. The real turning point was marked by a conversation the week before our final fling – the camp in Wales.

Joy hadn't turned up that morning and over lunch we were discussing the finances of the camp – who could pay what. It was well known that Joy had problems at home getting cash. Hil and I explained what we felt; that it seemed im- portant that everyone came on the camp, and if someone genuinely couldn't afford it we were prepared to subsidise individuals. What did they think, was that fair?

'Well my parents are all right for money, so I can pay,' said Alec.

'So's mine,' said Liz. 'I think it's right for you to pay for those who can't.'

At that moment Joy walked in. Inevitably there were witty comments.

'Sun rises earlier 'ere than Jamaica.'

'You ought to do them adverts for Dunlopillos.'

A month ago Joy would have retorted in kind, or flared up

in anger and provoked an argument. She said nothing,
just smiled and apologised for being late. She then looked
at the pie in the centre of the table that Tim was carefully
portioning out.

'Can I have some lunch?' she asked plaintively.

Alec blustered a reply, but Lester cut him short.

'Course there'll be enough for you.' And there was.

Next day she came in and worked at her maths for four
hours, with a short break for lunch.

In many ways her situation had been synonymous with
Debbie's: living with a Mum who was separated from Dad,
and the Mum being involved with her own fluctuating relationships. Both girls had very involved relationships of their
own and a demanding social life to cope with in consequence.
Both girls were attractive and intelligent. Yet Joy stayed
and Debbie didn't.

The concern of the others – particularly the boys (even
Clive who was a self-confessed racialist) was very moving.
Their co-operation in trying to draw Joy back into the group
was a good measure of collective responsibility. They reacted in the same way towards Judy.

From the day she'd started with us, shortly before half
term, Judy's attendance had been very erratic. There
were many reasons. As a late arrival, the 'group' was already formed so she had to adapt to us rather than the
other way round, and, though Lester and Dirk had the same
problem they coped with it much better. Judy was very
quiet and amenable superficially but this exterior concealed
a sullen wilfulness that had been one of the traits school had
been unable to cope with. Demure was an appropriate adjective. Being the most attractive of the girls, she soon
drew the boys towards her, but there was a tragic aura
surrounding her that seemed to prevent anyone from getting
really close. Home was a mess. Dad was on the point of
leaving and Judy never knew whether she'd arrive back in
the evening to find him still there. Coupled with her
mother's demands on Judy to look after the younger children,
there was little encouragement to make the hour-long journey
from her rural outpost into the city.

When she did arrive she joined in willingly, and we always
had the feeling that if only the school had been more accessible for Judy we could have tapped some of the obvious
latent potential. She would readily work at English and
maths with everyone else (subjects in which she matched
Joy's performance) and would often spend whole afternoons
sewing dresses or toys, or patterns from fabric.

But Judy demonstrated the impossibility of attempting an educational programme that doesn't take into account the home situation. Occasionally she would arrive with her little brother when her Mum had left her with the responsibility of babysitting. There was no way Judy could really 'learn' anything with us whilst surrounded by such tensions at home.

The day before the London trip, which she'd always expressed a keen wish to join, she came in very weepy.

'Dad's leaving home.' For some time he'd been involved with another woman and had been at best an intermittent visitor in his own home. Judy's Mum had always hoped it would 'blow over'. It seemed now he'd reached the point of decision. Maybe he'd have gone by the time she returned. Hilary went back with Judy that night to talk with her parents. Her concern was for Judy and what effect the marital mess was having on her. Dad refused to talk – rudely cold-shouldering a person he saw as another 'interfering social worker ... or teacher ... one of that sort'. It was a depressing visit. Hilary came away feeling that neither parent seemed really concerned about their responsibility for their children. Before she left she urged Judy to come the next day, sincerely believing a day away in London with the group would be good for her. But she knew there was little chance of Judy coming, and she was right.

Next morning Judy's mother phoned. Things were still unresolved and Judy wouldn't be in till later that week.

On Friday both Mum and Judy arrived after lunch, the latter very tearful, but Mum apparently sure that 'everything's been sorted out' and 'of course I'll see Judy gets here next week'. She didn't of course.

To complicate the whole affair, Judy was involved as a witness in a court case that necessitated police interviews and statements and attendance at court itself. For her, life was a mess.

And yet the group supported her. Perhaps it was partly because she was an attractive girl, but that apart, she did give a lot to the group on the days she came. Whatever the reason, some of the boys were concerned enough to visit Judy at home with Hilary. As the end of term drew near and plans were made for the Wales camp, it was clear to everyone that Judy was unlikely to come unless someone made a real effort to involve her. Clive and Lester went with Hilary to see her at home.

'If she doesn't come, she'll feel even more left out' (Lester).

'It's difficult though, leaving home if things are bad -
she'll just worry' (Clive).

Both boys knew how complicated was the home situation,
and they spent several hours at her house talking with Judy.

Though Judy didn't in fact come on the camp their effort
certainly wasn't wasted, since she managed a more regular
attendance the following term, and became more involved in
sharing activities with Liz.

Liz herself was the only girl who had become one of the
'group', and though she had her own problems at home, she
only missed two days in that first term. She gave a lot -
both in terms of a model to the others, as her attitudes to
school work and activities and job-finding were very positive - but also as a kind of mother to the boys. It was Liz
who'd step in to make tea or wash up if no one else would,
and though we hesitated to accept this, since it allowed
many of the boys to hid behind entrenched chauvinist attitudes, it certainly made for smooth running some days.

Tom Lehrer's quote 'life is like a sewer - what you get out
of it depends on what you put into it', summed up Liz's involvement with the group. She gave them a lot and was
ready to involve herself in anything, from coming to the
field with the boys ('Will it hurt the horse?' she'd said to
Clive, who'd gallantly offered her a place behind him on the
captured steed) to doing photography with Jim or Joy or anyone else interested, to redecorating the kitchen wall with
Judy in an attempt to cover the scribbled graffiti, to making
sweets as a present fro the group, to writing out the whole
diary in a legible way for others to read, to acting as a
spokesman to visitors about the strengths of the unit....
This last was a significant event.

Our 'school' was the only one of its kind in the county and
inevitably there was interest from the 'powers that be' to
see how well it worked and if there were any pointers for
development, since the number of potential candidates was
far in excess of the handful we had taken. (At that time
there were very serious discussions about setting up 'sus-
pension units' to cater for the very disruptive pupils that no
school would take.) The Chief EWO and Senior Adviser
visited one morning and talked to everyone. That is important. The kids must be involved in this process: it is all
very well for us as middle-class teachers to express our
rationale for why and how it works and what are the implications, but only the youngsters can say whey they individually reacted against school and what it is that attracts
them to us.

And of course comments varied tremendously from Liz's 'The atmosphere's different; you're treated as adults. In school it's sit down and start work and do as you're told – but here you talk more about what everyone wants to do,' to Lester's 'It's friendly here – you know one another. Schools are too big and they split up friends,' to Jim's 'It gives you a chance to think. For once it's somewhere you want to come; it's nice and if you've got problems there's someone who cares. If you're in trouble you can come here,' to Clive's 'It's OK – you can do what you want when you're in the mood, without having to stop and change every half hour.'

But they gave their opinions and maybe it had some effect, since the structure of the unit has been copied in planning the establishment of three centres for disruptive pupils. If only the form can be replicated as well, in terms of how it is approached, not what is approached, they stand a chance of succeeding.

It is the way that the 'curriculum' is agreed on that is crucial, not the content. The kids must feel part of the decision-making process. There must be room for their participation.

The Monday before we left for Wales, I arrived from a meeting to find all the group sitting huddled round the one heater. It was clear something was wrong.

'Clive's dog been run over.'

'Dead?'

Clive nods. 'Last night. I was walking home from the park, when this lorry came hurtling past, close to the roadside. I was on the pavement and I had Rex on a lead, but he was sniffing in the gutter and before I could pull him back the lorry had hit him. I carried him home but he was dead.' Clive's calmness and self-control was very impressive, but he was obviously upset and angry, and in need of support.

It was at times like this that the kids proved their previous labels so confoundedly inappropriate. The failures, the truants, the under-achievers, the school phobics, the hooligans, the maladjusted and the irresponsible were all huddled round the heater – eight people whom it wasn't worth bothering about.

Liz stretched her arm round Clive's shoulder. It was obvious he was close to tears. There was a silence, long and sympathetic, finally broken by Liz herself.

'Clive, shall we go to the Dog's Home?'

He looked at her through misty eyes, quite unembarrassed
by the depths of emotion.
'Maybe I'll find another collie.'
'Will you dirve us down?' asked Lester, who'd not said
anything till now.   'We could all go in the minibus.'
'If that's what Clive wants to do.'
Clive nodded.   'They can help me choose.'
Of all the group Clive was the most interested in animals
and very much wanted a job working with them.   The summer
before he'd helped out at a local Wildlife Park – eight hours
a day for five days a week, without any reward except the
very real pleasure for him of just being with animals.   'I
didn't do it for the money you see.'   He'd been enthusiastic
about a suggestion to try the zoo for a possible job and we
kept it near the front of our thoughts when thinking about
possible work experience placements.

The fortnight that followed the London visit was a productive period.   Their journey to London seemed to have gelled
their willingness to co-operate.   They were noticeably more
sympathetic and supportive of each others' needs.   Whereas
before, incidents like the playing of the radio at times when
some were trying to concentrate on letter-writing or balancing the petty cash book were commonplace, it felt as if
these were things of the past.

They worked together – at 'school' work, at cooking, at
planning the trip to Wales for which all of them (except Judy)
had already paid a contribution.   There was none of the uncertainty that had torpedoed the previous Wales expedition.
When Helen, a girl from the year before, visited the group
and stayed for lunch, she commented in amazement on all the
activity – 'All our lot did was sit around and smoke fags....'
What impressed Helen most was the spirit of co-operation
that contrasted vividly with the bickering and backbiting the
previous year.   It was evidenced in various ways: from
the sharing of projects, like Clive and Dirk who that day
were working on making a mosaic pattern for Dirk's girlfriend's birthday; and Lester and Liz who were cooking the
lunch in apparent harmony; and Martin who was putting the
finishing touches to his speaker boxes with Jim's assistance,
hampered somewhat by Jim's bruised hand.

He'd complained about it hurting for some weeks, having
bruised it in 'a punch-up' at his local.   Being terrified of
doctors he was adamant that it was 'all right' and Hil should
'quit going on about it'.   Sadly this characteristic – to
shrug off physical hurt – is only too common amongst these

youngsters. It is interesting to note that many of them, who would have clutched at any excuse to obtain a note releasing them from ordinary school, would turn up shivering with flu, or bandaged after a brawl, quite incapable of concentrating properly, but determined to be part of whatever was going on. Jim's disregard for medical treatment is a sad testimony to how some youngsters regard the 'welfare' services.

For Jim though, this particular 'accident' was potentially disastrous. Whatever job he started would most likely necessitate working with his hands, and whenever he tried to use his right hand his face would screw up with pain.

Three weeks passed before he agreed to go for an X-ray, which revealed a fracture on the mend, but slightly out of line. If Jim had gone earlier, it could have been re-set properly. Until he fractured it again, he'd have 92.6 per cent use from it - or whatever the guestimate figure was. It continued to hurt him until he left in the spring to start work 'roofing' with his Dad.

Nevertheless it didn't dampen his enthusiasm for going to Wales, and his own eagerness helped cement the commitment for the rest. For us all it was seen as the highlight to the end of term and the expectation (all-important) was that everyone would go.

In fact on the day of departure only Judy wasn't there, and given the confusion at home no one was surprised. It was one of those crystal days of December where the brilliance and promise of the day is almost hurtful.

We left after lunch: the journey to the farmhouse cottage in mid-Wales is a good four-hour journey with a half-way stop in Brecon. It's a long time - especially for kids with no sense of direction and timing who ask 'are we nearly there?' when we're passing Chepstow with 100 miles yet to travel.

Of course we map-read and play games and talk, and a four-hour journey is an excellent ice-breaker with ten people cooped up in a sardine can of a bus.

Excitement rose with the gathering dusk and voices joined in a chorus of songs as we drove through the valleys towards Lampeter with greying mountains impressively banked on either side of our oasis of evening light.

Rugby club songs with bawdy refrains are the pattern, if singing ever starts - though we try to broaden the repertoire with our well-intentioned attempts to introduce folky songs. 'Down by the Riverside' and 'Michael, row the boat

ashore' and 'The Drunken Sailor' do at least elicit unanimous involvement.   But something quite unique in our history of taking kids camping happened this time.
    After the well-known choruses of 'Three German Offi-
cers' and 'Dinah, Dinah show us your leg' had lapsed into
thoughtful silence, Clive started humming quietly to himself
- a tune none of us recognised.
    'What's that Clive?'
    'I'm not sure - "Fair Irish Lass", I think it's called.'
    'Do you know the words?'
    'Most of 'em.'
    'Can we join the chorus if you lead us?' I laughed, know-
ing from experience that the suggestion would die an embarrassed death.
    'One night in fair Larney,' he faltered for a moment and
then, drawing confidence from the darkness, continued to
sing; his voice growing louder and stronger with each line.
    It was beautfiul, though no doubt Clive himself would have
shuddered to hear such a description.   But the poignancy of
the lyrics and his melodic rich baritone brought me close to
tears.   I couldn't help but think of his school reports that
had described him as useless, and I felt angry for a moment
that at 16 such talent should go so unrecognised.   He sang
for several minutes - a love song with a sad ending.   As
his Irish lilt faded, the rest of the group broke into spontaneous applause.   Clive's teeth flashed in the half light.
'How about that one about "Blue-eyed Lilly" - you know it
Jim.'
    Jim did and the two of them shared eight verses of an
Irish ballad, leading us happily through the chorus.   In
sheer musical terms it was truly magnificent.   Both boys
had a natural ear for tune and pitch and it became evident
during the remainder of the bus journey that both knew a
very full repertoire of songs, gleaned apparently from various spells at Bristol's Assessment Centre.
    There was no doubt that by the time we arrived the har-
mony of their singing had enriched the atmosphere amongst
the group.   We drew up outside the farmhouse and the quiet
darkness closed in.
    Unloading the bus, arranging sleeping space, chopping
firewood, laying the fire and cooking supper occupied us all
until we finally sat down together round the large oak table
in front of a crackling hearth.
    It is almost platitudinous to describe the tremendous feel-
ing engendered by that shared evening in the old stone farm-

house, so very, very far removed from the centrally heated city estate homes they were used to.

We sang songs and played games and talked and no one asked where the telly was, or bothered to use the record player, conspicuously sited in the far corner of the room. It was long after midnight before we slept.

The next three days passed in a gentle whirl of activity, both individually and as a group. Clive woke early every morning to help the farmer down the road with his milking. The first day at 6.30 he sleepily refused to go and turned his face to the wall, but gentle persuasion soon won him over and the next two days he was up and away on his own leaving the rest of the group slumbering in their bunks. With his wellies and jungle hat and long 1930s-style raincoat (the sort that Christopher Robin wore when on an adventure) he looked every inch the farm labourer, and to watch him sponging the shit off the udders was to see a very different side of Clive from the urban school drop-out who'd been first charged for TDA at the age of 13.

The next day we went horse-riding. A motley crew of hats, duffle coats, cagoules and Wellington boots, cantering wildly over Welsh hills for two hours at £1.50 per head. Even Jim and Dirk, who were adamant that there was 'no way' they'd consider clambering on a horse, took courage and joined the carnival. Nine Bristol kids trotted out of the yard as a scenario for a Thelwell cartoon, and two hours later cantered in as John Wayne leading his cavalry troop. The ride dominated the talk for the rest of the day.

'Did you see me....'

'How about when....'

'What a laugh as Lester....'

That evening at midnight, after vegetable stew and a night hike, they were still re-living the high moments.

Predictably, the third day they slept late. Even adolescent energy has its limits and two late nights embracing a day of incessant activity had quite tired everyone, despite the plentiful refills of crips, Coca-Cola and other 'kek' that they, like similar groups, seem able and willing to consume in vast quantities without spoiling their appetites.

Perhaps we need to restructure our camps, because the pace for the leaders is pretty gruelling. To bed with the last and up with the first means a minimum of an eighteen-hour day 'on duty'. We tend to accept it as part of the camp – the total immersion in what the kids are doing – so that sleep and eating and activities are all shared. If our camps

were any longer we would need to take time off and have
stretches off-duty to re-charge. For four days though it
is just about possible to share everything.

Rutter's summary of the value of visits outside school is
worth mentioning:

It is joint working together over a period of time for the
same purpose, which helps to break down barriers. In
view of the conflict between staff and pupils, which to
some extent is an inevitable part of schooling, it may be
that joint activities between teachers and children outside
the classrooms may help them to appreciate the other
better and come to share some of the same goals. (6)

The last evening – apart from signs of withdrawal symptoms from those who'd run out of fags – was spent quietly
round the fire, hanging Christmas decorations, drinking
coffee, playing games, and just talking. The conversations
about living in the country, doing up old houses, farming and
living rough were interspersed with references to their own
home situations back in Bristol.

'Course,' said Liz, 'me mates would go spare if they
could see me now covered in horse-shit, draped in a grotty
duffle coat, no fags or make-up and not bothered about missing "Crossroads". I'll have to soak in a bath for a week
when I get back or me Mum won't let me in the house.'

'It's good just being away from people though,' added
Lester, 'so quiet you can really think for once. Do we need
to go back tomorrow? I'd like to stay here.'

His words nearly came true.

Next morning the crystal blue sky of the last three days
had changed to a steely grey. Swirling snow threatened to
block the road. The half-mile journey to the village to collect cereal and milk (having exhausted our supplies the night
before) took two hours and plenty of slipping and pushing and
skidding. At 10.00 there were two-foot drifts in some
places and still the snow was falling.

'Perhaps we'll be snowed in for a week,' cried Liz, glee-
ful at the thought.

Hilary and I exchanged glances and understood each
other's anxiety without needing to say a word. With no
money, no fags, no wood and no food, another day in the
farmhouse would probably stretch the fabric of harmony to
breaking point.

Hurriedly we packed up and piled into the bus and, crossing toes and fingers and clutching our mental rosaries, we
skidded through the snow to Lampeter and Llandovery till the

sanded reassurance of the A40 to Brecon crunched under our tyres.

Back in Bristol the sky was clear and blue and nowhere was there any trace of snow to be seen. It seemed quite unreal to think we'd nearly been trapped 120 miles away in the Welsh hills.

'Have a good Christmas – see you next year'. We dropped them at various homes. For the kids it was back to their mates and a night out on the town or in front of the telly. For us it was a hot bath and bed.

Chapter 6

Ancillary factors: resourcefulness, the fourth R

To describe our involvement with the group of youngsters over a term as if that was our sole preoccupation would be both sentimental and misleading. Anyone working in a similar way would understand the multitude of problems that face staff in 'Special Units', quite apart from the demands of the actual interaction with kids. The DES report on 'Behavioural Units' (1) eruditely describes the pressures, other than those at the chalkface, that the staff have to cope with: poor buildings, shortage of equipment, financial restrictions and lack of support, which all take their toll on staff energy. These difficulties are compounded by an isolation that probably represents the most significant problem of all.

The general pattern is for 'special units' to be staffed by two or three teachers (or social workers). The difference between two and three, though, is more than just a 50 per cent increase in staff/pupil ratio.

In the apparently loosely structured situation like our school at Bayswater Centre, it is very necessary to have two people 'on duty' all the time. That doesn't necessarily mean having two staff working together with the whole group: indeed the system of individual or small group work that is operated by many units precludes this possibility anyway. What it does mean is that one member of staff can concentrate on specific activities, whilst the other retains the responsibility of the 'overview'.

To give an example: we now run a weekly art session for all the group, one morning a week. The aim is that everyone will participate in some 'creative' activity. The two staff working with the group that morning divide their responsibility. One concentrates on organising the art pro-

119

gramme and the other on maintaining the 'overview'. This means that the art teacher can relax and give all her/his attention to working with individual youngsters, confident that the other member of staff is there to keep the whole session flowing smoothly – perhaps by taking aside the boy or girl who that particular morning is not committed to doing art, and whose need is something other than the prescribed activity.

Teachers in school are only too well aware of the limitations of their being both teacher and manager. The time available for personal work with individuals or small groups is very much restricted by the need to maintain overall control of the whole class. As a solitary individual leading a class of thirty children, it is pretty nigh impossible to relax to the point where personality becomes a significant factor in the teacher/learner interaction. Indeed if it is true that the important skills can only be learnt through close interaction with other people, then opportunities for teaching the really crucial things are very limited in school classrooms, because of the sparseness of the vitalising instruments – the people.

In 'Loving Us' Howard Case describes his experience in his own community school:

Our belief was, and is, that it is the education for human development begun by the parents which should be continued and enlarged, and if necessary improved by the larger community (not school) which the child enters as he goes out from his parents; and that learning is what comes out of the child's interaction with those around him; not what goes in, if anything, during a day's teaching. (2)

Where 'units' have just two members of staff, the reality of the situation necessitates them both being with the group of youngsters all the time. If the programme is a full five days a week, this means five full days with the youngsters, with no breaks during the day. In a closed situation like ours where the group arrive soon after nine and don't leave till after four, it isn't possible for the staff to retreat to a staff room for coffee breaks, or spend a lunchtime away from the school. This can be quite a strain, and is one of the peculiarities of such work that sets it apart from ordinary school teaching.

At the worst, it means there is no escape from the demands of the kids and no let-up from the responsibility of being 'on duty'. It is exactly the same situation as faces teachers taking kids camping or on extended visits of a residential nature. They are 'on call' the whole time – and it can prove a very exhausting experience, even for short periods! It also means that 'sick leave' is out, unless smitten by a really virulent infection. A cold or headache or a minor ailment that would normally qualify for time off don't really justify days away. In a large school you know your absence will be 'covered' by staff with free periods, which may be an irritating loss of preparation time for some, but is a service that you do at least provide for others in their turn – but with just two staff in the school, you know that if you're away the other will have to carry the show alone. There is no slack in the system to accommodate your absence. For a two-teacher unit this could be the most stressful factor of the job. For a three-teacher unit the idea of providing staff with time away from the group begins to become a possibility.

This time away is crucial for reasons other than stress release. The very nature of the work demands a large amount of liaison with parents and social workers or probation officers. Once you accept the social factor of the educational enterprise, it is no longer possible to exclude or ignore outside agencies, and indeed the complementary exercise nearly always proves worthwhile. It is arguable too, how effective we can be anyway, if we work in isolation from the families. If part of the reason for their disengagement with learning is rooted in domestic tension, then it is important to involve the family in the process of the school. Only their support for the enterprise will produce results; to ignore their contribution is to undermine the potential effectiveness of the work.

But it does take time to do a home visit or meet with a youngster's social worker.

There is also an argument (elaborated in Chapter 12) about the value of feeding the experience gained in special units back into mainstream education. In an article entitled Special Units for 'Socialism and Education' Mike Golby argues for the cross-fertilisation of unit staff in special units and staff in schools, through integration of unit staff on curriculum review bodies, school working parties, etc. (3)

That apart, there are obvious administrative demands of running a school. Its smallness of size doesn't diminish the number of factors that the staff have to take into account in maintaining a functional establishment. The upkeep of the building from its cleaning to its repair; the ordering and supervision of equipment and supplies; the record-

keeping of attendance and weekly and annual budgeting; the
negotiations with LEA officers over such matters as finance,
timetable alterations, referrals, and health and safety; all
require consideration that only time away from the kids can
allow.

To give an example: we have an arrangement that we cook
our own lunches. In our early days, when we were reliant
solely on our own fund-raising, we restricted our expenditure on food to £1 a day, plus whatever money the kids
could put in. The fare was nearly always bread and cheese
washed down by mugs of coffee (which became tea as prices
escalated!). With little variety in diet the group munched
their way through piles of doughy white sliced, bound in
pairs by strips of rubberoid Cheddar. But at least the
youngsters made the sandwiches themselves – though there
were always arguments about who had the 'topper'.

The first year that we were assured of LEA support for
running costs, we decided to experiment with cooking our
own meals. The problem, as every parent, or anyone who
has handled a saucepan, knows is that preparation of food is
time-consuming, and becomes expensive as the recipes
become more elaborate. School meals are by tradition
heavily subsidised, and the system of 'free' meals enables
'poor' kids to eat without paying. It has its drawbacks,
but at least it is one of the more equitable facets of English
schooling (although the administration of the system is not
always fair, according to reports circulated by the Child
Poverty Action Group). (4)

To enable us to afford to provide equivalent meals to the
'school dinner' meant us doing one of two things – either
forking out 20 or 30p a head each day from our own budget
and buying our own food from the corner shop, or taking
advantage of the school meals service for which we qualified. The former course of action would have cost us upwards of £10 a week, and since almost all the kids were in
the 'free meals' bracket the latter course was obviously to
our financial advantage. Though we would still have to
collect money from one or two in the group (which itself was
one of the biggest causes of argument on 'off' days), at
least we'd be spared the drain on our limited budget.

We decided to try the school meals service. Then came
the problems. The biggest hurdle was our decision to
become self-catering: the easy course of action would have
been to accept the 'meals on wheels' service that is provided for off-site units and small schools like our own. It

was very difficult to explain our insistence. We wanted the
group actually to participate and share in the activity, knowing from instinct and experience that mealtimes could be one
of the most significant periods in the day. Our insistence
met with one or two raised eyebrows from those who saw
such an exercise as just unnecessary interruption of the educational programme. Wouldn't we spend all morning preparing the food? Were we qualified to cook? What equipment had we?

This last question highlighted another stumbling block.
At the time we had nothing to cook on apart from a second-
hand Baby Belling. Our inventory for utensils consisted
of a few old saucepans and a dozen plates.

The cards were stacked against us ever beginning.

Fortunately, some of the people who had visited us could
testify on our behalf to the value of our meal preparation
exercise, and there was general willingness to trust our
judgment that meals on wheels were not the answer. But
how to proceed? The first suggestion proposed was for
ingredients to be delivered directly, but this would have in-
undated us with a paper work and preplanning requirement
that would certainly have swamped us, and given us a storage problem that we certainly couldn't have coped with,
being completely fridgeless! The alternative suggestion was
to attach ourselves to a local school that already handled
deliveries of food, and receive our ingredients through them.

In the event this was what we decided to try. The nearest school was a primary school half a mile away, which
meant us collecting the food at the beginning of each day, on
the way to work. It was a regular chore that involved,
understandably, a certain amount of waiting around. The
school kitchen ladies themselves were very helpful and
understanding – and without their assistance the arrangement
would have foundered pretty quickly. It was an added workload for the canteen organiser to have to see to the measuring out of separate small quantities of food for our little
gang. Since her ordering was done a fortnight in advance,
it meant us trying to give her warning of days when we'd be
out on a visit, which could sometimes be quite difficult given
the volatility of the group. Despite all those constraints,
that part of it worked well, though occasionally there were
minor disasters like when the tray of tinned tomatoes
spilled into the custard powder on the journey between the
two schools, or when the labels for salt and sugar became
confused for a rhubarb tart.

The other problem, of what to do with the food when it arrived, was harder to resolve.

A visit from the school meals organiser produced an understandable shudder at the facilities for food preparation. On every point we scored a zero. No cooker, no proper cooking utensils, no crockery, no storage space.

'This place is quite unfit for food preparation. You need a proper kitchen if you're cooking for twelve people.'

We couldn't help but agree! Yet there was no alternative. Our choice was between abandoning the idea or making do with what we'd got.

'Well, it's completely unsuitable. You'll be a breeding ground for rats and mice and goodness knows what else.'

We omitted to mention at that point the visit from the pest control officer a fortnight ago, which had resulted in two dead mice under the sink.

Though her sympathies lay with what we were doing, she was understandably unwilling to contemplate putting new equipment into such surroundings. Three days after her visit we received a consignment of concentrated washing-up liquid - which two years later we were still squeezing our way through.

For the rest of that year, on the tiny stove with its two rings and a small oven, we boiled and stewed and baked and roasted a variety of meals for the group. Our starting point was always whatever ingredients were provided by the school. Because it was a primary school, the quantities were generally woefully inadequate, and we always supplemented it with white sliced bread (and occasionally uncut wholemeal) from the local shop.

The problem of payment was never really resolved. Though most of the group qualified for free meals, there were three who should 'officially' have paid for their food. But the difficulty in collecting this money was out of all proportion to the sums involved. Whereas in schools there is a suggestion of discrimination sometimes against those on 'free meals' it worked the other way with us. The three who had to pay resented the non-payment of the others, and only one of them ever readily volunteered the cash. Nearly always it had to be cajoled out of their pockets and often the resulting arguments and moods negated the positive effects of a mealtime spent together. We tried alternative arrangements like trying to collect the money on a half-termly or monthly basis direct from the parents, but this ran into predictable difficulties when competition for payment of other bills was at its fiercest. Generally, we ended each term writing off a large slice of their contribution as 'bad debt'.

The above illustrates one aspect of the rather cumbersome administrative and liaison work that took up staff time. In this particular case it was certainly self-inflicted, but other aspects of the administrative workload like maintaining full receipted petty cash transactions, which had to be returned on a weekly or fortnightly basis, were chores imposed by the requirements of the bureaucratic system of which we were becoming a part.

The food-preparation exercise highlights a feature of such work mentioned already – that from the time the group arrive in the morning to the time they leave in the afternoon, the staff are on duty without breaks, unless they come to a clearly co-ordinated arrangement otherwise, that takes no account of the unpredictability of each day's events. With just two staff the nature of the work generally precludes the taking of time off – unless the session is highly structured. This situation is fine if the session is going well, but after a morning of recriminatory arguments, or when morale and energy are at a particularly low ebb, the stress of having to stay involved at lunchtime, knowing that the first opportunity for a break isn't till three or four o'clock, can be very draining.

It is the nature of the work of course, but the stress is compounded by lack of support from the colleagues and ancillaries that staff in a large school would take for granted. Whatever teachers in a large school might feel about some of their work-mates, there is a degree of cameraderie that defuses the stress of the job. The more tangible support features like a closed and separate staff room to retreat to, a meal service run and administered by paid ancillaries, a caretaking and cleaning back-up service, coupled with the less obvious, but no less crucial, support provided by an administrative team led by the headteacher, all ease the burden of the actual contact work with the pupils.

In small group situations like ours there is none of that. The personality of the staff has to be such that it can cope with long stretches of isolation, with support actually time-tabled for at set meetings. Without support from outside, it can sometimes be very difficult to maintain a balanced per-spective – and of course the value of discussing the work with experienced and interested people from other 'disci-plines' is tremendous. Most units have some kind of advis-ory/support team, and we are fortunate in having a group

(drawn from probation, social service, child guidance,
careers, special schools, magistrates and educational welfare and the advisory staff of the LEA) who are prepared to
meet with us regularly to appraise the work and offer advice
backed by solid experience.

The most important preparation in this sort of work is
yourself. In the fully exposed situation within which the
teacher is operating, the presentation and preservation of
self and identity is all-important. The staff's personalities
and appearance and responses are their prime teaching aids,
and these need to be refreshed and recharged for each day.
It is too easy to forget the responsibility to yourself that is
the prerequisite for anyone to work in this sort of way. It
is too easy to become so drawn into the job that you allow too
little time for re-charging.

During the period described here, we were at an interesting transition period between a state of complete independence (with concomitant financial uncertainty), and a state of
full LEA support (with concomitant restriction). The transition itself was no easy matter and required considered and
careful negotiations.

The process of substituting statutory support for private
funding is not achieved overnight. There are frustratingly
long periods between decisive meetings when nothing appears
to be happening and a feeling of isolation thickens and har-
dens. It is no use being aggressive. Those working within the system can be as frustrated by its delaying bureau-
cracy as those criticising it from the comparative freedom
beyond. It is difficult to know when to persist with requests or when to desist; when such requests are seen as
over-pushing and continued inquiry becomes counter-productive. The difficulties of this transition period can be illus-
trated by a further example.

We had begun the unit as an experiment, supported completely from our own fund-raising efforts, in a building negotiated through our own contacts. Our first base was woefully inadequate, being the crypt of an abandoned cathedral.
Its drawbacks were multitudinous - no natural lighting, no
heating and a solid silence that compounded the isolation of
all of us embedded in the womb of the empty and echoing
building above. It was dirty and despairing in its drabness,
but posters and the odd bit of scrounged carpet at least gave
an impression of cosiness. The advantages were few - it
was unoccupied and unfit for anything else.

The cathedral itself was across a courtyard from an

attached primary school, the occupants of which had recently moved to freshly built premises some miles away. The
whole primary school complex with its classrooms and
toilets and staff room and offices were abandoned and
gathering dust. Each day we would cross the courtyard
and enter the womb of the cathedral, staring longingly at
the comparative luxury of the well-lit classrooms that were
barred from us by a locked door and a few panes of glass.

The problem was that the building was unsafe - which was
one reason why the previous occupants had moved on (or at
least a reason which they'd exploited to the hilt to expedite
their own move!) Hairline cracks in some of the walls had
been detected and metal plates had been fixed at several
points to check for further movement.

We were prepared to risk it, but, since we were now partially funded by the local authority, they expressed concern
at the hazard, and were unwilling to support our moving
across the courtyard until the building had been proved
safe. They would arrange for further surveys. We
waited. Three months passed and autumn became winter
and we were no nearer our anticipated move. As dirt
solidified and our entombment period neared a year, we
became increasingly depressed by the surroundings, restless to move on and frustrated by the delay.

The empty classrooms that enjoyed light with the real
world mocked us daily as we walked past. On occasions,
because we had a key to the building, we would wander
through, making plans for our hoped-for occupancy, scru-
tinising the tiny metal plates whose hidden messages held
the clue for our future. We could see no movement. The
building seemed so incredibly solid, it was hard to believe
it was threatening to slip downhill.

December arrived and still we heard nothing.

The Monday before the Christmas term ended, five boys
in the group, who that year were particularly fractious and
irascible, came to blows. Bottles and plates and books
became handy missiles against threatening chair legs. In
the ensuing discussion, once fists had unclenched, it was
clear that the surroundings were affecting the kids as well
as us.

'It's all we're good for isn't it?' commented Royston,
who'd been suspended from school for a list of crimes that
had culminated in the final act of swearing at a senior mis-
tress. 'No one really bothers do they - we're the rubbish,
so we can live with it. Even the bloody rats give this place

a wide berth.' His last comment wasn't strictly accurate,
since an unidentified rodent had been spotted lurking behind
our box of tea bags and had been chased from the room by a
volley of darts. His comment drew unguarded support from
the others ranging from Barry's 'bloody shit-hole' to
Annette's 'it's a bit depressing - always dark and dingy'.
'Why the hell can't we move into the school?' We explained
again, aware that the reasons echoed rather hollowly in the
dingy vaults.

'Why don't we just move in, whilst they're deciding? I'd
rather slide down the hill than enjoy this living death.'
Royston rapped his shoes on the gravestone slate. It was
a feeling with which we sympathised strongly.

The day before term ended the heating in the crypt packed
up. The ancient, inefficient gas fire spluttered to its
grave.

Whether that was the last straw or not is hard to say,
since we were obviously searching for any reason at that
stage. That last day of term we spent moving our assorted
bits of second-hand equipment across the courtyard. We
notified the LEA of our squat, expressing our contrition,
and giving our reasons for the move. It elicited a prompt
meeting at which the dangers of the building slipping down
the hill were pointed out yet again.

'I'm sorry, but the alternative of staying in the crypt has
become quite unbearable. It may not actually be dangerous
in there but it's certainly unsuitable and unhealthy. Please
don't ask us to move back.'

Though the confrontation clouded our relationship with the
LEA for some months, we never regretted it. It really was
like being released from prison. Some months later our
squat was given official sanction and a degree of security.

In retrospect it seems rather insignificant. The primary
school itself was dirty, unheated and uncared for, and nothing like the kind of base we'd constructed idealised fantasies about in our mind. It was only marginally less cold
and more welcoming. The difference was psychological
more than anything else - something about being part of the
world and visible, as opposed to removed from it.

This feeling of isolation was a recurrent feature of our
early days. Now in 1980 with a building that accommodates
more groups and activities than just our own school, which
hums with people coming and going, and which echoes activity from nine in the morning till the early evening, it is
hard to remember the loneliness we began with, and the om-
nipresent feeling that no one particularly cared.

And, of course, why should they? We had after all
chosen to do the job. No one had forced us to give up
securely paid and supported teaching posts to engage in
this peripheral activity of picking up the tail-enders of the
system.
It is difficult to ignore this nagging feeling of being out of
sight and out of mind. Once the school was 'accepted' by
the LEA as a responsible project worthy of their support,
our hopes of finding suitable premises rose dramatically.
After all, we were only asking for a small house with a
garden and, as everyone in Bristol knows, there are empty
houses galore, many of them owned by the council. So the
frustration at being cooped up below ground with no feedback
from anyone that anything was happening was fairly predictable. Of course, we knew there were meetings at which
premises had been discussed, but it was all very vague.
We felt that once we'd moved across the courtyard again
we would be forgotten about till a crisis precipitated some
action from the LEA. We were quite right really. Nothing
did happen until the church, who owned the site, gave us
notice to quit, because they'd attracted another tenant in the
form of the Steiner movement. That was five terms after
our initial occupation of the premises. During that time we
were offered two alternative sites. The first was an abandoned warehouse in the twilight industrial area by the canal,
which smelt strongly of the rancid butter that had once been
stored there. A building more unlike our requested home
couldn't have been imagined! The second was suggested as
a prompt response to the crisis of our imminent evacuation.
'Can you spare an hour to look at a possible place this
afternoon?' I was asked one wet Thursday morning, two
weeks before we were due to move out. 'Next door to a
church that's being refurbished - a set of meeting rooms.
It might be all right as a temporary base.' We drove down
to the site together and parked in front of the old chapel.
A mud-spattered workman acknowledged our arrival with a
shake of his head. 'Can I help you mate?'
'Yes, we're looking for the new annexe to the church.'
He pushed his cap back on his head. 'You mean the meeting room? Yes round the back there, follow that path.'
We ducked under the scaffolding and trod gingerly across
the wobbling duckboard. Behind the church the scaffolding
gave way to a wall of breeze block. Two brickies were
laying the 56th layer. We stood in the middle of their half-
completed edifice and called up to the men above. The rain

had eased off, there was a hint of sunlight in the background.

'Where are the meeting rooms?' we asked.

The brickie pointed his trowel at the four walls, still wet
with cement. 'Should be finished in four or five months,'
he explained.

Fortunately we were able to laugh.

As a point of information it took us one more 'temporary'
move and a further year before we finally reached the
hoped-for base. Our experience is not uncommon. Working with the tail-enders, it is not surprising if the premises
offered are everyone else's cast-offs. Choice sites are
earmarked long before they actually become vacant, and
LEA officers are perhaps as powerless as anyone else to
expedite the waiting process.

So it's no use being aggressive when support isn't easily
won or given. The difficulty for staff in such units is that
they do lack the administrative and advisory support that is
a common feature of most comprehensive schools. Their
often unconventional approach, which is essential to any
success with the youngsters, can unfortunately create conflict with an LEA administration not geared to deviations
from the accepted norms of comprehensive schools. It requires a two-way effort to ensure that all the appropriate
administrative procedures are followed, at the same time
maintaining the essential flexibility of such units.

In 'In and Out of School', when describing the grind of
fund-raising for the ROSLA Project, we discussed the involvement of the LEA, and took great care to spell out the
extent of their support for the venture. At the same time
we did make an observation about how seemingly impene-
trable an LEA can often be to the outsider, and how unexplained delays can create a state of helpless frustration.
The observation was meant to be helpful, and of course is
supported by many officers and advisers themselves, who
would very much like more time for the 'human' face aspect
of their work. Yet even though the manuscript was read,
commented on and approved by the LEA before going to
press, the book in print was described in one quarter as
'downright offensive'. It is hard, when you have described
officers as 'obviously and genuinely concerned' and when
you remember the lonely frustrating months and years of
minimal support and no funding, not to retort in kind.

Perhaps we should have called in the local press at the
point where rats were destroying our meagre supply of

coffee and sugar in the dank and dismal crypt that served as our first base. Our classroom facilities at that time were certainly 'downright offensive' to the humanity of the children and staff. But newspaper headlines and abrasive criticism would only have evoked reciprocal action.

The sincere hope would be that LEA officers concerned with provision for centres like ours would be sufficiently involved actually to understand at first hand the problems faced by staff working in such areas of education. It requires a managerial approach beyond the style of the boardroom autocracy. Equally the staff need to recognise that certain administrative procedures have to exist and be followed in order for an organisation to function at a level beyond anarchy.

It does help not to precipitate confrontation, and even small things like donning a jacket for meetings is a gesture worth making. The last became something of a joke with the kids who knew that the presence of my herringbone tweed announced my imminent departure for some round-table negotiations. In actual fact it is difficult to preserve an acceptable informality with the kids, alongside the required formality of being within a system - albeit on the periphery.

This attendance at meetings is a crucial stage in the transition between voluntary and statutory status. Budgetary allocations are not decided at individual whim. At the stage described with this group, though the staff were paid by the LEA, they still had to find their own running costs. That is not a complaint, because the agreement at the time was clearly understood, but it certainly added a considerable burden to the workload. To raise £1,500 is no easy task! However in terms of links with the LEA, who work a system of corporate management, there was always a sense of individual concern. So although we knew that discussions about funding and staffing had to be made at committee level, and that the appropriate procedures would inevitably take time, we were helped by personal reassurance that we hadn't been completely forgotten.

Staff working in peripheral establishments like our Bayswater Centre are in a strange position. They certainly enjoy a degree of freedom often envied by their colleagues in larger schools. But the price of that freedom is a knowledge that every small addition, be it equipment or finance or staffing, has to be struggled for very hard. Such additions are never easily or automatically gained, and requests for increased allocation of resources must be coupled with

a level of informational feedback not demanded from the
comprehensive school. Accountability is the name of part
of the game of course, but it is of added importance for the
ongoing development of the work to keep people informed of
the day-to-day developments. That itself is a time-consuming task, but to those working in the administrative
offices, be it audit department, personnel, physical resources, building or advisory services, it makes a difference to know what is meant by the peculiar mnemonics that
describes the unit. A monthly report, or an annual journal, that circulates through the LEA office may help clear
the communication channels for the future. In an educational situation where the yardstick for success is not exam
achievement, the responsibility for establishing credibility
still lies with the staff.

Doing your own thing on your own is one tack, but is
guaranteed to cause conflict and rejected applications for
much-needed support. The argument, much vaunted by
those like the White Lion School, that such 'alternative'
schools should receive state support as a right has much to
commend it. But with our present system that right has to
be won through education committees and that process requires patience and time.

Chapter 7

Spring term

After a break of three weeks for the festive season, we were
understandably apprehensive about the first day of term.
Would the effects of last term be as skin deep as a coat of
floor polish, with a fresh application needed immediately?
Would their shyness, their level of self-confidence and their
introspection have regressed to their original levels? We
approached the first day hesitantly, preserving our own thin
veneer of confidence for the outside world.

Trepidation was unwarranted.

Everyone arrived on time and in good spirits. The first
two hours before lunch we just sat and talked, without making
any attempt to direct them into doing 'work'. It was good to
see them talking to each other about what they'd done over
Christmas.

'We had our Gran down most of Christmas – she's a real
laugh. Forgets where she is half the time, we kept having
to explain to her why there was a fir tree in the corner of
the room, where the telly usually went.'

'No telly over Christmas?'

'Oh yes, put it in the other room so it didn't get kicked
in.'

'Did you see ...?'

'Yes, goodennit.'

And so on.

Clive and Lester had met up during the holiday to 'shoot
pool and get steamed up'. Nearly all the boys had been at
work somewhere: Alec on a building site; Dirk on a fair-
ground; Jim helping his Dad roofing under an assumed name
to avoid legal problems of being under 16 with no insurance;
Clive plastering with his Dad (on the side); Lester window
cleaning with a mate with entrepreneurial spirit. Only

Martin had spent the whole Christmas at home, surrounded
by family demands. 'Boring,' he announced laconically.
'I'd rather have been here at this dump.'

Discussion about jobs was to characterise many of our
conversations in the first four weeks. Having formed a
group and having attempted to redress the balance of self-
confidence and expressiveness and such like, we now had to
prepare them for the 'outside' world.

The sanctuary of our school had only a limited life now,
and for some who were eligible to leave at Easter the world
of work was mere weeks away.

Leaving school and starting work is the modern version of
the initiation rites performed by primitive tribes at the transition between child and man. Not for them was the long-
drawn-out twilight of adolescence with its uncertainties of
roles and expectations. But nowadays at least at 16 to
leave school and start work is to become a man, and without
exception all our youngsters wanted to do just that.

The sad thing – and it's no news to anyone – is that youth
unemployment is the highest since records began and for
many kids – particularly ours – the chance to become an
adult through the work situation is sadly limited. It's no
longer 'what job will you do when you leave school?' but
'what will you do with all your spare time, if you're on the
dole?'

The syndrome of staying in bed late because there's no
reason to get up is only too common: of missing the midday
papers and so not bothering to look for vacancies and so
deciding it's not worth buying the evening edition; of hanging
about at home, bored, because friends are at work or equally impoverished and isolated in their homes some distance
away; of finally going out at night – to a disco or a pub and
eking out the ration of dole money that's left after giving Mum
a fiver, to relieve the monotony of the day, then returning
home late at night, knowing there is no need to get up in the
morning.

Our aim, ideally, is to help them find work; in reality we
know that some won't, so we concentrate on giving them a
taste of the 'adult' world through work experience situations. We have to be schizophrenic in our approach; prepare them for work by work experience and job counselling,
whilst equipping them to cope with the traumas of unsuppor-
ted unemployment.

The organisation of work experience is a time-consuming
business and can only be done at the human contact level.

Consequently it means writing letters, generally to firms
and businesses, and following letters with personal telephone calls. If school and work were inter-related there
would be no need for such delineation between what is 'educational' and what is 'work'. Reference to the Tvind
school described in Chapter 1 demonstrates that it is quite
possible to relate theoretical learning to practical work –
and work that is both personally fulfilling as well as finan-
cially rewarding.

The difficulty of linking work and education within the
school is that the pupils' attitude to real work is to see it
as something that can only take place outside school – which
is merely a reflection of societal attitudes. Children's
attitudes to school and work are formed and reinforced by
parents and peers who see school as school and work as
something different from school. So although we could
provide work experience within our walls, it is only actually meaningful as work to most youngsters when linked with
financial remuneration surrounded by adult activity. The
fact that many production-line processes expect an infantile
level of intelligence and ability is not important – it is _real_
work none the less.

So we aim for work experience – based on a balance between the kids' aspirations and what is practically possible.
That first day, over lunch, we talked about work experience
and their individual preferences.

Only Lester had anything arranged – a fortnight at the
racing stable in Berkshire that he'd fixed up before Christmas. At least it was a spur for the others. If Lester
could do it, so could they.

For Clive there was a possibility of a placement at the
zoo; for Jim it was likely that a friend who ran a one-man
garage would take him on as an assistant; for Liz there was
a chance to help out at the corner shop.

It seemed a hopeful start and encouraged the rest to consider their own situations realistically and make an effort
to look around.

The following day we'd arranged an interview for Clive
and I took him up to the zoo with Liz and Dirk as moral support. They stayed in the car whilst Clive and I searched
for the Head Keeper. Finally in his office he waved us
into a couple of chairs and directed questions at Clive,
whose nervousness worried me much more than it did the
Head Keeper. As the man explained afterwards: 'I've had
kids come in, and sit for an hour without saying a word

except for nods and grunts. At least he asked a couple of
questions. Honestly, I've had some right ones in here.
You wouldn't have thought they were at all interested whether they got the job or not. I'll take him on trial. If it
works out there's a possible job at the end of it.'

'Full-time?'

'Yes – we've got a vacancy in the bird house. If he
proves himself here, I'll hold the job for him till he can
leave school.'

Clive's confidence soared that day and, as he recounted
the interview to Jim and Dirk, it was obvious that he really
wanted to do the job.

That same evening I went home with him to explain to his
Dad, who also seemed very pleased. Mum hadn't got in yet
from the jam factory where she worked, but Clive promised
to talk it over with her. I left his house quite high that
night. When Clive had first come to see us his future had
seemed pretty grim, with borstal training a likely next step.
Perhaps he was beginning to steer a safer passage.

Our optimism was short-lived, because the next day Clive
didn't come in. We should have taken it as a warning sign,
since it was the first day he'd missed during the last six
months. But we were preoccupied with making arrangements for Lester's own work experience placement at the
racing stable, and it wasn't until Friday evening that I was
able to go round to Clive's house. I found him sitting in
front of the telly with his girlfriend Tina (herself home for
the weekend from an approved school) but he gave no explanation as to why he hadn't come in – just shrugged his shoulders and avoided the question. The insurance form he'd
been given for his parents to sign was still unfolded, but
since Dad was 'out somewhere' and Mum still at work, I left
with a reminder to bring it in on Monday, because he was
due to start the following Friday.

Lester, meanwhile, had been preparing himself for his
two-week trial apprenticeship at the racing stable near
Wantage. His wild enthusiasm for horses made it such an
ideal opportunity. If he worked hard he'd very likely be
taken on as an apprentice when he left school. As the end
of the week approached, though, he grew progressively
more nervous and worried about not having the right
clothes, or whether he'd fit in with the other apprentices.
To allay fears about the former, we kitted him out with an
assortment of old clothes and Wellington boots, and to give
him confidence about the latter we pointed out how well he'd
fitted into our group.

'Funny,' he remarked, 'before I came here to you, you
know, I couldn't stick at anything.   That was partly why I
had to see the head-bangers – that, and the fact my Mum
couldn't control me since her and my Dad split up.   The
head-bangers thought I was nutty.   So I came here.   To
begin with I thought you were a load of head-bangers too and
then I realised we were just as nutty as each other.   Ever
since then, it's been great.'
    By the end of the first week four of them were fixed up
with work experience placements – Lester at the stable,
Clive at the zoo, Liz helping out round at the corner shop,
and Martin at the largest fishing tackle retailers in Bristol.
The last was one of those lucky coincidences that you dream
of but never actually expect to happen.   Martin had a real
passion for fishing and that particular shop – Veals – was a
regular port of call on his way to an afternoon's rod-dang-
ling at Saltford.   He'd stopped off there with Hilary to buy
maggots, and having mentioned to her several times before
how he'd like to work there if he had the chance, she asked
the assistant if there were any jobs going.   Not only was
there a vacancy, but the manager was in, and by the time
Martin had paid for his packet of maggots, a work experience
place was already fixed up – with every likelihood of a permanent job at the end.
    For Martin that was a turning point.   His original fanta-
sies of becoming a pharmacist had taken a battering by various rejections from the local drug chains, who had pointed
out that the minimum qualifications required were four 'O'-
levels, and he'd become quite downcast at the realisation of
the tremendous gap between fantasy and reality.   So a job
at Veals, close to the world of his beloved fishing, restored
the tarnished dreams.
    Every Thursday that term he spent the day from 9.00 to
6.00 working as an assistant in the shop, selling bait and
tackle, advising customers on what to buy, and helping with
stock orders and such like.   Three weeks after he'd started
he came in early on the Friday morning after his day at work,
flushed with excitement.   'Know what,' he offered, without
waiting to be asked, 'the manager and assistant manager
were out yesterday – they left me in charge of the whole of
the maggot distribution for the South West.   All day.'   He
recounted the story with pride.
    Martin's success though was balanced by our failure in
other directions.   After our optimism at the end of the first
week about the four who'd already fixed up work experience,

a phone call from Lester's mother to say he'd left for the
stable after a night spent in floods of tears brought us back
to earth. Clive rubbed salt in the wound by declaring two
days before the event that he certainly didn't intend going to
the zoo; it was too far away, he'd have to get up too early,
it was too cold, and so on.

I bit my lip, intending to discuss the matter next day when
Monday-morning blues had subsided. He didn't turn up
though – either then, or the next day and since he was expected to start at the zoo by Friday I drove round to his
house. I was confronted by a tense, uncertain boy, and a
concerned mother, who couldn't understand why he'd changed
his mind – 'except that I think he don't want the weekend
thing, because of his girlfriend. It's the only time he sees
her.' Clive confirmed, after a long discussion, that he'd
agree to do a three-day week stint instead.

It was frustrating that neither Clive nor his mother saw
the golden opportunity he was on the point of chucking away.
For someone with such a love of animals and genuine interest
in wildlife, a job at the zoo was a perfect beginning. The
pay may not have been fantastic, but the work itself carried
all the rewards and satisfactions that many middle-class
wage earners take for granted as being a natural condition
of work. Clive was unlikely to be offered anything else
like it. And since vacancies at the zoo were pretty infrequent, the chance to get a foot in the door through work experience was well worth the effort.

The zoo really wanted someone who could start full-time
immediately, but since it was now almost February and
Clive was due to leave school at the end of March, they were
prepared to negotiate a compromise and take him on a part-
time basis – paying him for weekend work. The Head Keeper
was very sympathetic and helpful and quite prepared to make
out a special case for Clive which made the whole thing even
more delicate.

The other problem that Clive presented was the obstacle of
travel. He was uncertain which bus to catch, or where to
get off. Too often we are deceived by the kids' veneer of
bravado and confidence into thinking they can cope with
something so simple as asking about bus routes and times.
For many it is a real problem – asking the way of strangers
or travelling to strange areas. So I offered to pick Clive
up on the first day and drive him to the zoo.

By the time I left, his old enthusiasm had re-asserted
itself, but I was worried that Mum's overprotectiveness at

the difficulties Clive faced in starting the zoo job were
rooted in more than just natural maternal concern.

On Thursday, the day before starting, Clive came in in
good spirits and was very positive in his contribution to the
planned activities – even so far as to volunteer to wash up,
so that Alec and Dirk could get off early to the snooker room
with one of the students. Friday morning dawned and at
7.00 a.m. it was still dark as I drove along Clive's road on
his council estate. The grey sameness of the streets was
blanketed in a thin mist. Clive was at the front door,
dressed and ready to go, before I'd reversed the van into a
parking space outside his house.

He was very excited and talked non-stop as we drove
through the lightening streets. At the zoo I pointed out
very clearly to Clive where he needed to catch the bus
home, and we went through the 'employees' gate together.
At the bird house Pete (who'd actually been on the project
two years before) was already chopping loaves of bread
into a sack. He promised to take Clive under his wing and
help him round that day, 'I'll see he's all right, don't
worry,' Peter reassured me. I had to smile, remembering
Pete himself had been in exactly the same position 18 months
previously.

At lunchtime, when I picked him up so he could join the
rest of the group, I found him dressed in purple overalls,
chopping meat and clearly enjoying himself. 'I'll come
tomorrow,' he promised: which message I conveyed to the
Head Keeper, who was clearly relieved that his problem of
being under-staffed was going to resolve itself.

Clive, the man, in real keeper's overalls, strutted round
the room at lunchtime – full of what he'd done and what the
job involved. To emphasise the seriousness of his work he
declined a second helping, saying he needed to get back to
the zoo, because there were animals to be fed.

After leaving Clive at the zoo gate and arranging to visit
him there on Monday morning to see how he was getting on,
I drove on to his home to explain the situation to his parents. Only Dad was in, half asleep in front of a flickering
telly, and I urged on him the importance of Clive not being
late to work on the next day.

'Don't worry – I'll see he's up in time.'

I had to leave it at that, having arranged to be out of
Bristol that weekend. I hoped that his parents were supportive enough to see him through.

Back at the office to tidy away letters before locking up,
I found a message on my desk:

'Lester's Mum rang.
Left the stable.
Arrived home late last night.'
The one consolation was the knowledge that Liz seemed to
be coping very well at the shop and Martin - the future maggot organiser for the South West - had been ecstatic about
his first day at work.
Two days away was a welcome break. On Monday morning, sorting through the weekend mail that had accumulated,
the phone rang. It was Clive's Mum. Before she spoke I
knew that it must be bad news.
'He didn't go to work on Saturday ... ill ... collapsed
... seen doctor ... arranged another appointment for
today.' Her explanation was garbled, but the message
itself was very clear. Clive had shied away from going to
the zoo.
Why? Nervousness?
Mum couldn't think of a reason. I wondered if Clive was
putting it on to avoid the reality of starting work. After
all, his Dad has been 'on the social' for years now. I'd
hardly replaced the receiver when the phone rang again.
This time it was the zoo wanting to know what was happening. I explained the situation and that I would be calling
round the house later that evening to try and sort it out.
The Head Keeper was very understanding and expressed
concern for Clive's well-being.
Six o'clock at Clive's house found both Mum and Dad in,
with Clive lying on the sofa in the 'front room'. Both
parents seemed very worried.
The diagnosis was epilepsy, and Clive had apparently had
a minor fit. Now on a prescription of phenobarbitone, he
was going to see a specialist next week for further consul-
tation. Till then he'd stay at home. The boy himself was
downcast and introspective, so I stayed with him a while
and played back the tape of a sing-song I'd recorded the previous week with Lester. It brought back memories of the
camp in Wales and the fireside in the evening. We hardly
discussed the zoo job. There seemed little point. If it
was epilepsy, they wouldn't take him, since he'd have to be
escorted while with the animals. Their worry would be of
him collapsing in a cage. I drove away feeling very sad
for Clive. The perfect job was now quite beyond his reach.
I wondered how he would channel his disappointment and
frustration. He would need something....
After leaving Clive, I called in to see Lester. Though he

was out, Mum was at home, and very angry because Lester
had taken a fiver from her purse. 'That's the last straw
... I'm washing my hands of him ... he can go his own way
... serve him right after all I've done ... I'm not going to
take any more.' She related various past misdemeanours,
which only fuelled her conviction to be rid of Lester. My
own suggestion that maybe he was feeling he'd let her down
by leaving the job at the stable; that maybe his sense of
failure could only be ameliorated by more, rather than less
affection, sounded rather hollow and unconvincing. It certainly drew no sympathy from Mum. 'Rog, ever since I
split up from Lester's Dad, I've had to cope with Lester and
his sister on my own. It hasn't been easy, especially when
he knows he can run to his Dad for money if I refuse him.
If I try to discipline him, he just walks out on me without
listening. As well as doing my job, I have to look after
this place on my own - and he never lifts a finger to help.
What would you do?'
I had no answer.
It just underlines the need for support outside the school
situation. Whatever good we do, whatever advances we
make during the hours the kids come to us, can be so easily
undermined by what happens outside. It doesn't surprise
us. The reasons that they drop out of school in the first
place are rooted more in the home than in something endemic
in the school itself. Unless we make a connection between
school and home, much of our effort is a wasted endeavour,
easily upset by the over-riding reality of domestic tensions.
All we become is a pleasant interlude between crises at
home.
It's too easy to grow complacent when self-confidence and
reassurance appear to flourish in our setting. It is too
easy to be fooled by the outward veneer, forgetting that
being with us could be of very little lasting significance for
some of them. In those cases where our links with home
have been good, where parents have understood and accepted what we're trying to do, we have achieved much more,
which only bears out what educational sociologists have been
saying for years about the value of parental support. It's
a time-consuming process, though, and after a day's work
it can become a resented burden - especially when it sometimes means a drive through rush-hour traffic just to find an
empty house and everyone out - at work, or bingo, or down
the shops.
In those days our home visiting was sporadic and gene-

rally of the emergency sort in response to crises. We
have progressed from that stage, though, so that contact
is more regular and less urgent and may be done for no
other reason than to keep parents in touch with what's happening. It is the value of having a team of three instead of
two (see Chapters 6 and 11).

The next day, though Clive was still conspicuously absent
(and we explained what had happened), Lester at least had
turned up, full of enthusiasm to join in. He was quite
happy to discuss his experiences at the stable and passed on
useful information to the others about interview techniques
and job-hunting. There was a kind of 'man of the world'
authority about him that day, and though he was obviously
pleased to be back there was an aura of a man in transit –
ready for the next adventure, or work experience situation.
It helped the others and was a good introduction for the new
girl Angela, who started that day.

Angela, and Simon (who joined us a few days later), were
the last we intended to take that year. Our original intention had been to limit numbers to ten, as we were still in a
state of transition and uncertainty, particularly in terms of
premises and staffing – and were unwilling to stretch ourselves too far too quickly. But Debbie's departure had
created a vacancy, and since there were indications that
Alec was slipping by the wayside, we felt it reasonable to
take a couple more. Our overall number was eleven now,
but because of the work experience situation it was rare
that all eleven were ever in together. We were dubious
about what we might achieve with the two newcomers given
the time scale involved, but both had impressed us with
their enthusiasm for joining and with the particular urgen-
cies of their respective situations. Angela was the stereo-
typed tomboy, with close-cropped hair and the then fashion-
able baggy trousers and skin-tight, midriff jumper that was
acceptable masculine attire. Compared to her clever, artistic, attractive elder sister Jenny, who had demonstrably
succeeded at comprehensive school and who was guaranteed a place at Drama School after 'A'-levels, Angela had
failed miserably. Her parents were apparently very caring
and concerned, and in this respect it was quite an unusual
referral. Dad was quite prepared to fork out expenses for
'anything that would make Angela happy and help her'. And
in her turn Angela was very fond of her parents, though
bitterly jealous of her elder sister. It was a classic
crisis of identity for Angie. In terms of academic achieve-

ment and social skills she was a poor comparison with her
sister, and her attempt to deny her own femininity (though
she was physically very attractive herself) could well have
been a reaction to Jenny's aura of success that oversha-
dowed her own activities. Ironically, in academic ability
and expressiveness she was more capable than anyone else
in our group and could easily have taken exams if she'd
wanted. But she didn't. Angela was determined not to be
all the things chauvinistically expected of women, and was
more enthusiastic for adventure and risk than any of the
boys with the exception of Dirk (with whom she soon struck
up a friendship).

For Angie the first day was a good beginning. She
helped Judy with lunch and was ready to engage in conversation round the table - showing little of the reticence that
had characterised previous newcomers to the group.
Being a Tuesday and the afternoon earmarked for driving
lessons, there was the usual debate about who should go.
Predictably, because Joy had only appeared in time for the
food, the boys were adamantly against her going. 'Not
good enough, you know, coming in at dinner time and expecting to do just what you want,' was Lester's comment. 'I'll
do my English at home don't worry,' retorted Joy. 'Yeah,
but you ain't going to get to college with no CSEs - you
ought to do your work this afternoon.' Joy scowled at him,
and waved her knife menacingly.

'Try night school,' interrupted Jim, 'you might be up for
that.' They let her go though - and invited Angie to join
the driving 'class' (something we'd discussed with them the
previous week as a way of involving her with the group).

Our concern at the work experience programme after the
events with Clive and Lester was countered by successful
placements for three others. Jim started work with our
friend who owned his own car-repair business. His interest and ability at working on cars had been tested and
proved on our old Anglia that he had lovingly re-painted and
tinkered with to make it road-worthy for a trip to Wales.
Complete with overalls and nonchalance he arrived promptly
for his 9.30 start. I drove him to the garage, less than
half a mile away and at 5.00 he reappeared and, with a certain amount of pride, described what he'd done that day:
'Brakes, rocker box, batteries ... he let me help him underneath a Jag ... I'll start on the yellow car again this week,'
promised Jim.

Judy, whose enthusiasm for anything was grudgingly won

and whose erratic attendance made serious planning a problem, had agreed to follow up her professed interest in playgroup work by going along to a community centre where she could help on such a scheme. Living as remotely situated as she did, it was really very difficult for her to be realistically involved in what we could offer. An hour on the bus with a long walk at either end was asking a lot. It's a sign of how desperately she needed to be involved that she so often actually made the journey, despite inclement weather or unpropitious vibes at home.

For Dirk, the most physically developed of the boys and the one most eager to demonstrate his prowess, a placement as driver's mate with an acquaintance who did removals was to be the perfect sop to his masculinity. To be able to phone us up and apologise for his absence because 'I've got a job on with Billy' was status indeed. That is not meant to be patronising. It is sincerely very important that the kids take on adult roles - where they are asked to contribute in a responsible way that is actually valued. Work experience at least goes towards satisfying one of the basic needs listed by Fleming that was discussed in Chapter 4. (1)

By the end of January only Joy and Alec of the original group had not had a go at work experience, and there was a noticeable aura of increased responsibility in the attitude of some like Martin and Liz who were gearing themselves up to a full-time job. Though Clive and Lester had abandoned their placements, we never suggested or even really regarded their action as indicative of a failing on their part. In fact in group discussions we took pains to stress that work experience was a chance to try out jobs. Giving up was not necessarily a bad sign, if they had at least gained some insight from the experience and benefited from it. In Lester's case this was certainly true, since he had discovered that work was actually demanding and that his normally carefree attitude and lackadaisical approach was not guaranteed to win an employer's approbation. The stables comment on Lester was to describe him as 'lazy', which matched his own description of the place as being run by the 'Gestapo'! In Clive's case, the inability to return to the zoo in the near future was obviously not his fault. The zoo were very sympathetic but couldn't really wait around 'in case', so we agreed to write off the placements to enable them to advertise the job. The only annoying thing was that neither Clive nor his mother had bothered to contact the

zoo, though I'd specifically asked his Mum to do it - if only
for the sake of good manners and possible future referrals.

In Joy's case work experience seemed less crucial somehow, since she was determined to enrol for a college course
and was adamant that she'd pass the appropriate exams.
Given the domestic situation and the pull of her fun-loving
nightlife-seeking boyfriend, it was quite surprising that she
persevered, regularly bringing in homework that she'd con-
trived to do in the most unpropitious surroundings. In her
case we weren't nearly so concerned about arranging job experience as we were for Alec, whose infrequent appearances
were decreasing alarmingly.

Though Alec had only come to us very grudgingly in the
beginning, resenting as he did the birthdate rule that had
trapped him for an extra year, he was the one most in need
of remedial help, in a straight educational sense as well as
in terms of the social skills that he lacked so gauchely.
Alec was more illiterate than any of the others, apart from
Jim, and he possessed none of Jim's 'savoir faire' and wit,
which, in Jim's case, were strong compensations. Alec
was terrified of exposure and was a classic example of those
kids who try to conceal their illiteracy and associated fears
under superficial bravado. For those who believe in a
direct correlation between illiteracy and vandalism Alec
would have proved a perfect example. He was so lacking in
self-confidence, and yet so full of swagger and aggression,
which just masked the little boy underneath. Though almost
irresistibly attractive to many of the girls, he lacked the
social skills to make anything more than a superficial 'Drop
'em or I'm off' relationship.

On his own Alec could be gently encouraged to practise
his reading and writing, but for both teacher and pupil it was
a laborious process where Alec needed almost constant encouragement. On occasions he would persevere for as long
as half an hour, but any potential distraction from the others
in the group had to be anticipated and diverted.

Generally he took every opportunity to 'skive' and in this
sense he was the only one of the group who saw us as synonymous with school and authority. In his eyes we were there
to be endured not enjoyed, and as his official leaving date
drew nearer his rate of 'knocking off' increased. The
crunch came when Hilary went with him for an interview at
a warehouse. Alec was even jumpier than usual before the
actual interview and when the employer presented him with
an application form he just freaked out completely and

clammed up. It wasn't surprising really, but that day must have destroyed part of his fantasy about his own job prospects. The damage to his confidence is hard to estimate but his attitude and behaviour at school deteriorated noticeably.

By the spring term we reckoned that the kids ought to have reached a degree of understanding about what the school would offer and where we stood in relation to their own situation and aspirations. We expected them to see the real value to themselves of their attending the school without us having to nag or needle.

This seemed a reasonable assumption after six months, and generally it proved accurate. Our attitude was that there was plenty to do if they were interested, and we were willing to do it with them if they shared the initiative - but if they weren't going to do anything useful, then they might as well just go home. This approach had worked well. The unspoken contract implicit in their continued attendance meant we could do a lot of real work. With Alec, though, it meant licence to knock off. If we weren't going to chase him up, so much the better. He announced his 'retirement', told us we could 'stuff this place', he'd 'had enough', and walked out.

When he hadn't reappeared after several days we visited his home. Alec was out but we found a concerned Mum and Dad at home who had no idea what was going on. From then on Alec only reappeared sporadically, and never with any sense of commitment or intention to engage in anything seriously.

Alec's plight crystallised our thinking about what might be the essential elements of any appropriate curriculum for these kids. The factors we identified would be essential for any children of course, but there is a reasonable expectation that for middle-class kids some of the 'skills' included in our list will have been learnt at home. With our youngsters, though, and indeed many of those still attending comprehensive school, it would be unwise to make assumptions about overall competence.

For us it was the first time we made a serious attempt to analyse exactly what we ought to be teaching in a methodical sense. We started by listing the skills that we felt we had to ensure the kids were equipped with - like asking directions of a stranger, finding out where to buy something in a department store, how to use a telephone, what information services were available to them for job-hunting or recreational pursuits or consumer spending. Some of these may

seem trivial, and indeed it is hard to imagine that there are
people in this country who hesitate to catch a bus to a
strange area of their own city because they don't understand
bus timetables for the return journey, or they can't read the
destination headings or they're too scared to ask the way.
Of course, in itemising a list of skills, the essential point
about teaching methods is that the way such a curriculum is
approached is more crucial than the content – because the
strategy of the teaching/learning itself teaches many of the
skills that are included in the list.
For example, in planning an overnight camp, where the
emphasis will be on self-sufficiency and adventure training,
it is quite possible to overlook the fact that the preparation
for the camp can include crucial elements of your survival
skill list. By accepting a strategy that involves the youngsters in selecting sites, writing letters, preparing menus,
estimating costs and so on, you inevitably cover skills like
using a telephone, addressing strangers, planning co-oper-
atively, not to mention basic numeracy and literacy. It is
strategy that is fundamental, and staff need to recognise the
value of the time-consuming process that meaningful participation by the youngsters requires.
It was at this point in our evolution of thinking that Simon
arrived. He was absolutely illiterate, having a long history
of illness and truancy which had culminated in a situation of
personal rejection by his peers at school, who ostracised
and abused him because of various misdemeanours committed
by an elder brother who was now 'doing time'. At home
there was just Simon and his mother and from Simon's description it sounded as if his Mum relied on him to do most of
the housework as well as the garden. 'I gets home sometimes, and she's too bloody idle to even open the door for
me; and that's after spending all day in bed.' He was keen
though – really keen to try anything. Initially we were very
wary of such unusual earnestness, which we half felt must
be a demonstration more for our benefit than as an indication of real enthusiasm. But it was genuinely true that
Simon wanted to practise his reading; he wanted to take the
opportunity to go on visits; he wanted to find some work experience. In fact the proof of his commitment is that two
years after leaving us Simon still regularly attends the evening literacy classes organised for our 'graduates' – and is
actually improving his reading, as well as his social skills.
The latter certainly needed developing. His apparent
aggression – the jutting jaw, the roughly confident manner

of speaking, the brash matiness that jarred rather than
gelled made Simon an obvious butt for consensus humour.
   He was tough in a physical sense, with an energy store to
match, and he was quite happy to shift heavy loads almost as
a recreational activity. Simon's approach to life had much
in common with the proverbial 'bull at a gate', and the job he
most wanted was one where he would use his physical ability
outdoors. To restrain Simon inside for any length of time
proved quite difficult. Though he would try and concentrate
at a task inside, like practising reading, his enthusiasm always faded fairly soon. To have tried to steer him towards
an office or factory job would have been a cruel disservice.
   Simon was keenly interested in gardening. Nearby was a
garden centre who were prepared to take him on a work experience basis once a week. The first Friday I went with
him it was early in March - a clear spring morning. He'd
already met the boss, so there was one familiar face at
least. I left him listening to directions about where to start
clearing some of the ground in preparation for transplanting
seedlings. At lunchtime I called in again to see how he was
getting on. Simon was nowhere to be seen, so I knocked on
the door to the boss's office. He smiled in response to my
raised eyebrows. 'Bloody marvel, that kid,' he said, 'I
can't stop him working - he's cleared half the site already.'
He pointed down a gully, and I could just see Simon manfully
wielding a shovel, stripped to the waist, tossing earth over
his bare shoulder.
   That first impression was no flash in the pan. Simon
stuck at the placement doggedly every week, regardless of
weather. For the people at the garden centre he was an un-
doubted asset, with his willingness to work hard at anything
demanding. They certainly benefited from his strength.
For his part, Simon began to learn something about garden
centres - and by the end of his time there he could recognise
numerous plants and shrubs, and talk knowledgeably about
appropriate soils and planting strategies. And he enjoyed
the work. He was no mug though and took the proffered
couple of quid they gave him each week 'for expenses' with a
wry acceptance. He knew they were doing well out of him,
but he reckoned he could earn himself a job out of it in the
end.
   He was quite right, because though that particular garden
centre couldn't offer him one themselves, the reference they
gave him enabled him to land a job at another elsewhere.
Considering his personal job prospects when he came to us,

and the employment situation generally, this was no mean
feat.

What Simon acquired as well as gardening knowledge and a
reference was a degree of polish. His rough edges began
to lose their abrasiveness. He learnt the value of polite-
ness and calm speech. These were very real skill acquisi-
tions.

The shift in emphasis to 'jobs' that term caused concern
amongst the kids about the sort of reference they'd get from
the school. Of course one of the things that worried them
was that they weren't at 'school' in the normal sense of the
word. How would employers react to them being at a 'special unit'? This is only one of the more obvious dangers of
labelling kids. To counter it, we did often have to do a lot
of explaining to potential employers. Which is fair enough
perhaps. After all why risk taking an oddball when the
market is already over-subscribed with 'normal' kids, all
with equally good qualifications?

Given the imminence of leaving and concern over references it became a frequent topic of conversation - 'What would
we say?' Our answer was to throw the question back at them
and enlist their involvement in assessing their own ability in
terms of a reference. The initial emphasis was on 'good
points'. As a group we spent several mornings discussing
each individual in turn. The perception of some like Lester
and Joy quite surprised us. Their assessment of character
was uncannily accurate. It was a productive exercise, and
apart from the obvious and necessary boost to confidence, it
made them look more closely at the others in the group, so
increasing Response-ability and Awareness. Of course, it
wasn't all back-slapping. They were critical of failings,
but the atmosphere in which such criticism was couched was
generally supportive.

The only one who found it too much to cope with was Clive.
Following the zoo experience he had re-adopted the truculent
attitude that had characterised his early days of the autumn
term. He began to miss days without explanation; he was
often aggressive, particularly so to Hilary; he was generally moody and unpredictable. The rest of the group showed
remarkable restraint. 'It must be pretty hard for Clive -
knowing he couldn't take that job at the zoo because of his
epilepsy.' 'It's more than that though, isn't it? It rules
out lots of other jobs too, like driving for instance.'

These comments by Joy and Lester were reflective of the
general attitude. Their concern and sympathetic handling

of Clive was really quite moving.   The sad thing is that it
didn't seem to help Clive much.

To be honest, there were things about this 'epilepsy' that
didn't add up, and we had an intuitive, though unprovable,
suspicion, that someone at home was exaggerating the problem for reasons we couldn't quite fathom.

The facts were apparently straightforward.   Clive had
had a couple of attacks, the doctor had prescribed some
tablets and Mum had arranged for him to see a specialist.
The prognosis was 'petit mal' with the possibility of further
attacks, so the job at the zoo was firmly ruled out.

But Mum was apparently encouraging Clive to consider
jobs like window cleaning with a friend of hers or working
on a farm (with Clive's uncle) - both of which held an element of danger for someone prone to blackouts.   We were
frankly suspicious that Clive's rejection of the zoo had more
to do with Mum's animosity to the idea than with petit mal.

We decided to test the hypothesis by banning him from the
Tuesday afternoon driving session, pointing out that if his
Mum considered it too dangerous for him to work at the zoo,
we felt it was equally dangerous to be at the wheel of the
car.   The next day he came with a note from Mum.

'It's perfectly all right for Clive to drive.   He will be
quite safe and I agree to his going.'

'So it's OK then,' Clive stuck out his jaw aggressively.
'I'll be driving this afternoon.'

Our refusal was met with anger and silent obstruction.
Hunched over the fire, Clive made it quite clear he wasn't
going to co-operate with anything unless we agreed to his
driving.   For once none of the others, not even his 'mate'
Dirk, took any notice.   During the afternoon Clive slipped
out quietly.   We noticed him leaving, but thought it better to
pass no comment.   Instead I'd visit his house to talk things
over.

Two evenings later, I had time to spare to do just that.
Clive's Mum answered the door and, before inviting me in,
beckoned me to one side.

'He's still on the tablets, Rog.   I'm afraid he gets very
fed up, which is why he didn't come in yesterday.'

'What's going to happen then?   About jobs, for instance?'

'Well I don't know.   He's got another appointment with the
doctor in a fortnight, but there's this job window cleaning
he could do.'

'He can't window clean if he's suffering from epilepsy -
not if it was so bad he couldn't go to the zoo.'   I was
slightly irritated.

She merely shrugged in reply. 'Well there's places at our factory.'

I stifled a groan. The thought of Clive - the boy who loved the open air, and animals - being cooped up inside bottling jam seemed almost cruel.

In the front room Clive smiled up from the sofa. He was obviously pleased to see me. The 'mood' of two days before was quite forgotten. We sat and talked, plied with sugary tea prepared by Mum.

'The new kid's settled in all right, hasn't he?' Clive was referring to Simon. 'It'd be good for him if he can stick at it - especially the work experience, eh?'

'What about yourself though?'

'Blown it, haven't I?' Clive smiled wrly. 'Still me uncle said he'd take me on.'

'The farm?'

Clive nodded. 'I've spent a lot of time there already during holidays, I could live in during the week and come back at weekends.'

Despite the brave front, Clive was clearly quite depressed. I suggested a return visit to the Welsh farmhouse with Dirk and Lester (his mates) as company. We'd work on the place between jaunts out. His enthusiasm was quite moving as we discussed possible dates - the end of the following week.

For Hilary and I it would mean splitting the group, but given the loose knit of the work experience mesh, it could be coped with quite easily.

In conversation Dirk and Lester were both very keen. Dirk arranged release from his work experience and Lester made a point of seeing his Dad to ask for some money to cover costs.

On the agreed date Dirk turned up early, complete with sleeping bag and small holdall.

'Sandwiches for the journey,' he explained.

There was no sign of the others, but since we'd agreed a lunchtime departure we weren't over-anxious. Dirk helped me with the petty cash whilst we waited, and seemed to take notice as I explained how and where the money came from. 'It's a lot of work innit?' he grunted, sifting through the pile of receipts. 'But I suppose it's worth it to keep the place running.'

Clive and Lester drifted in together just before midday. Neither of them were carrying a sleeping bag or anything suggestive of an overnight stay.

'We aren't going,' Clive was the spokesman. 'I've got a job on with a mate.'

Gentle probing and persuasion evoked no response whatever. Inside I was very angry, not really believing the story of the job, yet quite helpless to expose the fantasy.

The two of them were quite immutable and even Dirk was perplexed by their obstinacy. It didn't cool his own enthusiasm though. We left after lunch.

For Dirk, the truculent, awkward and often aggressive adolescent, it was a complete break with his image. Those three days at the farmhouse he sweated and worked (and drank beer) with a determination that quite amazed me. It was a clear vindication of the principle of group pressure influencing conformity of values. He was with three adults who had gone to work on the farmhouse and the expectation was simply that Dirk would join in. Nothing was discussed about behaviour. We just assumed he'd pull his weight, which is exactly what happened. He did a tremendous amount of physical work for long stretches; he joined us in the pub in the evening; he shared the chores of cleaning and cooking without any questioning or dissent. We were mates together.

What was interesting to note was how the effect of those three days carried over back to the school. In the month that followed Dirk was a very reliable ally in organising the week and managing the day-to-day events of the week. When he wasn't 'on the job with Billy' he was in on time, ready to join in (and even initiate) whatever we planned for the day.

The real test of his new-found commitment came during the week after we'd returned from Wales. Clive had spent the Friday night of the weekend we'd been away in a police cell. The story, pieced together from his Mum's comments and a long conversation with his social worker, was pretty alarming. Having stolen a car and been chased by the police he'd taken a roundabout at speed, written off the stolen car and damaged both police cars. Though he himself was unscratched, two constables had been treated for injuries and the police were obviously in no mood to be lenient. Their intention was to 'throw the book at him'.

We talked it over with the whole group, wondering what we could do to help. Their reaction was interesting: mostly very caring, because like us they understood the pressure on Clive to prove himself. Having lost the opportunity for his ideal job and having realised he could well be barred from driving for a long time because of his epilepsy, his fantasy

world had been rudely shattered. With two props to his
virility – work and a car – both denied him, he was in a very
vulnerable state. It didn't surprise any of us that he'd
stolen a car.
But was our understanding sufficient rationalisation?
Could his state of mind justify and excuse what had happened?
There were one or two in the group who felt quite strongly
that Clive had gone too far.
'I know I oughtn't to say it, but he should be put away,'
was Liz's comment, which summoned up the mixture of concern and criticism that many of us felt.
Dirk was mostly silent. He regarded himself as Clive's
mate and was clearly ambiguous about what stand he should
take. Later that day I took Dirk aside. We felt it was important we talk with Clive, and I wanted Dirk to persuade
him to come up. He saw the point and agreed to call round.
On the last day of the week, Clive appeared, cocky and un-
remorseful about what had happened. He proceeded to re-
live his excapade with the stolen car to anyone who would
listen, but fortunately his anticipated audience didn't mate-
rialise. They all had other things to do.
With Clive there, my intention had been to call in his
social worker and have a serious discussion, spelling out to
Clive the reality of the situation: that Detention Centre was
on the cards and only a tremendous effort on his part to sort
something out for himself was likely to alter that fate. When
I told Clive I'd planned such a meeting for later that day his
attitude changed immediately. The cocky, confident young
man changed into a tense, neurotic boy and it was quite clear
he was set to run off. In desperation, to hold on to Clive
till his social worker arrived, I asked Dirk to help persuade
Clive to stay at the school.
The effect was disastrous. He relayed to Clive my concern that Clive should stay, which the latter construed as
meaning trouble. Within minutes he'd stormed off, angrily
accusing me of trying to get him put away. I was furious
with Dirk who also turned on me with 'I'm not going to see
my best mate shopped' and stormed off himself.
In the space of five minutes I'd successfully alienated 20
per cent of the group. So much for trust. I was in no
mood to pull punches or choose words carefully. I followed
Dirk down the road and caught him by the bus stop. For
Clive's sake, Dirk had to convince Clive to come in and talk.
We were the only people who could do anything to help and
there was no way we could help if he ran away. Emotion
flowed very freely.

'Do you trust me?' I asked finally. Pause. 'Yes,' he
grunted, and we parted with a handshake. I walked up the
hill critical of my own bad handling, but relieved that the
door hadn't slammed shut completely.

Next Monday I woke feeling very cold. By midday I was
shivering under four pullovers, and left the group. By two
o'clock I was in bed. It was the first time I'd been laid
low that year, and highlights the delicacy of the staffing
provision with such a small staff team. At that time we had
no appropriate arrangements for sick leave. If one of us
went ill the other had to cope, alone. It was as simple as
that, except that the pressures on the sick person to return
quickly were pretty strong. The net result was that we
didn't go sick – unless it was physically impossible to remain
vertical. It's not a question of heroics. Running a group
in the way we do is very demanding, because from the time
the kids arrive to the time they leave there's no let–up, no
time off during the day to re–charge. With two staff it is
possible for one to 'ease up' and freewheel at points, trusting the other to provide the momentum. If you're on your
own you can't ease up. So we don't go sick!

Because I'd asked Dirk to get Clive in the next day and
because I wanted to see him apart from the group I had to go
in. The four of us – Clive, his Mum, his social worker and
myself – met that afternoon. John (the social worker) laid
it on the line for Clive about what would happen. Detention
Centre was almost certain. The only way out was if he
fixed himself up with a job before the court appearance, so
that John could recommend a fine instead. Clive listened
calmly. It was his mother who kept interrupting with questions and comments. In her mind she'd got it all worked out
for Clive. Her overbearing insistence was a testimony to
Clive's problem. The joint statement from the social
worker and myself that this time Clive had to stand on his
own two feet and make his own decisions was as much a message to her as to her son.

With the court appearance set for three weeks hence,
Clive would have to work fast. The onus was on him completely. He made a hopeful start next day by writing half a
dozen letters to panel–beating firms and collecting their
phone numbers to follow up later that week. Sadly though,
the spark soon fizzled out. At the end of the week he
phoned through with the news of a possible job – 'My mate
says he can fix something up at the garage where he works.'
Clive had done nothing else though and had clearly given up.

'I shan't go to court anyway - I'll not be around when the
case comes up.'

Perhaps we should have helped him find a job. But we
felt it important that this time the responsibility for self-
help was entirely his. He had our support and he could use
us, but this time we weren't going to be directive. So we
did nothing more than to visit twice in the next fortnight to
see what was happening.

Depressingly and predictably, he was 'sent down'.
Three months Detention Centre with six weeks possible re-
mission for good behaviour.

I visited him there two weeks before his release. I
asked the kids if they wanted to write a letter or send a
present, but their attitude had hardened. There was an
emphatic refusal to do anything.

'His own bloody fault. He didn't do anything to help himself did he?'

'Fucking Div!'

'Should've got longer,' expressed the span of feeling.

It was a depressing visit. The aim of Detention Centre -
to give kids a jolt - was obviously successful up to a point.
I met a shaven-haired, cowed boy who lay on his bed in his
cell the whole time I was there, recuperating from an 'accident' in the gym. He wouldn't tell me what happened. 'I
ain't going to get into trouble again,' was an expression
that made me wonder if Detention Centre had actually achieved something for Clive. But there's no follow-through -
no support to stops kids re-offending. The rows of bored
faces in the classrooms and the corridors made me wonder
if it has to be done that way.

In terms of treating TDA merchants there are alternative
approaches that have worked. The experiment referred to
in Chapter 5 is one example. (2)

Long after the event Martin referred back to the incident
in a discussion about what else we could have done for Clive
at the time. His comment still left the question unanswered.

'Clive was doing all right till that epilepsy business. I
think he faced up to it the wrong way. What made him
worse was having to give up his job. And that day, after
it had happened, when he came back to school, he was
obviously worried what people would say. You could see
it in his eyes. He didn't know what to say, or do.
Which was why he got mouthy. He didn't mean to be like
it, it was just his way. But we thought then he was just
a big-headed cunt. I don't think you really understood

what was happening to him either. Hilary wasn't really
in a position to do anything about Clive - cos women tend
to give in easier.'
As the Easter term drew to a close we attempted to assess
the progress of each individual in the group. For Clive in
Detention Centre, and Alec who'd abandoned us, and Debbie
who'd dropped out in the Christmas term, it was pretty
clear-cut. For Liz and Martin, who were fixed up with
jobs through their work experience, it was also clear-cut.
The difficulty as always, without the yardstick of exam suc-
ccess or other tangible measures of achievement, is to evaluate and recognise the gain to the youngsters of a placement
at school. For the two who had chosen to leave at Easter -
Dirk and Jim - we had cause to feel some measure of satisfaction.
Both of them had developed self-confidence and an individual style that possessed a good deal of charm. The
aggressive approach of the former had mellowed with time
and the withdrawn, boyish insularity of the latter had
matured into a self-possessed, articulate and humorous
young man. In terms of job opportunities both were 'fixed
up', Jim with his Dad, and Dirk as a tyre fitter. They were
of the breed who would survive anyway.
Of the remainder, Lester, Joy, Judy, Angela and Simon
would continue with us into the summer term. Along with
Martin and Liz they wouldn't actually start work until the
official leaving date at the end of May.
Before term finished there were three events worth mentioning. The first, an incident of stealing, brought Hilary
and myself into direct confrontation with almost all of the
group, and our handling of it exposes an area of potential
weakness in our basic approach.
Two weeks before term finished, some money was taken
from Hilary's purse. This was the first time money had
ever 'disappeared' that year and the event came as quite a
shock to the two of us. For those people who would criti-
cise the woolly-haired liberalism that permeated the school,
this incident of stealing would come as no surprise. But it
did to us, because of what it meant in terms of trust. We
had always felt, and it had been much discussed with the
group, that we should be able to function as a group without
having to lock stuff away. The petty cash could be left in
its tin, the equipment and tools could be left around, and
none of it would disappear. That was our expectation and
this trust had always been respected and reciprocated by
the kids. Till the money disappeared.

Our response was to call a meeting and explain what had happened. We expressed our concern about what it meant in terms of breakdown of trust and group loyalties. Initially their joint response was a mixture of hostility and concern. Hostility because they resented and couldn't understand why we weren't taking a tougher approach. 'I'd get the police in,' was Dirk's comment, which was fairly representative of the group feeling. They wanted very much for the thief to be identified - and it was hard to believe from their demonstrated indignation that any of them could have done it.

Their suggestion for preventing similar recurrences was that everything of value be locked away, including purses and handbags. We talked it through, explaining what it would mean if we operated such a system. Our emphasis was on the importance of trust and openness. We wanted to go on leaving money around, because we wanted to be able to demonstrate trust. As a group they accepted the principle and agreed to try our method again. 'But if money goes missing again, don't blame me,' was Dirk's parting remark.

We continued not locking valuables away and deliberately kept the petty cash tin freely available (though we resolved amongst ourselves to keep a more watchful eye on its contents and usage!) Nothing disappeared again that year, but we remain open to criticism of our handling of such issues. The temptation factor for kids with a history of theft is quite considerable, and some would argue that it is both unreasonable and irresponsible to expect them to be able to resist the impulse. And of course it is a temptation, but if our messages of trust and responsibility mean anything at all they have to be tested and proved to work. Even inveterate thieves have to learn not to pinch from their mates and have to work out some sort of morality for their own conduct.

The 'morality' of stealing raises some interesting points. For people with little money and a social pressure (emanating from the media) to demonstrate material success in the absence of any other possible achievement, the temptation for working-class kids to steal goods is much greater than for their more socialised middle-class peers who are imbued with the values of deferred gratification.

And of course, in the 'adult' world, the middle and upper classes steal less obviously by fiddling tax returns or falsifying expense claims. Which is less honest - the shopkeeper who buys shirts at a £1 each and retails them to kids at £6 a time, or the skateboard seller who profiteered out of the 1978 craze by selling wooden boards with wheels (that cost several pounds at most to make) for upwards of £50 or £60?

Where is the morality in a shop-window display that tantalisingly tempts, out of reach behind half-inch plate-glass, or the rows of confectionery cunningly placed at supermarket check-out counters? It's an interesting digression.

In the two years since that incident there has been only one other case of theft in the school, and that involved a lad 'on the run' who broke into the school after hours and emptied the petty cash tin of its contents. His need at that moment perhaps justified the desperation of the act. None of the group begrudged him the fiver anyway.

The second important event concerned Angela. For two months she'd been attending quite regularly, though floundering around unsure what to do and not really able to concentrate on any particular thing for more than a few minutes. It was hard for her, coming in so long after the rest of the group, but whereas Simon (who had joined with her), had taken advantage of the opportunities presented, Angela seemed incapable or unwilling to be that committed. After two months she knew us well enough to feel safe in the group and her growing 'flightiness' was beginning to unsettle the other kids. It wasn't hard to see why she'd caused such problems in school!

We talked it over with her one evening. She recognised her own problem quite openly. 'The trouble with me is that I start something, then change my mind and give up – I've always been like that.' We agreed to try a formula to get over this. Angela would begin a woodwork job (something she really wanted to do) knowing that within minutes she'd lose heart and want to give up; at which point we'd persuade her to carry on, she'd resent the coercion and get angry back. We'd have a confrontation, shout at each other, and then laugh because it had turned out exactly as we'd expected. As a spur to motivation we went down to the local hardware store and bought a coping saw – a tool she needed for the particular job in mind. Next day she made a start. Nothing went according to plan.

At lunchtime, two hours later, she was still at it. Even Simon's flagging enthusiasm for his own job hadn't deterred her. There had been no arguments, no irritation, no confrontation.

It would be sentimental to suggest that was the turning point for Angie but, for once, she'd achieved something she could be proud of.

The third event was another trip to London. For some like Jim and Dirk this was to be the last occasion they'd spend with us. For others like Angie and Simon, still relatively new to the group, it was an opportunity to be involved in arranging something more substantial than lunch rotas or local visits. For the rest it seemed a fitting way to end the term together. We went by train again. The British Rail party rates offer specifies a group size of twenty, but fortunately they are flexible enough to accommodate 'special cases'. One glance at our motley crew is enough to understand why we don't travel in groups of twenty.

It rained all day. The bus from Paddington to Picadilly steamed with damp bodies. We dripped into the Design Centre to gain a brief respite from the downpour and then braved the onslaught from above to walk along Whitehall and then to Downing Street. The Thames seemed wetter than usual, but the cockney commentary on the boat raised a few laughs. From the Tower it was up to the kids. They map-read us through Covent Garden to Soho and Carnaby Street. The former had them goggle-eyed and giggling, the latter had them wide-eyed and haggling. Though they plucked up enough courage to enter some of the more interesting book shops, none of them were so venturesome as to ring the various bells for Diane or Lesley and ask for French lessons or massage. They preferred to preserve their male egos intact. Fantasy took precedence over reality.

We lingered too long in Carnaby Street - probably because the rain had eased for the first time that day - and joined the rest of the half million people rushing to Paddington for the 6.20. Pulses raced as the seconds ticked by between stops - 6.10, 6.15, 6.20. It was 6.25 when the doors opened at Paddington underground. We flashed past the 'This way to District and Circle Lines' and raced up the exit stairs to the main station.

'Platform 6,' shouted Lester. 'Over there.'

We pelted across the platform. The train was still in. Above us the tannoy apologised for the delay to the 6.20.

Gathering breath in the sanctuary of our reserved section, we watched London disappear into a twilight March mist. It had started to rain again.

The conversations on the return journey centred around how to re-structure the programme for next year. Led by Jim, they concentrated for a good hour on a thoughtful appraisal of what had or hadn't worked that year.

'The hardest thing was having to organise things. You expected us to handle the money and join in discussions and things and we'd never done that before.'

At Bristol Temple Meads we said our goodbyes to Jim and Dirk, and the rest of the group, who would return in two weeks' time, sauntered off with them into the night. No one remarked that it had stopped raining.

Chapter 8

Self – analysis

What progress are we making? Are we approaching it in the right way? What is the best thing to do now?

Such regular self-questioning and self-analysis is very necessary. The easy yardstick of examination attainment is not appropriate for many of our youngsters, even if they do actually opt to take exams.

We need to be very clear about what we are hoping to achieve and very aware of what our methodology is. For instance, if we were engaged in a straight behaviour modification exercise, we would need to be quite clear about our desired goal and about the method we intend applying. For instance, what kind of token economy would we operate? What system of praise and reward?

Though we recognise the need for some of the youngsters to modify their behaviour if they are to fit compatibly into society, we don't have a planned system to effect this regulation. We appreciate that behaviour modification tech—ue niques have been shown to produce results. Reports like 'The Highfield Experiment '(1) present a convincing testimony to the effectiveness of behaviour modification techniques. This is not the place to debate the pros and cons of such approaches. Our feeling is simply one of criticism for any method that merely succeeds in a closed system with carefully defined parameters. We are extremely dubious about an approach that regards children as malfunctioning machines which can be corrected by a rigid servicing that ignores the personality inside the machine.

In describing his school at Aycliffe (2) near Darlington, Masud Hoghughi comments that 'No one has any idea what treatment works and how well. What we know about disordered children could be written on the back of a stamp.'

His yardstick of assessing progress is that 'we expect all
the children we treat to emerge with fewer problems than
they have when they arrive, and above all, not to have acquired any more'.

Perhaps Mr Lyward provides part of the answer to what
approach is likely to succeed:

Finchden Manor shows the strength of a treatment rooted
in life and demonstrates the might of disinterested love.
... How much disturbance in children and adolescents is
to be traced solely to external things? No one is to be
taken seriously who denies that overcrowding and bad
housing may have a bad effect on children. But it is as
foolish to assume that people will become happier and more
peaceful through an improvement only in their environment
as it is to assume that environment has nothing to do with
disturbance of heart and mind. The change in environment at Finchden Manor may have affected the boys; but
the real change they found there was in its atmosphere and
spirit. (3)

The crucial feature, it seems to us, in any remedial/pal-
liative/therapeutic programme is whether the pupil/client/
person can continue to grow and develop as an individual
after leaving the institutional framework, without the props
of the programme he participated in.

We start with acceptance. We take the kids as they come,
with whatever clothes they choose to wear, with whatever
habits they import like smoking and swearing. You can't
say to youngsters 'we're going to treat you like adults' and
then on their first day impose your own values and judg-
ments, rejecting theirs.

This acceptance is crucial. In varying degrees the kids
have come from homes and schools where acceptance is lacking. In some cases there is positive rejection.

In 'Adolescence, its Social Psychology' (4) Fleming describes the need for acceptance as the fundamental need on
which our personal security is built. We agree with her,
and don't feel this is just a wishy-washy liberal attitude.
To achieve anything our kids (and indeed any kids) must feel
safe at the school, must feel that they are accepted as the
individuals they are. This is not to say that we ignore rude
or anti-social behaviour, or don't engage in social training.
Of course we do, but not until we have created an atmosphere
of security first.

Our acceptance of them is the prerequisite for their acceptance of themselves, which is the first of the four areas of

adjustment that Fleming reckons adolescents have to make if they are to mature quickly and successfully. To begin with they have to accept the reality of their physical appearances and intellectual capacity. In most cases they actually have a very low self-image, so our acceptance of them is a crucial step in raising their self-perspective.

Of the group described here only Liz and Dirk came to us with much of a self-image. They were both confident of their own abilities, and critical of the schools' responsibility for the deteriorating situation that had necessitated them leaving. Wherever the fault lay, their perspective was that it certainly wasn't with them! The others demonstrated the 'I'm no good' syndrome in varying degrees, from the immediate outward rejection of the idea of taking exams, to their unwillingness to try anything new in case they failed yet again.

It took Martin two months before he'd go round to the corner shop to buy food unaccompanied. 'I ain't showing meself up in there', expressed a fairly common feeling. This fear of being 'shown up' is endemic and testifies to the vulnerability of their self-image. By the time Martin left he was quite prepared to use the Yellow Pages and make inquiries of a range of electrical retailers in search of parts for his hi-fi system.

The second level of adjustment is the acceptance of oneself in relation to others – recognising that one's status varies from one group to another, so that as an experienced rider you can be the leader on horseback, but as a nonswimmer you can accept the assistance of others with your floundering strokes without feeling disturbed by the fluctuation of status.

When Jim first came to us his conversation was at the basic level of just shouting. In any discussion he had to be the loudest and most forceful, asserting his opinion or attitude very strongly. He would only join in activities that he had initiated or which he knew he could do well in – like working on the car or building benches. If he couldn't be the leader, he wouldn't join in.

By the time he left Jim was able to take advice from Liz about how to improve his writing and spelling without getting angry or resentful.

The third step, the acceptance of others as they are, is perhaps the easiest in which to measure progress. Initially all the kids tend to be intolerant of the strange and the different, and prejudice runs very deep from Clive's hatred

of black people, to Lester's dislike of "ippies', to Jim's
hatred of teachers, to Debbie's underlying vitriolic feelings
against all men.

In the first weeks strangers to the group evoked quite
weird responses, ranging from the aggressive acting-out of
outward rejection to sullen withdrawal and ignoring of their
presence. The early visitors had a pretty rough ride, but
by the visit of the policeman, described in Chapter 5, attitudes had begun to mellow somewhat.

The important aspect in all this is the emergence of their
ability to be personally objective about others - to realise
that friends may actually have shortcomings, and that people
they dislike may have good points.

The magistrate before whom Jim had appeared in court
visited us shortly before the end of the spring term. At the
mere suggestion of her coming there was a noticeable stiffen-
ing of backs and a thickening of the atmosphere. 'I'll put
bloody salt in her coffee and jam in her handbag', was
Angela's idea of a welcoming gesture.

Would she be coming if she wasn't interested? What was
the value of her interest? Would it help her to do her job
better to know more about us and more about the kinds of
youngsters we worked with? What could we learn from her?
Something about how the kids were perceived from 'the other
side' perhaps?

In the event six of them sat with her for over an hour and
talked about early school experiences, and what they perceived as the reasons for their ultimate referral to their
present school. Angie served the coffee, and the plateful
of biscuits disappeared at a comparatively sedate pace as
they talked and listened.

'She was all right,' was Lester's summing up. 'Thought
at first she was a bit stuck up, you know, but she joined in
didn't she ... and even drank our grotty coffee from those
dirty mugs, without even testing it to see if Angie had salted
it like she'd planned.'

I looked at Angie questioningly, who just giggled in reply.
'I couldn't do it in the end, Rog - not once she'd smiled at
me - it'd have been a bit tight.'

An important aspect of this acceptance of others as they
are is to recognise that friends may actually have shortcomings and yet still be friends regardless. Equally important, and of particular relevance to their domestic situations, is the acceptance that people they dislike may actually have some good points. The Mum who Liz hated did at

least cook her meals and wash her clothes and help her with
telephone calls in connection with job applications.

The fourth stage Fleming describes – the acceptance of
others in relation to oneself – is hard to measure and hard
to recognise. It requires a considerable degree of self-
assurance to accept that others may have a different point of
view to oneself which is quite reasonable and which can only
be appreciated if seen through their eyes and in the light of
their experience.

It would be immediately beneficial, for instance, if the
kids could understand why their Mums (and Dads) get their
hair off when they're late home at night, unannounced and
with no prior warning. Having spent two hours after dark
wandering the streets of an area notorious for a series of
particularly vicious rape incidents, Liz still found it hard to
understand why her Dad belted her when she got home long
after the promised hour.

In Chapter 4 reference was made to Fleming's categorisa-
tion of acceptance as just one of the four basic human needs –
with the need for expression, the need to discover and the
need to contribute usefully and responsibly as the other
three. In the context of looking at causal factors for the
'abnormal' behaviour of our youngsters it was useful to
refer to Fleming's analysis.

But what does it actually mean in the context of our self-
questioning about progress and 'success'? How does the
foregoing analysis of acceptance relate to the group described in this book? Where had we fallen short and what could
we have done better than we did?

The fundamental error we made on occasions was not to
practise what we preached! In teaching acceptance you
have to demonstrate it as well. Telling is not teaching and
our whole attitude must reinforce our expressed concern for
acceptance and responsibility. Being human and under
stress we didn't always live up to this. On occasions like
the time Joy found herself up-ended on the floor after a particularly needling confrontation it is important to recognise
the fault openly. There is considerable value in accepting
one's blame openly. It doesn't need a 'sackcloth and ashes'
martyr's approach, and in fact can usually be done easily
and lightheartedly. But our consistency is important as
teacher/demonstrators not teacher/preachers. There is no
doubt that for some pupils we will become models for identification. It is inevitable. Adolescents are searching for
identity and some of our kids are bound to fix on us as the

model to build on. What is potentially dangerous is that the kids may lack any other adult model at all – so that our values and morality and conduct become the only model for identification. If there is a lack of parents or other respected adults the only models are peer-groups and the media, and self-education along those lines may not necessarily be a very productive process. The only other group of adults with whom the child is in touch are teachers, and it is particularly for those kids 'at risk' that inter-individual contact (what takes place between one pair of blue eyes and another) is absolutely crucial. (5) The human contact element in teaching is vital, and it is recognition of this aspect that dictates our policy of bringing other people into the school to work with the kids. Many of them are students as described in Chapter 10, but many are people with no formal qualification. Respected adults can come in any shape, size or grade of certification. The important thing is their presence and their awareness of what their presence/influence could mean and what the consequences of their own behaviour and demonstrated attitudes might be on the basis of that influence.

What, though, is the reality of this? Beneath theories about identification, and hypotheses about stages of acceptances, is there a real process taking place that is of value to the kids who come?

At this point it is interesting to reflect on their own perceptions of the year. We interviewed the group described here the year after they had left us. The point of this was to try and discover from the youngsters what attracted them to the school and what it was that they (the consumers) found most useful with the benefit of hindsight, and what lessons we could learn from their comments. All the group, without exception, felt that what they saw as the 'adult' atmosphere was very important.

'It was different right from the start. We were treated more as adults'. In school, it's sit down and start work, but here you talked much more about what everyone wanted to do' – Liz.

'Some kids need a chance to wake up and get into gear. That's where schools go wrong. You need a chance to get ready. Here, by the time you'd had a cup of tea and a cigarette, you felt more like working' – Martin.

In their terms, of course, adult atmosphere would be equated with laissez-faire; being able to do things in their own time. Yet, surprisingly, they accepted a degree of structure, and all of them responded to English and maths and commented on its usefulness. In truth, of course, such slots presented a framework of security – recognisable subjects they could cope with which weren't so frequent that they became overbearing. The atmosphere of our school is permissive in some ways compared to their previous schools, but at least it produces a positive attendance and a willingness to work, though the work pill sometimes has to be sweetened by fun activities.

The work that the group described here would accept readily was initially that which revolved around English and maths and jobs, though subsequently they were prepared to work for less tangible motives like presenting reports of the school for others to read. On one level this close-minded attitude to learning just English and maths is indicative of a very immature attitude; yet at the same time it is a realistic response to an objective assessment of their abilities and needs – and what role education should fulfil for them.

From their comments it is clear that we could have introduced even more structure than we did. To be given choice and apparent freedom to select can be very threatening for young people.

'I'd have liked to see more ideas given. If people are given the opportunity to do whatever they want – they don't realise what it is they do want. When you asked us what we wanted to do, it was very hard, because we didn't know. We needed to have more ideas from you' – Lester.

'You should have had more of a timetable ... trouble is though that would have made it too much like school, and some of 'em would have stopped coming' – Joy.

'You should be a bit tougher. It would've been better for some of them if you'd made us work harder, but then you can't make people learn. If they want to do it they'll do it. You can't force them. Of course you can persuade people some things are worth doing, but if you don't like school or the subject, it really doesn't matter how hard a teacher tries – you still won't get 'em to listen. Somehow you've got to be tougher in a gentle sort of way' – Dirk.

The reality is that with youngsters who see education as a job preparation agency (a view no doubt supported by their parents) the finer points of a school curriculum, like history or geography, are lost. Education to them has a utilitarian value: if it's no obvious help, then it's no bloody use.

Accepting this starting point and recognising the needs of these youngsters – with general deficiency in some basic 'social skills' area – the problem from an educationalist's perspective is how to use their willing participation in certain defined activities to achieve goals beyond just the immediate one of enjoyment. Somehow bridges have to be built and crossed.

At one level, of course, this is where the high staff/pupil ratio pays off. Children learn the most important skills from the ways in which respected adults go about solving particular problems, and by working on problems with people they look up to who are trying to solve the problems with them. And that is the crux of it.

Learning to read is one of the most fundamental skills, and though it's one of the few really vital skills that schools purport to teach, there is significant evidence that children learn to read (or not) before they start school; because what is fundamental in the reading process is an understanding first of all of the value of books and printed matter.

Child development follows a regular pattern. Lying, crawling, kneeling, stumbling half-upright, walking, talking – the development always occurs in the same order, though the time scale between mileposts of achievement differs from child to child. Yet there is a natural progression that characterises all development and a baby must master the ability to crawl before he can walk, must gurgle incoherently before he can talk, must clasp and unclasp many objects before he can catch and hold a ball thrown to him. Dexterity in one activity is a precursor for learning dexterity in the next. As with scientific discoveries, 'ripeness' of mental and physical ability and perception is a necessary condition for further development. Archimedes could only make the discovery about displacement and specific gravity because he had already mastered skills like that of manipulating abstract concepts of volume, or the ability to observe trivia acutely. Likewise, children can only learn a new skill if they have sufficiently mastered prerequisite skills. Which may explain the difficulties faced by some of our youngsters when at 15 they are still unable to read or converse at a level commensurate with their chronological age. The frustration of appreciating a deficiency whilst lacking the prerequisite skills to master it must explain part of their behavioural nonconformity.

It makes the task of teaching such skills like reading very difficult, because it requires an understanding of the preceding and very necessary stages that need to be mastered first before the youngster is 'ripe' to learn to read. Moti-

vation and curiosity are two such prerequisites; confidence
that 'having a go' at something new doesn't always necessarily end in failure is another. The 'apathy' of some of
our youngsters merely disguises an unwillingness to put
themselves at risk: what is the point of trying something
different if you know from experience that it won't work?
It is confidence, then, that is a prerequisite for master-
ing other more formal skills. Are we successful in teaching confidence?

'My mates all think I've changed. I'm not so quiet. I
think I'm more self-confident. I'm much more ready to
take part in anything. You know at my other school, I
wouldn't have a go at new games or go on visits. Now I'd
jump at the chance' - Lester.

'I still get nervous at interviews but at least I know more
about what's involved in getting a job. I know what to ask
for and I'm not half so worried' - Judy.

'Before I came I hated going up to strange people and
asking them things. I didn't even like going into shops.
But now I don't mind. It doesn't seem to worry me' - Simon.

'I went to London with my mate last week' - Jim (who had
not been outside Bristol till we took him away on camp).

Self-confidence is linked with self-acceptance and developing a certainty about your own strength and weaknesses.
Perhaps we could have done more to focus on this aspect.
In group sessions several times we talked specifically
about individual 'good and bad points', but these occasions
were very infrequent.

Lunchtime discussions - our one guaranteed group activity
of the day - were often used to highlight individual achievement. With a captive audience (intent on such an enjoyable
pastime as eating) concentration is at a maximum.

Quite apart from the boost to self-confidence of the kids
actually succeeding in preparing an acceptable meal for a
dozen people, the act of sharing food and talking and joking
and listening strengthens the security of the 'group' and the
identity of the individuals in it.

Self-acceptance is crucial when it comes to job selection.
This is one aspect where we feel we can assess tangible progress. Most of the youngsters have totally unrealistic job
expectations when they arrive. Though not on a par with
the joke about the unemployed labourer who registered as a
brain surgeon, they nevertheless have wildly distorted aspirations. Careers as mechanics, playgroup assistants or
long-distance haulage drivers, and college courses are fre-

quently mentioned in the first weeks by kids who, at that
point in time, possess neither the academic qualifications
or social skills even to nibble at the bottom rung of their
expressed career interest.

Part of our job must be to replace fantasy with reality.
The process can be a long one because it means a realistic
appraisal of personal ability, which inevitably results in
lowering of sights. Through discussions with those in
work, through meeting prospective employers, and through
work experience itself we whittle away at constructing realistic possibilities from the tower block of fantasy. In a
supportive environment that is aimed at generating self-confidence it can be done.

The next chapter, dealing with the final half term with the
group that remained, expresses the reality of the job situation.

Chapter 9

Leaving school:
the final term

In many ways our success at finding the kids jobs is actually
failure. Because we provide individual attention, we can
negotiate with employers on their behalf and support them
through the traumas of the first day at work. But their
ability to find jobs is unrepresentative of their peer-group
generally and our success could not be replicated nationally,
even if every school-leaver had the individual attention ours
receive, for the simple reason that there aren't enough jobs.
So in one very important sense we are failing, because in
our school we can avoid the problems facing many teachers
and youth workers – of how to prepare kids for unemployment. Of course, we offer sops like everyone else: introducing them to leisure activities they can make use of with
time to spare. But these are sops; there is no substitute
for real work as long as society equates school with being a
child and work with being an adult so that not to move from
school to work is to remain trapped in the half-way house
between child and adult.
One problem, though, is that we actually regard a lot of
the jobs open to them as demeaning and degrading. Consequently when Jim came in excitedly one morning to tell us
about the job he'd got in a local garage 'valeting' cars we
experienced quite conflicting emotions. We were pleased
he'd got a job – the entry permit to the adult world – but we
were bothered at the nature of the work itself – at its lack of
prospects and opportunities for self-fulfilment.
But what is the alternative for a kid like Jim with no exam
credentials and few social graces? In 'Learning to
Labour', (1) Paul Willis provides an analysis of how working-
class kids are destined to get working-class jobs. His
appraisal of the situation supports the 'conspiracy theory'

view that education is an agent for social control, with pupils being schooled to respect the status quo and accept their position within society, no matter how low. In the old days, of course, inherited wealth and privilege was an acceptable system, and schooling was only available for a minority elite. Nowadays, though, automatic access to wealth and status by mere accident of birth is not quite so acceptable; so it has been necessary to devise a system of universal schooling that disguises the passing on of wealth and privilege to a selected elite under a banner that purports to offer equal opportunities for all.

This perspective regards the whole educational system as merely existing to reproduce the existing relationships of production, so that, in reality, there is no way of improving working-class life-chances or job opportunities generally through a process of universal schooling as structured in Britain. Kids' failure, both at school and in work, is inevitable because only those with certain predispositions are going to succeed.

The contrasting liberal democratic perspective sees all kids as having an equal opportunity to take advantage of the educational framework that is offered to all, but some choosing by default or laziness to accept a low run on the job ladder. The educational system allocates human resources within the occupational structure of society through the exam system, and anyone can use it to improve their life-chances and class position. But working-class kids don't generally. This perspective sees the kids failure as their fault or their ineptitude.

But whatever the perspective the reality for these kids is still the same: limited job prospects or no job at all. Generating awareness of the political nature of the economic structure that they are part of may help them to understand why they are only going to be offered low-status jobs. But it won't improve their job opportunities, unless the dissatisfaction engendered spurs them into some sort of remedial action. We don't believe in playing that game.

What we do believe is that we must operate at two levels. We must help them find jobs. Finding kids to fill vacancies or finding vacancies to fit kids is a very basic level of working. It is a fundamental approach in a money-dominated society where jobs provide cash and status. Given the existing situation, it is hard not to work just at that level, expecially with the sort of youngsters who come to our school.

But at the same time we must operate at the level of trying to develop their self-awareness, so that they are critical enough to choose a job appropriate to their recognised skills.

What is the reality for the group we have followed through most of a year?

By the beginning of the spring term two had left to start work: Jim with his father and brothers, and Dirk as a tyre fitter. Both of them would be earning 'good' money. Two of the group had fallen by the wayside. Debbie's departure was now history and Clive was en route to Detention Centre. Alec had opted to go on the dole, but did actually start work on a building site within weeks of signing on. It was the only way he could afford to go on running his motorbike once his Dad had stopped his allowance! Occasionally at lunchtime he would call in, helmet in hand, grinning from ear to ear and a good deal less jumpy than he'd been in the past. He provided a suitable demonstration about work being a ritual initiation from child to adult.

We started the summer term with seven of the original intake left, though our overall number was higher, since we had already begun to introduce new members to the group – those youngsters with whom we would continue working the following year.

Predictably, things had happened during the holidays. Joy's step-father was inside for non-payment of fines and her Mum was desperately short of cash; Liz's Dad was 'having very nasty arguments' with her Mum and she was worried about them splitting up; Martin's Mum was back 'in hospital' again – one of the psychiatric institutions that encircle the city; Angie's Mum was also in hospital, awaiting a lumbar puncture to cure back trouble, and her Dad was often away lorry driving. That first day back was the day scheduled for her Mum's operation and Angie herself was understandably in a very anxious state of mind. Simon's description of the holiday presented a monotonous picture of days spent running endless errands for a mother who was 'too bloody lazy to get out of bed to feed the meter!' Judy's domestic situation hadn't altered at all, and she was desperate to escape from the claustrophobic tension at home. Only Lester didn't seem weighed down with problems. The City Supporters Club had certainly benefited from his extra time, though it was doubtful whether his Mum had drawn much consolation from his increased liberty. He'd done nothing to help at home.

Amidst these tales of woe what was encouraging was their readiness to talk about it, and not just with us. They chatted amongst themselves, and seemed to draw support from the attentiveness of the others in the group.

'You can always sleep at my house.' Lester's offer to Judy may have had more to do with his own attraction for her than his concern at her domestic situation, but at least it represented genuine interest.

'I'll come with you to the hospital – we could pick some flowers from the garden.' Liz's words encouraged Angie to _do_ something instead of worry.

The value of our work can be measured by such incidents. It would be a wasted effort if at the end of the year, when our support is withdrawn, the kids are left floundering and revert to their original state of introspection or lowered self-confidence. Our success or failure could be evaluated perhaps by what use they make of the springboard we offer. Have they the strength of mind and self-confidence, derived from self-acceptance and self-knowledge, to strike out alone or with the others in the group? To see them using each other for mutual support and to know that after they've left us they keep in contact, knowing there is strength in their mutual friendships, is very encouraging.

At this point in time in 1979 we are witnessing yet another group in the throes of leaving. For three of the girls the Wimpy Bar in the city centre or the coffee lounge in Woolworth's has become the meeting place for their own form of group therapy. As they pass through their traumatic phase of leaving and having to stand alone, they are able to use their established friendship to protect their fragile confidence. Occasionally they ring one of us to let us know the things they are doing. Despite individual fears they are working through it.

It is easy to belittle the potential maturity of adolescents. Their status as children doesn't preclude their experiencing 'adult' awareness and friendships. As Martin put it one day, when trying to explain reasons for dropping out from his previous school: 'People think that nothing happens to kids what happens to grown-ups. If I say I'm depressed, people think I don't know what the word means.'

That first day of term we listened to their problems and told them ours: that we were likely to be pushed out of the building we'd used as a base all year. The owners of the site had become increasingly concerned at the growing dereliction of the rest of the building which had now been vacant for eighteen months. Having received an offer from another organisation to take over and use the whole enormous site, they were obviously likely to accept. It would necessitate us moving on, especially since we'd not been ideal tenants in our upkeep of the few rooms we did use. In truth, we hadn't done very well, since the responsibility for all the cleaning had fallen on us. We had an old broom and a dust-pan and appropriate cleaning fluids, but no one really liked cleaning, so it was a job everyone avoided or shirked when-ever possible. In a non-residential situation it is easy to do. Squalor can be coped with for short intervals, if you know you can escape from it later. We did have a sweeping-up rota, and there was a shifting responsibility for main-taining functional toilets, but the building had taken a bat-tering during our year of occupation. All this was talked about.

'Where would we move to?'

We didn't know, but we assured them we'd do our best to hang on in the building until they'd all left. We would not willingly move out before the half term when they could officially start work or sign on.

The next day I was late into school. Telephone calls in the office base a hundred yards away held me up. When I finally arrived at the entrance I found Lester, mop in hand, fiercely scrubbing our only carpet. Pools of soapy water bubbled across the grimy floor. 'We're cleaning up,' he announced. 'Then we won't have to move,' added Angie. They really meant it and put their energies behind their words. I gathered up more brushes and buckets from vari-ous corners of the office up the road. Lester finished scrubbing the carpet and moved on to mopping the floors; Simon began to remove the graffiti from the kitchen wall in preparation for painting over it. 'Clive, the Fonz' and 'City Rules' faded into obscurity. Their concerted effort amazed us. By lunchtime (prepared by Liz mostly, after Martin had cooked some bread rolls) the place was looking very different. Their enthusiasm carried through until late afternoon when we all piled into the nearby swimming pool to soak off accumulated sweat and grime.

Before the end of the week there were other notable 'highs': Simon vowed he was going to spend an hour every day practising his reading; Joy went off for an interview at the local technical college and was offered a place; Martin came in from his work experience full of the fact that they'd put a definite job offer for him in writing. He was the man

of the moment in his striped suit and matching tie. 'Would
you come back next year and teach fishing to the group on
an odd day off?' we asked. 'No fear,' was the pat response, 'I'm not coming to teach bloody delinquents.'

The time before the last seven could officially leave
school was short. Six weeks to half term. In that period
we had to concentrate on job finding and counselling, and
what other essential survival skills we felt were appropriate. The atmosphere was easy, with none of the tension
that had characterised various weeks in the previous two
terms. There was a general mood of confidence and optimism and enthusiasm for participation. Joy's guaranteed
place at college and Martin's job offer spurred the others to
do something themselves.

It was interesting to see their willingness to concentrate
on academic work. English and maths periods presented no
problems. It was as if, knowing the end was in sight, they
wanted to make the most of the time before the opportunity
finally disappeared. Simon persevered at his hour a day
(and subsequently joined our evening literacy class to practise reading). Angie, having formed friendships with some
of the Danish girls from Tvind who had stayed at the school
that memorable fortnight in February, brought various
'teach yourself' books and set to learning the language.
She made faltering attempts to write letters, half in English
and half in Danish, and talked of her intention to travel there
herself. In fact it was Angie who made us see the need for
a more organised learning programme. For the first time
Everett Reimer's concept of 'educational resource networks
that link teachers of specific skills with learners who wish
to acquire that skill' (2) had real relevance to our situation.
Some of them were beginning to want real learning and
Angie's interest in Danish was a good example. We were
able to put her in touch with an acquaintance who had spent
some time in Denmark; he was able to offer her direct
tuition about vocabulary and accent.

In this respect - the following up of individual interests -
we are exceptionally well placed. As people who have
lived in the city a number of years we all have our own contacts, and can cater fairly well for most requests from the
kids to follow specific interests. Guitar playing, electronics, fishing, cycling, are just some of the examples. Our
hope would be, of course, that they would have the confidence to pursue interests themselves, using the adult education network that proliferates in various corners of the city.

Martin's decision to join a local rifle club, after an introductory session there with one of the students, vindicated
this principle. It is worth noting about Martin that after
two years working in the fishing tackle shop, during which
time he rose to be more than just a mere general dogsbody,
he decided he wanted to go to college. His ambition with
us had always been to take various exams at 'O'-level with
a view to becoming a pharmacist. He is now on the way
there, having swapped a guaranteed £45 a week with paid
holidays and fringe benefits like free maggots, for the uncertain security of student life.

Martin in fact proved a solid rock till the time he left.
During the last few weeks, when he could easily have let
things slide and taken a back seat, knowing he was all right
with a job, he demonstrated the sort of commitment that was
a valuable lesson for the newcomers to the group. Punctual
and reliable, he cooked and cleaned, and practised during
the allotted English and maths slots, helping others like
Simon who were light years behind in terms of social skill
acquisition.

Sadly, the opposite was true for Liz. The knowledge of
a certain job at the corner shop where she'd been doing
work experience made her restless and disruptive. 'Tain't
no point in being here now, I might as well leave until I can
start work properly,' summed up her attitude. She was
quite right in one sense, but we knew that her defiance was
partly a response to the up and down situation she found herself in at home with Mum and Dad continually rowing. We
owed Liz quite a lot for her support and commitment that had
been such a model to the others for the earlier part of the
year. Without her enthusiasm and participation much of
what we'd attempted to do would have floundered. So we
contained her aggression and spent a lot of time just talking
and drinking coffee – one of the few activities she was prepared to contemplate without fuss. On the last day she
came in particularly early, a good hour before the rest.

'Wanted to say sorry,' she said. 'I've been a silly cow,
haven't I, for most of this term. Dunno what came over
me.'

The saddest event before the term finished was Judy's
removal from home into an assessment centre. We'd known
for a long time about the difficult home situation and that
she'd been staying out late many nights and sleeping away
from home at various friends' houses. Occasionally we met
some of these 'friends', who could certainly have been des-

cribed as very 'dubious' characters. It wasn't that unlikely that Judy was on the fringe of a criminal gang.

With our limited staffing resources there was little we
could do, given the distance from Bristol that she lived.
We could make the occasional visit, but in support terms it
was a drop in the ocean. Her situation highlighted the need
for our being able to work with the whole family. Seeing
Judy in isolation from her Mum and the domestic conflict was
almost a waste of time. Predictably it wasn't long before
she appeared in court on a theft charge, and on Mum's rec-
ommendation (because she referred to Judy as beyond her
control) she was transferred to a girls' remand centre where
she stayed until she left school.

In some ways her stay there helped, because she was
visited regularly by different members of the family, and
there seemed to be a general improvement in the relationships within it and more understanding about Judy's predicament. She left there to start work in a laundry – which was
a beginning at least – though the demands of the job bore
little relation to what we knew of her aptitude and ability.

It was because of pupils like Judy that we realised the
urgency of securing additional staffing. Work with many of
our youngsters is only of any real value if we are working
also with parental consent and involvement. Indeed, if the
causal problem lies in the home, it is almost fatuous to try
and effect a patching-up operation in isolation.

And of course, part of the measure of our success should
be to ensure that younger brothers and sisters don't follow
the same stormy route to our door – and that can only happen
if parental handling and understanding alters in perspective.
So we do need to involve parents right from the start. That
can only be done, for the reasons outlined in Chapter 6,
with a minimum pool of three staff.

With Judy gone we were left with just five of the original
group – two of whom, Liz and Martin, were fixed up with
jobs.

A coincidental return of Dirk and Jim on the same day, on
a day off from work, spurred Lester and Simon into action.
The comparative maturity and poise of the two young 'men'
was quite remarkable. A month in work had stabilised
Dirk in particular. Completely gone was the aggressive
pitch to his voice. He very reasonably gave an account of
his job and the value of good self-presentation at interview.
In teaching terms that day we had two excellent allies.

Simon's energetic involvement on his work experience day

at the garden centre bore fruit in terms of a job offer.
Though vacancies were very limited, they assured him of
employment as soon as a position fell free. Meanwhile, he
would work there on a part-time basis and tend the allotment
that he'd carved out of a piece of waste ground at the end of
the deserted playground.

At any 'interview' Simon would have been deemed almost
unemployable. He was pretty inarticulate and grubby and
aggressive in appearance, with a disturbing shiftiness in his
eyes. He would have put most potential employers right off.
But this unfortunate 'disguise' was a thin veneer over a
caring, sensitive person. Given the opportunity, Simon's
inner man would take over. The work experience placement
at the garden centre had enabled this to happen – and there
was no doubt of his value as a worker. Stripped to the
waist, wielding a shovel, sweat glistening on rippling
muscles, he was the epitome of the Mr Atlas adverts for
whom young ladies are supposed to cherish wild fantasies.

Before Lester left he was offered a choice of jobs – window
cleaning with a mate, or labouring with a building firm.
Despite his chuntering about dislike of physical effort, he
chose the latter. Six months after he left us he was still
there with them, and had a vision of five years' hence when
he had teamed up with a mate as self-employed doing interior
decorating. The irony of this would not have been lost on
his Mum, who'd never managed to persuade Lester to lift a
brush to help her when she'd redecorated their home from
attic to basement.

Only Angie presented real difficulties in terms of work.
Her own internal confusion became more apparent as the
leaving date approached. It wasn't really surprising. She
had still not accepted her sexual identity and right to the end
demonstrated the frustrated tom-boy who had been trapped by
the accident of being born female. Angie would have been
much happier as a bloke; she wasn't at all interested in
being 'feminine'. Heaven to her was roaring around on a
motorbike, with greasy overalls and enough money to keep
the tank topped up. The problem for Angie, was that,
being a female of her time and class, she would inevitably be
offered predominantly 'feminine' jobs, like in a shop or a
factory. Jobs as a car mechanic or builders' labourer,
which she would have much rather preferred, would be
denied her by most employers. We don't tend to adopt a
patronising chauvinistic attitude – and we don't see roles as
exclusively male or female (as is borne out by our approach

to the communal sharing of all activities) but in Angie's case
the best help we could have been was to enable her to realise
her femininity.

We never really succeeded. But she made it in the end,
after she'd left us. Working in a stable, thirty miles from
home, she prevailed upon her Dad to buy her a motorbike.
One step away from heaven at least!

Half term came and those who could leave did so. (3) We
were left with the core of the next year's group and time to
question the value of the three terms' involvement.

In statistical terms there had been some glaring 'failures'
- Clive in Detention Centre, Debbie on the streets, Judy in
a remand home. On the other side of the balance were the
'successes' - Joy on a college course, and Martin doing the
job of his choice.

But statistics are a mask really. In terms of self-acceptance and awareness Clive may well have advanced the most.
He'd certainly experienced and demonstrated real caring
involvement during the year. And Martin might have 'made
it' without us!

In any work of this nature - without the criterion of examination achievement - it is hard to talk in terms of success
and failure, as those who have written other personal
accounts would also testify:

Only in later years do we begin to become conscious of
the contribution various influences have made to our own
maturation. No one can know the contribution he makes
to others, for those are selected by the recipient, con-
sciously or unconsciously, and cannot be chosen by the
giver. (4)

What we want here is for our work to be taken seriously.
Judging us on how many children we get back to school is
to entirely misconstrue the point of our work. It carries
with it the idea that we can cure these children and that
what we are doing is somehow irrelevant to children who
are still at school. Have we failed if we do not get children back to school? But the children here are learning,
participating and choosing - isn't that what a school is
for? (5)

It is salutary perhaps to ponder about what would have
happened to most of them if they hadn't come to the school.
At best: nothing but boredom and a wasted year of doing
sod all. At worst: acute frustration leading to delinquency
and court appearances. Would Clive have been the only one

in Detention Centre?   After all these are the total school
refusers, the complete tail-enders of our educational
system, and in their way they have already caused a lot of
headache to a lot of people.   It's easy to forget history and
expect too much too quickly.   The balance between forming
relationships and pushing towards some sort of structure is
hard to maintain consistently, and we are still learning.

Chapter 10

Student involvement

A cornerstone to the school's effective functioning is its
staff/pupil ratio. With the eleven youngsters in the group
described here there were two full-time staff. This may
sound like Utopia to those teachers – particularly in primary
schools – with class sizes of forty or more. But there are
children for whom even a ratio like our 1:6 is not enough.
Some youngsters need individual attention in large doses.

At 15, adolescents who lack the 'cultural capital' to take
advantage of a society dominated by middle-class values are
in a dangerous situation, with regard to society as well as
themselves. It is more than just a matter of acquiring survival skills of the sort described in 'In and Out of
School', (1) though these are of course important.

The cultural heritage that public schools pass on as an
inevitable by-product of their schooling process is reinforced by family values back home. Likewise, youngsters from
middle-class families find the ethos of comprehensive school
and home quite compatible. But for working-class youngsters there is a contradiction between the cultural values of
the school, as epitomised by the teachers, and the values at
home. The cultural capital they take to infant school on
their very first day is either inappropriate or inadequate
compared to that of their middle-class peers. Right from
the start, therefore, the school would have positively to
recognise the need for small group situations to bridge the
gap between certain pupils. 'An ideal universal pedagogy
would take nothing for granted, and would not count as acquired what only some pupils had inherited.' (2) To pena-
lise the underprivileged, the school has only to neglect to
take into account the cultural inequalities between different
social classes, so that by 15 the problem has intensified and

the useful cultural capital of some youngsters is still at a minimal level.

With a year to go before starting work at 16, it is only really possible to transform the position through small group situations. Whatever the compromises between idealism and reality, it is vital to equip the particular youngsters we receive with a skeletal survival kit that includes a measure of cultural capital acquired from us.

The response to our plea for more small group situations in comprehensive schools is often along the lines of 'Well, if we had your staff/pupil ratio, then we'd be able to do that too.'

And so they would, and should, and could if only the self-imposed barriers of 'professionalism' did not exclude a skilled and willing personnel resource outside the school gates.

The bald fact is that if, for the first ten years of their schooling, working-class kids are constantly discriminated against, then at 15 many of them must have individual attention.

Take the example of what is probably the most threatening situation for teachers - an awkward, aggressive adolescent in confrontation. In a classroom there is a whole choice of options open to the teacher, ranging from excluding the pupil to giving him or her full-time personal attention.

To be realistic, though, it is often impractical to give attention in a large class, and exclusion is the inevitable immediate response to a threatening pupil. The problem for both teacher and class is removed, but sadly the problem itself smoulders and intensifies the other side of the closed door.

It is difficult to blame any teacher for such a reaction. Schools, as they are structured, don't allow enough time for the preventive work that might anticipate and defuse such an outburst before it arose, and often don't allow for any alternative except punitive exclusion.

Some schools are experimenting with classroom 'sanctuaries' where pupils can be sent, or can choose to go, to get away from confrontation situations. But even there it is implicit that the pupil is the one to blame. The general expectation of both pupils and teachers is that if the head comes along to find a youngster excluded from the classroom, it is the actions of the pupil not the teacher that are thrown into question.

In our situation we are dealing with some youngsters to

whom the exclusion technique has been liberally applied and
for whom outside our doors there really is nowhere to go,
except a home that might be locked or unwelcoming. So our
idealistic intention is never to have recourse to such an
approach. Having two staff working with the group means
that if an explosive situation develops between one member
of staff and a youngster, it is possible for the other to step
in and defuse it. If the explosion occurs between two
youngsters we are near enough (i.e. no barrier of desks) to
defuse it as friends. Sometimes, though, the inevitable
happens: one of us is in another room and tiredness or
frustration boil over to the point of confrontation.

Like the occasion when Alec arrived late and in a jumpy
mood to find us all sitting around the table doing maths. He
refused to join in and tuned the radio in to Terry Wogan
(one of our few rules was an agreement not to have the radio
on for certain periods of the day, like when we were doing
maths). His response to my request to turn it off, was a
grunted 'Fuck Off!'

Clearly, something was bugging Alec, something that had
probably nothing at all to do with me and had very little to
do with the group and had very likely happened last night or
that morning before he'd come. With hindsight, of course,
these perspectives become clearer, and an analysis that
maybe he'd been picked up by the police, or his girlfriend
had left him, or his Dad had belted him would probably have
been more accurate than the more immediate one that he was
determined to be deliberately annoying.

'Alec, we've all agreed that we don't have the radio on
when we're doing maths. Could you please turn it off?'

'You're always picking on me, aren't you? Just because
I'm in late. What about when one of the others comes in
late?'

'Alec, it's nothing to do with you being late. You're
interrupting what's happening here, that's all.'

'I like the radio on. I reckon I work better then.'
This mumbled interjection from Joy drew a chrous of assent
from several others. Hard-won concentration was beginning to flag. I moved to switch off the radio, since Hilary
was next door talking with a parent. This necessitated
leaving the group, and Joy, who only ever worked at maths
with someone watching over her shoulder, stirred restlessly
and looked longingly at the gas fire across the room.

Alec waited till I'd sat down before switching on the radio
again. He glared at me provocatively. It was becoming a

game which one of us was bound to lose. The others were
watching with keen interest, all thought of arithmetic pushed
well aside.

As I sat down the second time, a dart thudded into the
desk beside my hand. Alec's grin stretched from ear to
ear. Fortunately no one else was laughing.

'Alec, if you're not going to join us and you just want to
disrupt us, perhaps you should have stayed at home.'

'Too fucking right. I don't come here to be picked on.'

Something snapped finally. 'Alec, you're being a
bloody-minded little sod. Why don't you go outside for a
bit and cool off?'

'I fucking well will!'

The door slammed. Footsteps echoed down the corridor.
Alec stayed away until I went round to his house to discuss
the incident. It would have helped the situation if Hilary
had been there and available to 'go off' with Alec somewhere
else for a time, instead of him just storming out with his already black mood much darkened by the confrontation.

Fortunately, Special Schools administration recognise
the necessity of good staff/pupil ratios. In Avon, for instance, the accepted norm is 1:6. But as anyone who works
with these kinds of youngsters knows, even this is not always enough. Youngsters who have experienced ten years
of schooling that has constantly disregarded or criticised
their presence can sometimes have acquired the unenviable
personal handicaps of infant reading ages, low self-confidence and limited verbal expressive ability which need and
deserve personal attention to redress the balance.

So even the generous teacher/pupil ratio for 'special'
institutions must be supplemented by additional adult involvement. To this end we involve a number of students working
alongside us with the youngsters. The students are trainee
teachers from the university School of Education or trainee
social workers from the polytechnic. For the youngsters
they represent extra hands and more possibilities.

The use of students with the groups on the parent ROSLA
project is described very fully in 'In and Out of School'.(3)
For all of them such involvement with youngsters in an informal situation, where authority is earned, not provided,
by invested status, is a valuable preparation for their subsequent professional role. If they cope with our situation,
we reckon they will learn skills that can be effectively
applied in mainstream teaching – and reports from the
schools they move on to certainly suggest this to be true.

One problem for the students is that they are only involved
for a part of what is a full-time weekly programme for the
youngsters.   In their terms this presents difficulty of continuity.   The complaint, particularly from the student
teachers, is that they don't know what the youngsters have
done the rest of the week and that this ignorance sometimes
renders their own preparation worthless.   Our answer to
this is first to ask if they expect their experience in a comprehensive school to be any different.   After all with timetables constructed so that subject teaching is done in blocks
of three or four lessons at a time, it is quite normal for
teachers only to see a class once a week.   For some of them
that connection and its implication are hard to grasp.   Generally, their perception is that sich a situation is all right in
schools, but not with us.   Our hope is that they may actually
enter schools critical of this aspect and do something about
it, because the students are right to recognise that teaching
a class is a difficult situation when they don't know what's
happening to the pupils for the rest of the week.

Equally true is the difficulty of teaching a group of youngsters in school without being aware of what is happening at
home in individual cases.   The validity of an approach that
ignores domestic tensions or frictions is open to serious
question.   If people can only learn when free from worry,
then teachers must cope with pupil anxiety before presenting
'knowledge' for acquisition.

Of course this is the value of residential schooling where
domestic tension can be contained, and where life both inside and outside school is part of a connected progression of
events.   Such an approach to schooling is one way of reducing the differential caused by the unequal inheritance of the
cultural capital described earlier, and gives credence to the
ideas propounded by the Israeli Kibbutzim, where children
are schooled in a residential setting, orientated around a
social construction of an expanded family. (4)

However, the insularity that constitutes the advantages of
a residential school also reflects its chief disadvantage:
that the child finally has to return to his original environment.   The good work of many such community situations is
completely negated on the child's return home.   Residential
schools that are most beneficial would be those that provide
the child with the necessary skills (and inclination) to survive outside the walls of their protective sanctuary.

In such residential situations, though, at least everyone
concerned with the youngsters is aware of the intermarriage

between social and educational factors, and aware of the
necessity for taking account of the former in preparing the
latter. The value of a training placement for students at
Bayswater Centre is that such a truth is self-evident, since
much of their time is spent concerned with domestic issues.
But it would be unrealistic to pretend that it is easy to
transpose this awareness to a straight school-teaching situation. Their recurrent complaint about working in a par-
tial vacuum is a recognition of a very real obstacle. The
issue to debate is how this can be improved. For the students at Bayswater we point out several ways they can keep
themselves informed about what happens on days that they
aren't with the group. One is for them to read the daily
journal that the youngsters keep; another is to share information at our weekly seminar; a third is to ask the youngsters themselves.

It is possible to do these things in school as well. There
is no reason apart from 'time' why all the teachers of a particular class couldn't pool their curriculum plan for a half
term so that each one of them can see what that class of
youngsters is going to be exposed to, and, equally important, who will be teaching them.

An important feature of teacher training should be the
sharing of the experience of being taught alongside the
youngsters. To follow one class through its weekly timetable and participate in its activities and lessons should be
a basic experience of all trainee teachers. The exposure
to the variety of teaching styles and ranges of personality
that an ordinary class has to cope with would be an illumi-
nating experience.

When I was teaching science in a comprehensive school I
well remember one particular second-year class who I saw
three times a week. On two of these occasions they were a
delight to be with - interested, lively, motivated and co-
operative. On the third occasion they were usually fretful,
fidgety and argumentative. It didn't make sense, until I
discovered the lesson before mine was with an irascible,
ineffectual lady, on the point of retirement, whose lack of
interest and concern in the class was only matched by theirs
for her.

It would be interesting to try this sharing approach in
schools. After all it is only what 'integrated studies'
attempts to do. Naturally, it would require time allocated
for such preparation. But why not, if it makes a rewarding
difference? The very real barrier of 'time' could be re-

moved if those designing the timetable felt such collaboration and cross-referral important enough. The barrier is acceptability not feasibility.

In the hope that the kind of educational 'system' we are offering at Bayswater Centre will prepare the students for teaching in comprehensive schools and will influence their approach and attitude in their respective schools, we spend a lot of time with them in seminars outside their involvement with the youngsters. Inevitably in such an unstructured framework they need considerable support, particularly in the early stages, and we feel too that we must present and discuss with them the wider socio-economic context of the work of our school if we are to influence their approach to teaching itself. There is no doubt of the value placed on such an experience by the students. For people bred on a diet of academic fodder it isn't so surprising that such a practical placement is regarded as useful. After all it's the first time in sixteen years of their own schooling that they've soiled their hands with work (apart from the inevitable short periods during vacations, when impecuniosity necessitated the finding of work in a factory or on a building site). Maybe their enthusiastic response just illustrates the value of practical experience for <u>anyone</u> intending to teach, and reinforces the argument that teachers and teacher training programmes should not be divorced from the society in which they operate. The Chinese model where 'intellectuals' and 'bureaucrats' are required to spend regular periods of time in the factories and fields as well as in their offices has something to commend it despite its many drawbacks.

We are quite sure that the students benefit personally from their involvement at Bayswater. At worst they will enter schools less convinced of the value of belting recalcitrant pupils; at best they will appreciate the importance of our Three Rs, and will give pupils in schools the respect and responsibility that will be reciprocated in a majority of cases.

We feel that such placements as ours should be a compulsory part of any teacher training course, and this belief is borne out by the testimony of the students themselves. With our small group situation, in a less formal setting than school, where our emphasis is less on academic achievement and more on developing productive relationships, it is possible, with good professional guidance, for students to learn skills and gain insights that will very much influence and improve their approach to schools.

For the kids, of course, the advantage of having students around is tremendous; more interest, more opportunities and more people than they need to relate to. From their point of view the only drawback is that the number of students involved can be quite large - nine in a week for the group described in this book: which in the early stages means some confusion as to names and who's coming on which day.

From the staff point of view as well, student involvement is very rewarding, especially when they bring fresh ideas and a critical appraisal. Once over their shyness and particularly when things start going wrong as well as right, they can be very critical and their criticism is worth listening to.

In an attempt to tap this source of useful criticism for our benefit we contacted all the student teachers who had been involved with the school since it first began in 1975 and asked them a number of questions to which we hoped, with the benefit of hindsight and practical involvement in a real school situation, they could provide valuable replies. We were also curious to know whether involvement with our school had made any difference to their subsequent work or choice of jobs.

The full questionnaire sent to students, together with a tabulated analysis of their replies, is given in Appendix 4.

Though the 19 returned replies (out of a possible 25) certainly don't represent a statistical sample of all the student teachers' opinions, they do raise some interesting issues. In the rest of this chapter I intend to use their comments and criticism as a starting point for further exploration of our attitudes and approaches.

The questionnaire was divided into two sections, with the first part designed to elucidate the students' opinions and perceptions of the centre with reference to the pupils, and the second part intended to be an enquiry into how placement at the centre had affected their subsequent work in or out of school.

SECTION ONE

In studying their respective assessments of the centre, it is interesting to note how infrequently the students' comments are concerned with educational attainment - certainly not in terms of what most schools would describe as educa-

tional. Their remarks tend to be about behaviour and personality development of individual kids, rather than cognitive development.

This perhaps reflects <u>our</u> priorities. Though we recognise that the kids do need and often want 'education' in the
factual informational sense, and that their ignorance about
even the geography and history of their own environment is
alarming in its totality, we believe there are more fundamental 'subjects' to concentrate on first. This belief has
something to do with the lack of 'cultural capital', mentioned
already, that constitutes a general problem for many working-class children.

They are referred to us as 'school-phobic', 'school refusers', 'disrupters': disturbed adolescents in need of
treatment. 'Maladjusted' is another way of putting it. And
of course they are misfits, in the sense that they don't or
won't fit into the standard structure organised for the majority of school children. In some cases they very bravely
opt out, at considerable cost to themselves. But the fault
may not actually be theirs, since their starting point at age
5 may be so far behind or removed from that of their middle-
class peers that to enter the same race is a ludicrous exercise.

In his book about Newton Aycliffe School in County
Durham, (5) Masud Hoghughi, the Principal, raised a few
eyebrows with an assertion that this gap in 'cultural capital' is often actually exacerbated by professional interview:

The only justification for such intervention is to alleviate
problems, or at least prevent them from getting worse.
Too often intervention does neither. One boy here has
been in 19 establishments - that means 18 took him on and
gave him up as untreatable, or at least passed him on.
What does that do for a child?

Whose fault it is, is largely irrelevant for immediate
practical purposes. At 15 they are on the verge of leaving
school, and society will expect them to adapt and adopt and
cope with an adult role. Somehow in twelve months' time
their 'maladjustment' must be 'cured'.

In general terms for these children we can do one of
three things: (1) provide them with an alternative school
where they can fit in; (2) change them so they can eventually
fit into ordinary school or society; (3) change the schools
to accommodate them as well as the 'normal' undisturbed
youngsters. As a simplistic delineation the first is the
goal of the radical de-schoolers, the second is the goal of

the Child Guidance clinics, and the third is the goal of the
educational idealist and reformist.

We subscribe to a mixture of all three, which isn't just a
case of backing all horses so we can't lose (or gain) very
much.   We do provide the alternative, but unlike de-schoolers we would also hope to see schools change to suit the
needs of all people and not just an academically orientated
minority of school children.

Since schools have the existing hardware resources, it
seems more appropriate to develop an 'educational' network
from within, than by constructing makeshift alternatives outside.   This is not to say that education outside school is un-
important.   In fact, we believe quite the reverse.   We know
from experience that for many kids much learning has to take
place outside school because so many youngsters and adults
shy away from its institution.   But if schools looked and
behaved and seemed different, the situation could change.

A recent DES press release took up this issue, when pub-
licising a £100,000 follow-up study it was going to support,
on how desirable changes in schools could be brought about:

Unjustified absence from school can, then, be a consequence of other problems and it can also be their cause.
In such cases, special steps may have to be devised to
ensure that learning is by consent and co-operation between teachers and other members of the education service, and with social and youth workers; to provide an
education which depends less on conventional authority
and perhaps more on a form of contractual relationship
between teacher and pupil.   Using informal learning
methods and containing strong elements of social education ... or re-education.

But such special provision should be seen in educational
terms not as an alternative to school, but as an interim
measure, from which young people would normally expect
to return to normal schooling.   This task of reintroducing
young people from a separate unit back to normal full time
schooling needs special attention from both ends.   The
jump may be too great and sudden either for the young
person or for the school. (6)

It seems a pity that the state school approach, with its
superior hardware resources, and the alternative school
approach, with its relaxed atmosphere and generous man-
power resources, can't come together.

The Danish system incorporates a flexible framework
which allows for just such a collusion.   There is a tradition

in that country of tolerance towards educational alternatives and these are accepted as a recognised and funded
feature of the overall state-supported provision. Even
though some of them espouse curriculum models and structures very different to ordinary statutory provision, they
are regarded as acceptable within the established principle
of right of educational choice. In Britain there is no such
tradition. Though educational institutions notionally adopt
the principle that 'schools should prepare children for life'
most, in reality, concentrate on preparing children for
examinations, and this is the juiciest carrot for much in-
structional work that takes place in a school. Social education, or non-examination curriculum, forms a very small
part of most youngsters' timetables. Of course an indus-
trialised society needs engineers and technologists and
leaders of perception and learning; and universities as they
exist at present need to select from a vast range of appli-
cants, and selection is made simpler by exams. But only a
few will ever aspire to university applications and it is still
only a minority that even reach 'O'- or 'A'-levels.

So for the rest - probably the majority of school children
- this game of credential acquisition is not quite so important, for in their terms 'life', when they leave school, is
work or unemployment, and their preparation for this is
sadly inefficient. Many youngsters - particularly working-
class youngsters, for whom school is often a showcase of
alien values - need a realistic preparation for life, which
can generally only take place outside school given the structure and organisation of the system at present. It is only
through an alternative approach that puts the needs of the
pupils first that some kids are going to be reached at all.

Our first aim at Bayswater is to try and provide an alternative where they can fit in, and the best way to do this is
by laying emphasis initially on many things not considered
important at school, like talking and showing we value their
opinions, and at the same time under-emphasising those
aspects of schools, like subjects and unexplained rules,
that they have reacted against. The priority must be the
relaxed atmosphere of the centre and our attitude to their
taking responsibility; they must want to come and feel safe
and secure before they will feel able to do the risking and
exploring that is the prerequisite of further learning.

Only then can we concentrate on the second of those three
listed alternatives - 'Changing the youngsters, so they can
fit in.' We would prefer to describe the process as one of

trying to give them the skills necessary to survive in normal society. In one year these adolescents have to become adults. They need to learn how to survive in a world which imposes values they tend to reject. For instance, some might need to see that stealing, which one or two could actually regard as quite normal, is not a safe survival skill. They need to see that there are times when conforming can honestly make life easier and doesn't necessarily mean a loss of status. We must also concentrate on rebuilding self-confidence and self-esteem, on re-kindling a trusting and caring attitude to friends and others; on demonstrating the possibilities of leisure activities; on enabling them to understand access; on enabling them to understand that 'charm' is every bit as useful in the real world as examination credentials.

Consequently, it isn't surprising that the students, who play an important part in this 'cultural' adaptation, will inevitably see the unit as playing a largely non-educational role in the school sense, even though all the youngsters now sit CSE exams in a choice of at least four subjects.

Given this perception, it is logical for the students to define the potential benefit to youngsters' attending the cen centre in non-academic terms (Question 2). They regard appropriate admission criteria as resting on things other than previous academic attainment. Indeed although we certainly don't ignore past school records when selecting youngsters, we find it more important to try and assess potential interest and intellectual ability. It is certainly true that it helps the running of the group to have one or two youngsters already capable of CSE attainment when they join us. However, we frequently find that poor literacy and numeracy ability and low IQ measurements often mask tremendous latent talent.

The students' observations as to how the centre could harm some youngsters (Question 4) are interesting, since they appear to contradict the claim that a caring approach can only do good. Some of the students clearly disagree and in this they would be supported by the one or two youngsters who express a wish to have been sent away, rather than come to us. The explanation for that may simply be an urgent desire to escape from home. Domestic tensions and problems may be so overwhelming that a community home seems a blissful alternative. Perhaps, though, the wish to go away derives from a feeling of guilt. The youngsters have 'failed' in societal terms, have let down their friends, their parents, their relations and teachers – not to mention themselves. They may well see themselves as inadequate and worthy of blame. Their guilt (unconscious or not) needs expiating – either by punishment or by giving them an opportunity to make amends. For these youngsters perhaps our structure can be too liberal to be felt as punishment and it is hard for them to make amends in a way that would purge their guilt. For some, then, a more rigid approach would be appropriate. That sounds harsh but it need not be so in fact. Detention could be in a firm but therapeutic community, where the punishment is in the removal from home and restriction of freedom, but where at the same time they are supported in a caring environment that enables them to mature to a stage where they can make amends.

This is not an argument for wholesale detention of 'maladjusted' kids; but there are youngsters who feel that a spell in 'Detention Centre' before coming to us is a just sentence. If the result of their stealing a car or knocking off stuff is an immediate referral to our liberal sanctuary, this must be confusing for those who see their behaviour as deserving of punishment.

Whatever our own thoughts about Detention Centres, they have done some of our children some good in a strange way, but the support aspect which should surely be an important feature of the therapy is sadly lacking in most Detention Centres. Many youngsters, embittered by what they see as an overdose of punishment, feel the scales have tipped into an 'I'm going out to get my own back now' attitude by the time they're released.

The following is a transcript of a spontaneous tape recording made by two of our group about Detention Centre. One of the boys had spent a spell inside a few months previously, and during a session with one of the students he was encouraged to re-enact certain aspects with the other lad playing a complementary role. Kevin, the student, just let the tape run, and though the unexpurgated version may appear overdramatic, it contains a disconcerting element of brutality.

Week 6

P: Oh 'ello officers, is this our new DC boy?
G: Yes, we've just brought him in from the central police station. He's in for assault and other various things.
P: Right, c'mon boy over here! Stand on the red line. C'mon move! Now ... got any belongings on you?

S: No I ain't.
P: What d'you mean, no, you ain't? No you ain't WH-A-AT?
S: Sir.
P: Give him a boot over Albert.
S: (Screams as the boot goes in)
P: Now listen, perhaps that'll remind you to call us sir.
S: You ain't allowed to do this.
G: Look boy we're allowed to do anything we want in here, see?
P: This is a prison boy not any Kingswood recreation room. Now get over on the red carpet. Stand in between the lines.
S: Yes sir.
P: Hurry U-U-P!
S: Sir, I can't stand up on my own too much sir.
P: Stand U-U-P! Now ... run over there! Come on double quick. You should be back by now.
G: And don't go dripping blood over the clean floor.
P: All right, get into that bath. Two minutes. Hurry up! You finished yet?
S: No, not yet sir.
P: Well get out!
S: Sir.
P: Dry yourself, c'mon. Now put your clothes on. There's yer jeans on the floor down there.
S: I can't wear those, they're dirty old rags.
P: What? Give him a work over Bert. Now listen boy! Go on give it 'im Bert, bang his head a couple of times on that wall.... All right Bert, that's enough, you'll kill the kid. Now listen son, perhaps that'll learn you to do what you're told. YOU ain't in any community home now, so pick up your stuff. Run down the corridor. Quick, you should be back by now....
P2: Now son ... I 'eard you just come in 'ave you? They call me 'rhubarb' but I don't want to hear you call me that. That's my nickname see.
S: Yes sir.
P2: Now ... you don't like your Mum and Dad do you?
S: Yeah I do sir (P strikes S).
P2: No you don't son!
S: No I don't sir.
P2: What do you mean, you don't? You don't like your parents? (Strikes S again.) Pick up your stuff ... now hurry up. Run down that corridor. Now back! B-A-C-K! Right, stand to attention. C'mon!...

G: Parade. P-A-R-A-D-E 'shun! Right march off two by
   two. Hurry up!
P2: Follow me. Follow me. See that bed over there?
S: Yes sir.
P2: I want yours made up exactly the same as that. And if
    it 'ain't boy, when I comes back, God help you! Now,
    got all your stuff?
S: Yes sir.
P: Here's a piece of paper; check it off. If you ain't got
   none of that stuff you come and tell me son, right?
S: I can't read though sir.
P: What d'you mean you can't read?
S: I can't read sir.
G: Open your eyes boy!
P: You better start reading. After tomorrow you'll be at
   school, 'n you got your scrubbin' all of next week. And
   after scrubbin' you might get a job. So think yerself
   lucky. You'll get seven pence scrubbin' fees ... and
   that'll be enough to cover you son. Now ... get into
   bed and I'll wake you up in the morning.

Morning

P: Everybody up. Come on get your shorts on. Get your
   shorts on.... Get your shorts on son.... Get your
   towel.
S: It's only six o'clock sir.
P: What d'you mean only six o'clock boy? We've let you
   have a lay in. Now get up.... Right, come on,
   double up the showers. M-O-O-V-E.
S: Sir, the water's freezing.
P: Shut up.
G: What d'you think this is a holiday camp?
P: You ain't in a community home now. Come on, get out.
   Right, you down to your rooms, sweep them out, sweep
   the corridor, get your clothes on and make yer bed packs
   up. M-O-O-V-E!
   Line up. You should have done that by now.

Breakfast

P: Come on, get your trays. There's your tray son.
S: Where does my breakfast go sir?
P: Just put it in the big one and small one and grab yourself a cup tea and hurry up. Hey, you son, move yourself.

S: Why sir?
P: I said M-O-O-V-E.
   Now ... you ate yer breakfast yet?
S: Yes sir.
P: Well get outside there and line up for medical. We're
   gonna check to see if you got any fleas.
P: (Talking to a superior) Umm ... sir we got one of the
   umm ... medical boys for you for check up. (Talking
   to the new inmate) Right, come you slag. Get yer
   clothes off. Drop your pants.... Turn round....
   Pull em up.... Now son, what are you in here for, you
   scum? Eh?
S: Assaultin' sir.
P: Assault. You dirty slag! I've known little kids like
   you. You've been in and out ain't you? AIN'T YOU?
S: No sir, this is my first time.
G: We can see that boy!
P: Well, you're in here now ain't you?
S: Yes sir.
P: What do you mean yes? D'you think this place is gonna
   learn you a lesson?
S: Yes sir.
P: That's what they all says innit?
S: Is it sir? I dunno.
P: Well, you better start learning. You start circuit
   training straight after this medical. Right?
S: Right sir.
P: Right. Get out to your room. Get yer shorts and
   towel and M-O-O-V-E!

In the gym

P3: Right you load of slags, line up outside the gym.
    Move. Move! Stand in a straight line. No talking.
    Right into the gym on the red line. Move!
    Now boys, I'm Mr Delaney. I don't take no bullshit
    or rubbish about you can't do no fuckin' things ... you
    slags. Now get the circuit out. Come on, it should
    be out by now boys, move yerselves.
    You boy.... Come over here.... Bend over, touch
    your toes.... (Kicks S)
S: Uggh!
P3: Shut up and get back into line. Right this circuit's
    been done in three minutes. I hopes you lot's gonna
    beat that. When I says go, you go. Right?

S: (Throws up.)
P3: Move it!
S: I can't do it sir. I've just been sick.
P3: M-O-O-V-E! Come on, more press ups, deep down on
those squats, backs straight. Heads up.... Right,
hold it lads, into the showers.

In the showers

P4: Oi, when we was doing that circuit you cheated didn't
you?
S: No sir.
P4: You don't have to call me sir. I'm in here for the
same thing as you.... I seen you cheat.
S: I never.
P4: Yes, you did you little scum (he strikes S).
S: No, please don't.
P4: If I sees you cheating again that's what you'll get
(smacks him again).
G: Oy! You two.
P & S: Sir?
G: Stand against that wall.
P & S: Sorry sir.
G: I'll give you 'Sorry sir' (he beats S).
S: No sir. Please don't sir.
G: Right, extra scrubbing for you two. What was it all
about anyway?
P4: He cheated in circuits sir.
S: I never sir. (7)

As well as questioning the centre's appropriateness for
'delinquent' kids, the students also question its benefit for
the very withdrawn. In a normal school the silent child
should be a cause for concern but sadly, because of his
silence, he often remains unnoticed and ignored, whilst the
noisy child lays prior claim to the teacher's attention. To
'draw out' such children from their icy reserve is difficult.
Our situation, with its demand for 'group sharing' can
actually appear threatening and make it impossible for a very
withdrawn youngster to join in, so it could be harmful, by
presenting yet one more situation that reinforces feelings of
isolation.
    The only way out, it seems to us, in those cases, is for
individual attention away from the group. The LEA system

of home tutoring offers recourse to such a therapy, but
sadly the emphasis is placed on English and maths, which
seem rather inappropriate for youngsters who need something more fundamental than cognitive knowledge. Home
tutoring that concentrates on thawing the isolation first can
work. We have tried it, with limited success.

Royston, described in Chapter 4, was a good example.
His failure to attend our school necessitated the LEA making
home tutoring provision for him, and since we already had
contact with the family it was suggested that we organised
the home tuition. Because of staffing commitments at the
centre, visits to Royston's house were usually arranged for
the early morning. At the appointed hour, Royston was always to be found still in bed, having made no effort to stir
himself to wakefulness. He was assisted by a mother who
either connived at his 'laziness' or was unwilling to risk inevitable confrontation with her only son. The presence of
a television in his room certainly explained his unwillingness
to rise at 9 a.m., since he had inevitably watched the midnight movie the previous evening.

It would have been quite understandable if Rog (my col-
league of the same name, a coincidence which causes equal
confusion to staff and pupils alike),who was doing the home
tutoring, had given up at that point and left Royston to his
state of slumber. But he didn't. His first visits were
spent talking to a boy who remained impassively silent,
snuggled beneath a barrier of bedclothes. Eventually, Rog
persuaded him to rise from his bed before he left the house.
From then it was slow going, but the point was reached when
Rog was able to persuade Royston to be up in time for them
both to work on Royston's motorbike (a present from Mum).
This thawed the relationship and led to Rog being able to
steer Royston into the realms of literacy - through insurance forms and driving licence applications. Though consistently undermined by Mum between visits, he generated
enough social confidence in Royston for the boy to find a
job, and stick with it, after leaving 'school'. It is certainly doubtful that the statutory home tutoring approach,
with heavy emphasis on English and maths, would have lured
Royston from his bed at all.

Of equal concern is the students' comment that the informality of our school could be harmful. This expresses a
commonly held fear that a liberal approach can be difficult
to come to terms with for children who are used to orders
and structure, where decisions are always made for them by

'authority' figures. The confusion for them is that the
source of authority is very difficult in our setting. It is
not invested in our status as teachers, though initially some
of the youngsters' preconceptions of teachers affect their
perception of our authority as being just that. But it soon
crumbles when they can see we have few sanctions that we
wish, or intend to apply. The basis for their attendance is
not our coercion but their compliance, and our authority
derives from the relationship we form with the youngsters.
We try to develop positive reinforcement within the group,
which itself provides the support and the sanctions.

We recognise too that within the informal atmosphere it is
very necessary to have a structured framework. 'Doing
your own thing' is not a system of much help to young people
who are in real need of adult support and guidance. We are
directive but with their compliance to an agreed structure
and standard of behaviour.

It is not surprising that all the students noticed significant behavioural changes in the youngsters attending (Question 6). Indeed, it would be surprising if they didn't
change, given the high adult/pupil ratio and the interest
shown in them as individuals. What is interesting though is
that the list of 'transformations' reflects an emphasis on
'social' education. Confidence, awareness and responsibility are all necessary preconditions for a state of mind
that enables 'factual' learning to take place, and they are
more fundamental in a survival sense.

The students' comments about what was most helpful for
the youngsters is consistent with their perspective of the
'social education' bias of the school (Question 7). Their
emphasis is not on specific subject material, but rather on
social and vocational preparation. There is an almost
unanimous acceptance by the students that this is most important for the kids, which presents an interesting contrast
to the very different starting point for teachers in schools,
where it is the 'curriculum', not the needs of the pupils,
that defines the content.

Turning to their criticism of the structure and content of
the school (Question 8) most of their comments tie in with
earlier observations about the apparent lack of structure
and direction. In our early days this was certainly a jus-
tifiable criticism, and like other alternative experiments we
too have moved away from the 'no rules, do what you want'
approach to a semblance of order - recognising that children, like adults, need a structure to work within. The

important point is to distinguish between a structure that is directive by consent, or just simply authoritarian and hier- archical. For instance, we prepare an outline timetable and before they arrive we decide some rules that we believe will enable the unit to function more smoothly. We do not decide on things that are dependent on their personality and fluctuating moods - like dress or friendship or speech or behaviour, unless the latter impinges on other people's freedom.

Nevertheless, we do find it difficult to balance ideals about democratic participation with a real need for struc- ture and some regulations. Numbers make a big difference. In 'Small is Beautiful' Schumacher writes very profoundly on the importance of size to the running of truly democratic institutions, (8) and it is no surprise that the larger com- prehensives tend to have more discipline problems and dif- ficulties of alienation between staff and pupils than do smaller schools.

In offering suggestions about what they would change were they running the centre (Question 9) the students' observa- tions reflect personal priorities that present an interesting contrast to the perceptions of those members of the public or educational administration, who favour an emphasis on the Three Rs. The great debate has launched a shift in public opinion towards a resurgence of the importance of basic numeracy and literacy. We concur with that attitude, but, in line with many of the students, we recognise that some of our kids are still at square one, where 'social skills' need developing as an essential precursor to scrip- tural and numerical competence.

The final question to the students gives an opportunity for personal comment. The most frequent - that it increased their own awareness of adolescent problems - is a testimony to the value of the placement as a training resource, and at this point it seems appropriate to reproduce an extract from a student journal, appraising the centre half-way through his course. In considering the benefit of the centre, both to the youngsters as well as himself, he presents an opti- mistic perspective of its strengths.

An evaluation of Bayswater Centre after one term

My changing perception of the kids

Before the first meeting at the beginning of term, I expected
to meet a group of kids who were resilient, abusive, and
literally tough, both physically and psychologically.
   My first shock was the 'normality' of the kids.   Most
didn't have the tough image in a physical or visual sense.
Most of them, although obviously living in insecure situations, seemed very knowledgeable about life.   Sometimes
as a result of their comparative greater exposure to life's
harshness, I felt naive.   It has taken longer to become
aware of the psychological insecurity of the kids.   Gradually, awareness was made of their general lack of confidence in certain public situations.   Towards the end of term
the individual weaknesses of some of the kids have become
apparent.   For example: one boy's irresponsibility in
sexual matters and his inability to differentiate between a
sexual and platonic relationship with girls; and another
boy's fantasy world, symbolised by his idolatry of his
father.

Value of Bayswater Centre for the kids

(1) A genuinely caring situation is provided, in which the
kids' problems receive thorough attention – a very different
situation to the one the kids might otherwise be in: in school
assessment centre, Detention Centre, or just truanting.
(2) On more 'educational' terms, the unit fulfils a useful
function in providing information on problems likely to be
encountered in post-school life, and the agencies available
to be called upon to help.   This has spin-offs in getting the
kids to think ahead.   At the level of activities, improve-
ments could be made, I feel, in making greater attempts to
base explorations upon the interests of the kids themselves.
   Staff ratios are advantageous to help with any numeracy
and literacy problems, and the resources of the group are
wide enough to be able to provide facilities for further intellectual stimulation and the possibility of taking external
exams.   Thus at a cognitive/intellectual level, the unit is
potentially able to cater for individual needs.
(3) At the psychological level, the kids are forced to come
to terms with their own hang-ups.   This is done gradually,
and often by using the social pressure of the group as a
whole.

Besides psychological 'onslaughts', other aspects of
character are worked upon, by inculcating social consciousness and awarding some degree of responsibility;
both aspects find their forte in the group decision-making
which is an important part of the life of the group, and
which could be usefully extended.

It is this personality development aspect that an institution like Bayswater Centre is better able to provide than
any other school, and it appears to be doing this fairly
effectively.

Value of my experience at Bayswater Centre: a personal
account

First, since the conclusion of the preceding section appears
to be advocative of a behaviourist approach, my work on the
scheme has forced me to reassess my own analytical methodology. Rather than dismissing the behaviourist's 'therapy'
simply in terms of injections of an adjustment/conformity
drug, it must now be awarded at least some value as it
seeks to provide (through coming to terms with individual
hang-ups) some tools for survival. So the behaviourist
approach must not be totally discounted. I would maintain,
however, that its value must be assessed with caution and
within the context of a firm analysis and understanding of
the wider picture.

Second, the excursion into a sub-culture that the experience has afforded me, has given me an understanding of
factors influencing the lives of people who form the truant
and delinquent sectors of our society.

Third, I have obtained a good deal of information on the
various support services available to anyone working with
youngsters. (9)

The above underlines the force of our claim for inclusion of
such small group interaction with children as an intrinsic
part of any teacher training course. His comments reflect
what most of the trainee teachers feel. Two years later,
at the same point in his training, another student describes
his involvement:

This scheme is the only part of the course which offers any
real contact with children. For although as students we
are required to observe in a secondary school one morning

each week, the circumstances are very different and there
is little or no chance to participate actively or to control
what takes place. Teaching practice on the course begins
next term and I would like to quote extracts from the instructions I have received from my particular school,
which demonstrate the expected relationship between
teacher and pupils in this environment.

(1) Pupils should enter and leave classrooms in an orderly
fashion. No running, no pushing, no noise! If a class
arrives in a boisterous fashion, it is useful to send them
out of the room and have them come back again in a proper
fashion. You are establishing your standards.

(2) The teacher must clearly be in charge of the pupils.
Talk by the pupils should be purposeful, there should be no
giggles, no shouting, no grabbing things or persons by
pupils. No pupil should leave the classroom without getting
the permission of the teacher and should see that the teacher
is aware of his or her return.

(3) No teacher should set out to be liked. It is a teacher's
job to get children to learn effectively and if possible to
enjoy the process.

These are some of the guidelines that have been developed
in order to help the teacher maintain discipline and manage
large classes of children, which consequently places the
teacher/pupil relationship on a necessarily impersonal
basis. Because of the large numbers involved, few pupils
are able to benefit from individual attention. Some of them
show their opposition to this system by rejecting completely
its rules, regulations and aims. For them, school is seen
as a situation where one is forced to take in irrelevant
knowledge by external and alien figures of authority - the
traditional 'them' of working-class culture.

The problem then in schooling today is the fact that working-class children are not intrinsically motivated to do what
the school wants them to. The examination system and use
of discipline has only helped to destroy self-initiative and
self-motivation in the child. Many psychologists have told
us that play and curiosity are vital elements of learning and,
without these aspects being developed, intrinsic motivation
cannot occur. When intrinsic motivation is fostered, the
self-esteem of the child is increased and a desire to learn
encouraged. The major function of the teacher should
therefore be to foster the desire to learn.

The scheme has enabled me to form a less naive attitude
to the children who are disruptive in school and has helped

me to realise that such children are not just disruptive for
the sake of it, but usually have problems which they find difficult to cope with. Their attitude is often a result of problems either in or out of school, and emerges when they are
unable to solve such problems. For example, if a pupil
cannot read fluently, then he faces problems in that he may
have difficulty in understanding the timetable and does not
know (especially in a large comprehensive) where he should
be at a certain time, and arriving late means remonstrations
from the teacher. Obviously, continual reprimands lead to
a feeling of resentment and alienation from school, and the
desire to truant increases. This inevitably leads to more
problems, because the longer the period of truancy, the
harder it becomes to return to school.

Working with the boys has given me the opportunity also to
discover what interests children out of school and an insight
into current trends in youth and popular culture. Involvement in their subculture with its rapidly changing values and
stances is a way of expressing their rejection of a mainstream culture that has rejected them. Paul Willis in an
article entitled How working class kids get working class
jobs explains that within a school

the boys' opposition to the school and its agents were very
powerful determinants of what amounted to an anti-school,
alternative or counter culture within the school. Member-
ship of this culture or the manner of your relationship to
it was very much more important to the non academic lads
than was the achievement of any formal aims of education.

He goes on to say that

It is no accident that much of the conflict bewteen staff
and pupils should take place on the grounds of school uni-
form/casual dress. To the outsider it might seem a fatuous argument about differences in taste. Concerned staff
and involved kids, however, know that it is a continuing
tussle about authority, a fight between cultures and ultimately a question about the legitimacy of school as an
institution.

Involvement with the scheme therefore, has led me to question many aspects of traditional schooling and I realise that
it cannot provide adequately for the needs of all children.
My experience is limited and it would be arrogant to suggest
radical changes in the system without far greater knowledge
of its workings, but I too have suffered the indignities and
humiliations delivered to children each day in the name of
education. Thus the greatest benefit I have gained from

this part of the course is the chance to meet children in a
less formal situation, free from the barriers of a teacher/
pupil relationship, which has enabled me to gauge to a certain extent what they expect, what they enjoy, and what they
hate about school. (10)

SECTION TWO

The second part of the questionnaire is predominantly concerned with how the students have applied the experience
gained from their involvement at the centre in their future
jobs.

The fundamental problem of relating their experience with
the youngsters at Bayswater to the very different situation
of a school classroom has already been discussed. What
the students feel it is important to teach, and what it is
actually possible to do in an ordinary comprehensive school,
are two very different things. Idealism is often swamped by
the flood of reality. The problems of implementing the 'art
of the possible' become apparent as soon as they start
teaching practice and find themselves confronted by classes
of thirty or more pupils. Approaches that they have been
successfully applying at the centre become no longer useful
in the classroom situation. To many students, any possibility of treating the youngsters as individuals becomes quite
ridiculous. In tutorials, when this is discussed, they are
adamant that it's mostly the fault of the local authority
system, which only allows ratios of 1:30 because of its insistence on small sixth-form classes (encouraged perhaps by
parents or senior teachers) at the expense of those in the
statutory age bracket. It is too easy to be glib and say that
in stating the obstacles to implementing innovation the students are just avoiding action. But how on earth do you
teach in a school in the way we can at Bayswater?

There are ways, and though this issue is discussed further in Chapter 12, there are a number of comments relevant
to make at this stage.

One approach that offers scope for social interaction in
school is programmed learning – a technique which can be
successfully applied for some subjects, with the youngsters
working either individually or in small groups using preprepared material, so that the teacher can move amongst the
whole class. This technique encourages an interaction between teacher and pupil that is basically centred round the

work material, but which can still allow time for the social intercourse, which many youngsters need first.

Programmed learning is an effective tool for motivated youngsters, and can certainly enable the teacher to spend more time talking to individuals than formal class instruction allows. Even so, the amount of time for social interaction is bound to be fairly minimal, however committed the individual teacher. In a one-hour lesson with 30 youngsters this works out at two minutes a child – a time boundary which would make any psychotherapist shudder!

A second approach is to introduce other adults into the classroom. The community around the school is full of people with skills and knowledge. It must be so, in any area. They won't necessarily possess BEds or BAs but they may well have something positive to offer that could complement the predominantly academic background of many teachers.

The union objection to this is that such a move might enable local authorities to disguise staffing cuts more easily, and would maybe even lead to an increase in teacher redundancies. There is also a fear that it might undermine teachers' authority by putting their 'professionalism' in question.

Yet if professionalism in teaching terms means to put the needs of the pupils first, then the 'all hands to the deck' approach for the pupils' benefit must be nothing short of very professional. Furthermore, even for those teachers who regard their role as primarily to teach a specific subject and not to engage in 'social work', the complementary involvement of outsiders to engage in social interaction is crucial – especially for those youngsters who need individual attention.

These 'outsiders' could work alongside the teacher under his direction and the teacher's authority would be enhanced rather than diminished, because he would still have the responsibility for organising the overall dynamic. For the occasional incompetent teacher, and those inclined to laziness, such a proposal, if implemented, would expose their lesson content to criticism and possible ridicule. For a committed energetic teacher it could be an exciting opportunity.

But the students, some of whom promise to be excellent teachers, still find it hard to grasp the connection between what is done and what succeeds at the centre, and what could be done and successful in a comprehensive school.

To some extent this is a criticism of a teacher training
course that offers limited practical guidance about teaching
methods to student teachers. New teachers are left very
much to fend for themselves, and though it is true that the
best way of learning the ropes is by climbing them, it is
also true that on-the-spot practical guidance would be very
valuable. Supervision of students on teaching practice is
woefully inadequate - the norm being two or three times a
term, rather than the two or three times a week which would
be of real help. Some schools have instituted the role of
professional tutor, but in the present climate of cutbacks
these posts will be the first to go.

When they do start their term's teaching practice, we are
in a unique position to help students discuss and compare
what is done at the centre and what is possible in school.
However, it is important that any suggestions or criticisms
are based on the reality of personal experience - that we,
as tutors, understand the problem of teaching in a comprehensive school. Our usefulness to the students in terms of
their self-preparation for school lies in our own real experience of what it is like to teach in school. There is no
point in our attempting to draw parallels between what is
done at Bayswater Centre and what could be done in school
if we only understand the latter as a theoretical exercise.
This is not to say didactically that experience can only be
gained first-hand - but it's a recognition that second-hand
observation of situations stand more chance of distortion or
misunderstanding. There is a strong argument for all college of education lecturers involved in tutoring students
about the craft and art of teaching to remain involved themselves with practical teaching. Even a morning session a
week in school would keep them in touch with the shop floor,
so that their tutoring of students would be based on an up-to-
date appreciation of the real issues facing young teachers -
class control, organisation, preparation, marking, preservation of status, winning respect and so on. It would make
their advice in seminars much more credible.

Additionally, the academic experience of college lecturers, with their up-to-date knowledge of educational innovation, would inject a positive contribution to staff rooms.
The example of Harry Ree, Professor of Education at York
University, who resigned his chair and returned to teach
French at Woodberry Down comprehensive school,is worth
highlighting. The Chinese tradition, where all academics
and white-collar workers spend time in the fields and fac-

tories to ensure their own work remains relevant, seems so
eminently sensible for a society that is governed by bureaucrats and theoreticians. As a nation of shopkeepers, we
all need to spend time on the shop floor.

After five years of running the centre – away from direct
involvement in mainstream education, my tutoring approach
to the student teachers was significantly altered after I'd
begun teaching science to a group of first-year 'low-ability'
pupils one afternoon a week in a local comprehensive school.
The problems of organisation and control, and constrictions
of time, conflict very abruptly with theoretical ideals.
Content and actual subject teaching become secondary factors in the early days of meeting a new group. Yet the
determination to try at least to make the content relevant
comes across to the kids in the end.

If schools are to remain relevant, they must be open to
change, and the force for that change could be the influx of
young teachers joining a school, with their fresh ideas and
enthusiasms, being allowed to introduce them under the
guidance of experienced teachers who really understand the
'art of the possible' but have not themselves lost their
idealism.

Which is why a placement at the centre is such a valuable
part of the students' course. There is an opportunity in its
unstructured environment to attempt to practise what is
preached by the prophets of relevant education. There is
an opportunity to understand adolescents in a context, which
can be coupled with the subsequent term's teaching practice
to put idealism into a practical perspective.

It is interesting, therefore, to see from the students'
replies how much – with the benefit of hindsight – their time
at Bayswater had actually affected their subsequent attitudes
to teaching.

What comes through strongly from their preliminary remarks, is that their initial expectations were often too high.
They were surprised at the 'backwardness' of the pupils,
at how ignorant and limited the kids were in terms of knowledge, and they realised how important it was that activities
were attempted in response to the kids' needs, instead of
what they (the students) might have felt appropriate.

The general message that comes across from the students
reflects an increased awareness of the problem facing these
youngsters through difficulties of home backgrounds and
personal weaknesses.

In terms of actual job choice (Question 4a), apart from the

depressing and laconic observation by one of the students
that she had no choice about teaching posts (which is a reflection on the uncertain employment situation), it is encouraging to note that, of those who were working in
schools, the majority had deliberately attempted to involve
themselves with 'difficult' kids. Since it is a recognised
fact that these groups in schools need the better teachers,
this is heartening. It is only by deploying good teachers
amongst all groups that there is any hope of redressing the
existing discrimination against working-class kids - which
after all is partly what comprehensivisation was intended to
do.

The 100 per cent affirmative reply to whether it had affected their attitude to 'difficult' youngsters (Question 4b)
shows every indication of increased sympathy and understanding, although, as some predictably point out, understanding a problem and handling it effectively are two different things. The very role that students must adopt
within a school can be an insurmountable barrier for children who are unable to see any teachers as human and are
quite surprised to discover they actually drink or go out and
have interests.

In their assessment of how their teaching was influenced
(Question 4c), the recognition that an authoritarian teaching
style was useless in school is interesting. There are two
apparently opposing schools of thought about this. One
supports the notion that children (or indeed anyone) will
not learn by intimidation, and the other claims that children
prefer a strict teacher who makes them learn. What is perhaps actually more true is a mixture of both; children need
a structure, which is imposed firmly, but within which they
can enjoy freedom from petty constraint.

The students' comments about their altered attitude to
children inside or outside the classroom highlights a basic
contradiction of school teaching (Question 4d). All youngsters need individual attention at some time, but without a
serious reduction in class numbers this is only possible in
an out of school situation. The irony is that though school
provides the structure for adult involvement and leadership
and guidance of young people, the actual opportunity to do
this is restricted to break times and after school. Lessons
themselves are often a barrier to real contact!

The 'not yet' response about involvement in promoting
changes is predictable (Question 4f). Probationary teachers are offered little opportunity to suggest changes. This

is sad, because though their experience may be limited, their enthusiasm and commitment is high, and too often, by the time they attain the giddy heights of responsibility posts they have lost or forgotten their useful ideals.

However, the optimism of the final questions (5 and 6) suggests that some are seriously trying to influence schools, despite a recognition of the obstacles confronting them. Staff attitudes, curriculum restrictions and parental pressure, combined with the clamorous rewarding demands of the already motivated youngsters make any attempt to re-negotiate schooling for potential 'school phobics' an uphill struggle. Yet, if nothing is done for these pupils, the cost in personal terms and to the community is very high - £14,000 a year for a residential placement to accommodate an embittered youngster is an expensive and belated alternative.

The firmly expressed confiction that something can be done - which bubbles through the final comments of the sutdents - is a hopeful note on which to conclude.

Chapter 11

Metamorphosis of a school: three Rs

The group described in this book left us two years ago.
Since then there have been significant changes.

Before visiting Tvind we knew from our own experience
that trust and responsibility were key links in any workable
curriculum. We knew too that the physical structure of the
building had to be suggestive of possibilities. An abandoned, rambling primary school could never be anything more
than a transient base, and would be treated as such by
pupils and staff. The building had to belong in some way to
those who worked in it. We knew, before visiting Tvind,
the value of relevant education and in a limited way were
endeavouring to apply it.

Visiting Tvind, though, was a shot in the arm. Upper-
most in our minds on the return journey were the questions
'What implications does this have for our own work? What
have we learnt that's of use?'

Perhaps the most important was that we had witnessed a
situation where our ideals of engaging youngsters in self-
determinism and participation were actually being practised.
What we had thought possible, but had experienced very
sporadically and often superficially, we could see was possible. Kids at Tvind could accept and cope with the responsibility of managing their own education, and could reach a
stage of consciousness where self-development and communal development embraced each other in a symbiotic partner-
ship.

Very simply it starts with expectations. By giving the
youngsters a role, they accept responsibility, and the expectation of the school is that this is so. The ethos is
established and communicated not just by the teachers, but
by those pupils who remain for another year. Like our

public schools, Tvind has developing traditions which will
be handed down from one group to the next.

Without doubt the residential setting fosters the environment for self-determinism and responsibility, and they use
that fact. The pupils are answerable for their actions and
are involved in the decision-making process.

The expectation is that this will be the case. So right
from the start they join in. As Annie Lundgand describes
in Appendix 3 they all feel part of the ideal and recognise
that they have a shared responsibility for furthering the
cause. So they accept group decisions like no alcohol or
drugs; they accept that they must be involved in a public
relations exercise of showing people round.

And because most of the theoretical work is linked with
practical work, and the practical work makes sense,then
there is enthusiasm and motivation for academic study.

In their case, education is not seen as a preparation for
life, but more as a participation in life. They live and
learn through living.

The problem with our own situation is that it is not residential, and so the youngsters don't have to live with the
consequences of their actions and in certain ways can evade
responsibility. A further complication is that to date we
have begun with a fresh group each year, so that every year
we have gone through an induction process, with attitudes
and expectations always emanating from the staff. At Tvind
they experienced that difficulty in their first year: Annie's
graphic account of the five-day meeting illustrates the scale
and seriousness of the problem. But since that time the
accepted ethos of Tvind is passed on by the pupils as well
as the teachers.

Before visiting Tvind we had felt this aspect was crucial
- establishing the tradition of responsibility. With the
group described in this book we did finally achieve a certain level of collective responsibility, despite unpropitious
surroundings and inadequate staffing. The same year as
visiting Tvind we achieved our ambition in terms of buildings. After a gruelling three years wandering through the
deserts of church halls, cathedral crypts, old primary
schools and abandoned caretakers' lodges we were offered
a large house in a 'respectable' residential area. For the
first time since starting the school we had a building that
was more than just a temporary base. The potential of a
large house and a garden were there to be realised.

Concurrently, with the support of MSC, we were able to

increase our staff team to three. For the first time we
could actually implement our principle of there always being
two adults working with the group at any one time.

For the first time we had the resources we'd been clam-
ouring for for over three years. The LEA had given us
enough yarn to weave the magic thread.

Bolstered by the Tvind experience and the observation of
other units like those mentioned in Chapter 2, we decided to
trust our ideals and make a fresh start, with responsibility
for organising and running the school being shared with the
kids right from the start. The emphasis would be on their
involvement with us in a pilot project whose success or
failure could influence the development of other such projects, or even influence mainstream education. Their participation with the hosting of visitors and the induction of
new pupils would be essential. The last, our equivalent to
the public school tradition, was crucial. We were not
going to dictate or coerce, it had to be co-operative.

We started with six 'pupils' a few weeks before the summer
term ended. We wanted a group who would have time to get
to know us and each other and share enough through the long
hot break to start the autumn term as a cohesive band. We
stipulated two conditions to the kids, that they should attend
every day and join in whatever activity was agreed, and they
would come on a three-day camp to Cornwall before term
ended. On that basis we would talk them into the group, and
if the subsequent three-week period was mutually successful, we would take them permanently on the roll for the following year. The six kids came to Cornwall.

We met them periodically during the summer break, by
mutual arrangement, to sit and talk and drink coffee and
plan our timetable for the next term. We drew up a skeleton framework bearing in mind the need to give time to what
we considered to be the essential Three Rs - Responsibility, aRticulation and Relevant education.

The kids accepted quite readily the value of setting time
aside for English and maths. They demurred at the suggestion of labelling any other periods by recognisable school
subject names: geography, history and French were anathema to them; the idea of artwork, under the heading 'creative activities', was not unanimously endorsed but did win a
majority verdict; games which weren't hockey and rounders
or PE met with varying degrees of enthusiasm.

They all saw the value of spending time 'working on the
house', doing decorating and minor repairs. They very

much wanted to allow time for talking. 'We don't want every minute organised,' expressed a common concern.

The following skeletal timetable emerged:

Monday	Discussion	Lunch	House maintenance
Tuesday	Creative work	Lunch	Project work
Wednesday	Maths	Lunch	Project work
Thursday	English	Lunch	Games
Friday	Visit	Lunch	Discussions

During the autumn term we stuck to it more or less. The Monday morning discussion period generally ran into lunchtime, but most of the group were willing to stay later than usual in the afternoon to work on the house to effect steady improvement. The lounge/meeting room was papered and painted first, and then, slowly, other rooms like the kitchen took shape and atmosphere.

The 'art' session, catalysed by Sue who came in once a week to infuse ideas and demonstrate know-how, flourished from a two-hour slot to an activity that embraced copious extra free time for some of the kids. The 'art room' became the focal point of interest at fluctuating times, reaching a high peak of activity during the early part of the summer term, when five of the kids prepared folders for their CSE exams. The combined stimulus of Sue, and the rather intangible reward of a CSE, stimulated a prolific outpouring of ideas and energy from the five involved.

In accepting the sessions for English and maths there was a mutual understanding that work at these subjects was inherently of value and the theme of responsibility and relevant education was a common thread in our approach to teaching these.

English at Bayswater Centre involves the kids in handling some (not all yet) of the correspondence for the unit: replying to letters, preparing information sheets and the occasional magazine, and keeping a record of what has been done individually. For those interested in taking the exam it meant practising essay writing and comprehension exercises, as well as preparing a folder of work in line with the requirements of the CSE. The 'School Project', an appraisal of attitudes to school that Mandy compiled from interviews with teachers, her friends and acquaintances, students and other staff at the centre, was more than just a piece of exam material. It was a very personal experience of a deep-felt concern. The finished product was a mature and interesting document, which stood as an ironic testimony to the latent talent that had nearly been discarded as worthless.

To make maths relevant is a harder task, since many
people can manage to live their lives without recourse to
more arithmetic than that demanded by fiscal transactions in
the supermarket. However, in handling the petty cash
book, which meant keeping a record of how the weekly allocation of £15 for 'incidental' items like petrol for the bus,
milk and tea and paper clips was spent, the group learnt
something about book-keeping, whilst their mental arithmetic was still kept alive. The exercise was demonstrably
useful. If the books didn't balance because they hadn't
collected sufficient receipts, then there would be questions
asked. If the sheets were accurately presented our petty
cash would be reimbursed from central funds by the appropriate sum. We could continue to spend. Without their
sharing the responsibility for 'doing the petty cash' we
would have no money for incidental expenditure – and the
lack of coffee and milk would precipitate a crisis that affected everyone!

It gave everyone – staff and pupils – some idea of where
the money was going. We presented a graphic record every
week of how much we were spending on equipment, travel
and stationery and food.

Collecting receipts became something of an obsession with
all of us. The 7p for the 'Evening Post', the 13p for an odd
bottle of milk all had to be receipted and recorded individually. It was a valuable exercise and paid dividends when
it came to organising camps, because all the kids had some
idea at least of what ordinary things cost. The petrol cost
for the trip to Denmark was estimated at £100 for the 2,000-
mile journey. We meticulously kept receipts and recorded
expenditure en route. The total bill was £93.33 (and if we
added to that the £2.75 for the oil can we'd have been well
within the limits of 1 per cent error!).

In truth, though, beyond the possibilities encapsulated in
fiscal exercises like book-keeping and budgeting, there are
few opportunities to apply maths in a practical way on a
regular basis. One-off calculations about how much paint
for certain rooms, or how much chipboard was required for
the darkroom were useful exercises. In our experience we
feel that maths is somewhat overrated as a school subject.
That statement borders on heresy and would be quite unac-
ceptable to a large number of those in the profession! But
in terms of practical application, much of the modern exam
syllabus is no more than mental acrobatics. The argument
that it 'trains the mind' is reminiscent of that put out by the

dying breed of classics teacher, justifying an allocation of
five lessons of Latin for every pupil each week.

Maybe it is true: but in our situation, we find that our
Three Rs offer just as much scope for exercising the mind.
There are notable examples. In running the playgroup,
in handling the influx of visitors,in discussions at Open
Days, in the play they presented for 9-year-old kids in the
adjacent primary school, our youngsters were put in the
position of being the people with something to give, be it
their own personalities, or their own ideas, or their own
experience. In activities like handling the telephone calls
and the petty cash, and cooking the lunch, the kids shared
the responsibility for running the school with the staff.

To link these activities with the requirements of the CSE
exam boards for English and maths was an exercise in Relevant education that demanded a lot from staff and pupils.
There were times when there was no apparent connection.
Then, as at Tvind, we had to recognise that some things
were to be done simply because of the exams. The responsibility for making that choice was theirs.

Half of them made that choice and ended the year taking
three exams each - English, maths and art. For kids who
have been written off as useless, this was really quite a remarkable achievement. The most significant thing was not
in the grade attained or the passing or failing. It was
obviously good if they did well, but in our terms the most
important aspect of their taking exams was what it exempli-
fied about their self-confidence.

At the beginning of the year the idea of taking an exam was
anathema to all, the mere suggestion caused embarrassed
laughter or evoked sullen silence. It was a ridiculous suggestion. They were obviously no good. Exams, relevant
or not, were quite beyond their limited ability. Their attitude wasn't surprising. If you're told you're stupid or lazy
enough times, it is hard not to believe it.

By January five of them were willing to try again, and set
time aside for preparing themselves for the ordeal. For
one or two it remained an ordeal, culminating in the ultimate
anguish of returning to a real school to sit the exam. That
was a serious problem, and certainly affected actual performance on the day. To be surrounded by the physical structure and atmosphere that they'd rejected so forcefully was
bound to affect them. On the day of the first exam we drove
them to the allotted school with a certain amount of trepidation. We parked the car and walked towards the entrance.

The assembly hall bell ringing in the hall must have exhumed
many buried fears.

As I pushed open the door to the main building, a grey-
haired woman stepped forward.

'Only sixth formers through here,' she commanded, quite
abrupt and unsmiling.

I blinked in amazement. She must have registered an
error of judgment, because she added 'and Staff?' in a questioning tone.

Behind me the kids were quite silent, listening to every
word. This was exactly what they remembered as the worst
aspect of school.

I held the door open and beckoned them in. 'This way –
and through that exit over there.' Hesitantly they shuffled
past. I smiled at the teacher. 'Staff,' I explained, and
left her in a state of puzzled silence, to join the kids as they
passed through the portals beyond.

It was a sad experience really, after all we'd done to re-
store their shattered confidence. Perhaps, though, it was
more significant to me than the kids. I was just angry that
she had not shown us the courtesy of asking first whether
she could help or show us the way. Her response had been
the pat one of a person in authority, with no time for step-
ping off the preordained pedestal.

At least we could laugh about it later.

'Your face – when she said "only sixth formers",' Mandy
giggled. 'I thought you were going to say something really
wicked.'

Of the 'exam results', art was the most successful, in
terms of self-development as well as ultimate grades.
Their interest in art was so infectious that it was common to
find the whole group engaged in the art room at times when
they could have been elsewhere.

Our intention has always been to develop 'resource' rooms
where there would be enough equipment and materials to
stimulate activity. We had always wanted to have 'doing'
rooms. And the art room, well stocked with paper and
paints, was a vindication of our beliefs in the value of such
a structure. The intention is to create a number of activity
rooms for woodwork, for photography, for music – with the
emphasis on an enabling atmosphere and ready access. So
that people can go and 'do' when the interest takes them.

To this end some of the 'project' work was geared towards
such resource development. With the help of students from
the university School of Education on Wednesday afternoons,

we were able to offer a range of 'projects' geared to individual interests. Electronics, gardening, photography and guitar playing were four of the most successful. Each activity involved one of the students with two or three from the group.

In photography, for instance, the student in charge taught the kids the rudiments of developing and enlarging, so that their celluloid encapsulations of camps and visits could be evocatively displayed round the building. Their experience and observation in the borrowed darkroom enabled them to think quite seriously about building our own. To date it is three-quarters complete. The woodwork and the wiring are finished, with the plumbing still unresolved. When it is finished we will spend the allotted sum of money on an enlarger and other accessories.

The involvement of students has been discussed. Since moving into a permanent site it has been easier to give them a role to slip into when they first come, and that has proved invaluable. The students need structure as much as the kids, and need to feel an equal sense of belonging. Our 'project' work has had definite parameters, with the building and the benefit to the group as a focal point for activity. So the minibus has been worked on, the garden cared for, and several magazines run off during 'project' time.

With student help we were also able to offer a games period - NOT organised hockey or lacrosse, but swimming and snooker, squash and weightlifting: all individual or small group interests that could be pursued outside our precincts. As a group they went potholing, horse riding and climbing, and at those times the mutual assistance offered by the more proficient to the less able was a moving testament to the value of developing response-ability.

From the start we have emphasised the importance of the 'group' and used this as a focal point for many discussions. We laid great store by 'group' decisions and their growing awareness of the strength and support associated with belonging to a coherent group. The 'group' acted as a motivator, as a restrainer, as a counsellor, as a kind of friend with many voices. It is this collective aspect of our work that underpins any success, and is what the Danes at Tvind had struggled towards so purposefully.

Belonging to a group demands response-ability and fosters maturity. It diminishes feelings of isolation and loneliness, and provides an opportunity for experiencing the excitement of working with friends towards a commonly agreed goal.

This is exactly what Rutter identifies as an important element in developing a good working atmosphere within comprehensive schools. (1)

So our Monday morning discussion meetings were more than just planning sessions where announcements and comments would be aired and recorded. It was a time to bring the 'group' together, and the one definite time in the week when everyone was sitting in the same room. It worked so well that we wondered about the value of such a session at the end of the week.

As long as we had access to transport and the weather was in our favour we would usually use Fridays for a visit - as a drawing together of the group at the end of the week. It worked very well, until our ageing minibus failed its MOT at the beginning of the spring term, and the opportunities for visits became somewhat restricted to places within easy walking distance or accessible by bus. On wet Fridays a very damp gathering of people would steam round the storage heaters, talking and drinking coffee and sometimes feeling, like us, frustrated by the lack of purpose in being together.

Coincidentally, we were approached by an emerging theatre-in-education group of actors, Bush Telegraph, about the possibility of their working with our kids. The organiser of the group had been a student with us several years before, and well understood the philosophy of our approach.

For three years I had shied away from introducing drama to the kids. Even though I had used it successfully with fifth formers in school, I was uncertain of the reception in our situation. Intuitively and vaguely I felt that it would be regarded as 'wet' or 'soft'. This year though there were two kids who actually wanted to do drama and their enthusiasm kindled enough motivation in the others.

Using various well-tried trust games Angie and Jefh developed a pattern of work with the group on Friday mornings, which provided the cohesive end to the week that we'd hoped for, and for which we'd previously rlied on the minibus. This is not to suggest that the Bush Telegraph team were merely a human substitute for our deceased minibus! Much has been written about the 'educational' value of drama, and how it can offer scope for self-expression for youngsters who experience difficulties with the written word. Though that is true, its value for all kids is obvious to anyone who has tried it. The opportunity it affords for self-exploration and for self-development are tremendous. Under the skilled

and intuitive guidance of Angie and Jefh, the kids emerged
from their shells and became confident people, prepared to
take risks and be extrovert. There were some quite amazing 'transformations'. The play they presented to a group
of primary children before the summer term finished, and
their willingness to spend a week of their summer holiday
involved in rehearsals with Angie and Jefh, indicates the
real value to them of the drama activity.

From Monday to Friday, for the first time since the school
started as a halting experiment, we had a structured timetable that embraced the whole week. Though it gave time
for individual interests, there were periods of emphasis on
group activities that we felt were fundamental to any lasting
success. Since the timetable had been agreed with the kids
at the beginning there was very little dissent about what we
were doing each day. Though there was an obvious reluc-
tance to leave the comfort of the coffee and chairs in the
common room for the comparative bleakness of the maths and
English room, there was usually a good-humoured acceptance of its validity. For the first time there was a prevailing atmosphere of commitment. Just arriving and being
were no longer enough. Doing and sharing were the expected
standards.

Apart from daily routines the year was punctuated by re-
cordable events of varying magnitude. The display that
greeted the visitors in the entrance hall for our open day at
the end of the summer term, listed the following:

Camping at Witheven Farm in Cornwall: 2nd to 6th October
Getting to know the Community: our Open Day: 13th
October
Danes visit us in Bristol: 15th-20th October
Visit to Heathrow: 14th November
London for a day: 13th December
Chris Gray (our third member of staff) joined us: 10th
January
Last Waltz: 31st January
3 Days camping at Minehead in a blizzard: 8th-11th Feb-
ruary
Godspell: 23rd February
Fun Raising (sic): 26th-28th March
Open Day: 6th June
Jefh and Angie and play: 8th June

Using photographs and illustrations the kids had prepared
a collage of the more extrovert events of the year. Mostly
they were activities which they'd shared as a group, with

the emphasis on fun and freedom. What is important about all the activities – the camps, the visits, the playgroup, the parties and the diaries – was their involvement in the planning and execution of them all. From the initial idea that circulated round the common room on a Monday morning to the clearing up after the camp or whatever, the youngsters accepted responsibility for being involved.

Each visit was fun, and in educational terms the learning by doing and participating amply justified the expenditure of time and energy.

The largest display was headed Denmark Expedition and, perhaps, more than anything else this year, it stood as a testimony to what the kids had achieved.

Conceived as an idea following a brief stay by a small group of Danes in the Christmas term, no one felt that a return visit to Odense was a serious possibility. For those youngsters who had barely ventured beyond the city boundaries, Denmark was no more than a name calling to mind either bacon or pornography. They had no idea about its whereabouts and no confidence in our declared intention to go if they wanted to. 'It'll never happen,' was a common cry. 'We won't ever get it sorted out, people will drop out at the last minute.' The experience of eleventh-hour oscillations in numbers for previous camps certainly gave grounds for doubt.

'If you get it together, we'll go.' The onus was on them, though during the early spring months we provided the encouragement and direction.

None of us, staff or pupils, had ever contemplated such a venture. Slowly though a plan evolved. The ageing minibus was put on a ramp and revivified. Letters went off: to the Danish school we intended to visit, to the respective embassies of countries en route for information, to the AA for maps, to the passport office. Menus were prepared. Equipment was repaired and sorted. A list was drawn up of all the things we had to do and each person agreed to take responsibility for organising several things.

Dates were fixed, the ferry was booked, the MOT was passed, the kids brought in their share of the money and parental consent, the route was agreed. The day before departure we sat in the common room surrounded by piles of food and equipment – all neatly packaged and labelled.

The Director of Education joined us that morning and listened as each person in turn ran through what they'd been responsible for organising. He was able to witness a

demonstration of the effectiveness of our emphasis on our
Three Rs. Two boys described the route and answered
questions about distances and times and camp sites. Two of
the girls ran through the menu – dried food featuring predominantly in every meal. The day before they'd spent £90 in
the local cash'n'carry. 'You don't like Alpen?' retorted
Ally to one of the boys who demurred at the suggestion for
breakfast. 'Well, I expect you can find a bit of grass to mix
with your milk!'

Eleven of us, with luggage, and food to keep us alive for a
fortnight, chugged away in our sardine can of a minibus
through Belgium, Holland and Germany. At the Danish
border the van was the subject of much merriment to the cus-
toms officials who had trouble accepting the validity of the
insurance certificate. 'From England?   All the way?
You're crazy?   I wouldn't buy this vehicle for 10 kroner!'
We knew, though, that the combined wisdom and expertise of
Bill (our caretaker) and the boys had rendered it mechanical-
ly sound and safe to drive (it had actually passed its MOT
three days before we left!). The rust holes were a mere
disguise!

It was then all downhill to ODENSE. We had an English
picnic, much to the surprise of all the Danish naturalists.
On arrival, the Danish people were very welcoming.
Everyone wanted a shower and a cry.   Adrian taught the
Danes how to play cards and the game of 'cheat'.   We all
wanted to go to bed early, but ended up staying up late –
with singing, led by Rog and Rog and Chris, who didn't
know the words and had to ask the Danes.   During the
night Jeff kept everyone awake, except Roger Newby, by
saying 'goodnight' and 'good day' and 'what Bruce Lee films
have you seen?' – all in Danish.

This is an extract from the magazine–style journal that we
kept daily and then typed out and bound together back at the
centre to provide an individual copy for all who'd gone.

The 'expedition' was an overwhelming success – quite justifying the exhaustion experienced by all concerned.   It was
a fitting end–of–term event for those youngsters who had
spent that year at Bayswater; in some ways it was our
'thank you' to a group of kids who had vindicated the trust
we'd placed in putting our Three Rs as a priority.   There
is no doubt in our minds of the weighting that Responsibility
must be given in planning any educational curriculum or
structure.   Young people must be active participants in the
process.   The group who came to Denmark proved it could
work.

What happened to them after leaving school?

Of the boys, one joined the Navy as an electrical engineer, one joined a firm of graphic designers, one became a mixer in a flour factory (earning as much as £100 weekly with copious overtime); one began training for forestry work through the Youth Opportunities Programme.

Of the girls, one joined CSV on a nine-month placement away from home in a strange city; one joined the Brook Clinic staff as a temporary assistant under YOP; one secured a place on a child care course at a technical college.

In terms of jobs they didn't all succeed. There were three drop-outs for a start – one lad who became involved with drugs and was removed to a more restraining community home, one girl who withdrew after one term, resisting all attempts from us to bring her back, and another girl who, having 'done her time' and reached the statutory leaving date, wasted no time in abandoning us for the delights of the dole queue. But it wouldn't be real if there weren't drop-outs, and these drop-outs shouldn't necessarily be seen as failures.

What was real this year was the vindication of our ideals about education – ideals that had evolved from initial flirtations with de-schooling literature, to be subsequently amended by personal experience and encouraged by observation of schools like Tvind.

With a permanent site and sufficient staff we have demonstrated that 'alternative' education is not just a wishy-washy concept, bandied around by radical dissidents. Our emphasis on the magic Three Rs has weathered the trial of a year's exposure to a group of kids whose only alternative to us had been home tuition or residential care.

The final test of its validity is being witnessed as this book goes to print. New kids are coming into the group. Three of them joined us for the Denmark trip. If our emphasis on responsibility is more than skin deep, the old group of youngsters will pass on to the new ones the values of the school – that there is strength and purpose in collective action; that learning by doing and participating is the pattern that works.

It seems to be happening.

Chapter 12

Conclusions: implications for mainstream education

The week before we left for Denmark with the group of youngsters we held a small open day for teachers. Through the in-service training programme organised by the university School of Education, we invited a small group of senior staff – mainly interested heads and deputies from nearby schools – to a seminar to discuss the work of the unit.

The title for the seminar was 'Implications for Schools', and the purpose of the day was to try and evaluate what aspects of our curriculum provision could be incorporated within mainstream education – or could be used as a basis for change.

We have always considered this aspect of the work quite crucial. The framework of 'special units' can never be expanded as a model to cater for more than a small minority of children. Apart from reasons of sheer expense, the intention of LEAs who have set up such units has never been to develop more than a certain number anyway. Many of them have been instituted merely as additional instruments of containment to bring recalcitrant pupils into line. Neither educational policy, nor budgetary allowances will permit a significant increase in the number of such units, and already there is a levelling-off in the number established each year.

However, and perhaps ironically, these educational outposts can offer the opportunity for experimentation that is denied to large comprehensive schools. There is some degree of truth in the assertion that though it is too risky to take chances with exam-oriented middle-class children, no one minds too much if you use working-class drop-outs as guinea pigs. Consequently, though these special units may have been conceived for very questionable reasons, they do at least offer a framework for exploration within the system.

With their relative financial security compared to the free
schools they can concentrate on developing innovative curriculum and structure unfettered by distracting anxieties
about mere survival.   If those running these units recognise
and accept this pioneering role, then there may be hope for
altering and extending the curriculum in mainstream education.   Unfortunately, the pressures of just keeping the unit
together and dealing with the mass of day-to-day problems
often precludes any outside involvement of the staff concerned.   The following comment from the head of one such unit
illustrates the dilemma.

'I am very much aware of the tremendous interest in this
Centre from others working in social work and education, but
quite honestly at the end of the day I've little energy left to
concern myself with such requests for visits or for information.   I try to do what I can when I can, but just running
the centre itself seems to occupy most of my time.'

Our feeling is that whatever the responsibilities of the
work with young people at Bayswater, we must try to maintain a dialogue with those in mainstream education, and allow
time for such intercourse.

Hence our open day, with its emphasis on what teachers
could learn from our experience that might be applicable to
the school situation.

This suggestion of 'change from within' may well not
appease the radical left, who reject what they regard as a
reformist approach, because their own perception of schools
is merely as agents for elitist control of the masses that
should be swept away.   And, of course, there is much in
sociological theory to support their view.

If we consider the historical evolution of educational
provision for working-class children, we can see the influence of conflicting factors right from the start.   Though the
desire of the nineteenth-century 'liberal' educators to
develop the numeracy and literacy levels of the 'ignorant'
lower classes was one significant motivating force, it is
also true that less altruistic motives predominated, like the
recognition by the ruling classes that mass education could
be an agent for social control.   For instance, mill owners
recognised that productivity would be increased and wastage
reduced if the loom operators could read basic instructions
for handling the machinery.   It could therefore be argued
that the educational expansion of the nineteenth century was
simply an urgent reaction from the upper classes to such
working-class movements as the Chartists or the Owenites,
who represented a real threat to the existing order.

Of course, if this is an accurate perception of the evolution of schools and their main function was (and is) to inculcate values acceptable to those in control, it is hardly surprising that working-class children fail within the defined structure. Indeed, some would argue that the actual intention is that these children shouldn't succeed. Though this 'conspiracy theory' is not necessarily supported by all critics of the present system it is certainly true that the system does reinforce class inequalities, and there is no doubt that working-class children do not succeed as well as middle-class kids.

In 'In and Out of School', written jointly with Dave Brockington, we discussed some of the reasons why working-class kids did less well than their middle-class counterparts. As well as pointing to domestic tensions, peer-group pressures and personal inadequacies, we included the school itself as one of the causal factors for working-class disengagement from education.

None of this is very profound, but it caused Max Morris when reviewing the book to accuse us of being slanderous in asserting that schools might actually be rejecting some children. Our resulting disappointment that someone concerned so intimately with education should be so aggressively defensive as to misconstrue our argument was cushioned somewhat by a passing remark from a friend to the effect that if Max Morris didn't like the book it would probably go into a second printing – which it did within a year, we were relieved to note.

I find it sad that there is such an unwillingness amongst many of those running the schools and the administration to admit anything less than 100 per cent success. Perhaps it is an inevitable reaction to a society that devolves increasing responsibility onto schools and demands increasing results at the same time. But until the few brave voices, who publicly recognise the existing deficiencies, are joined by the many who remain silent, our schools will continue to discriminate against a large slice of the population.

Of course schools fail some children; so do parents, so does society and so do some of the individual children themselves. These assertions aren't just derived from parochially limited personal experience. Research since the war has highlighted the influence of social class and family background on educational achievement. For instance, Maurice Craft's book 'Family, Class and Education', (1) succinctly analyses a number of studies which have investi-

gated the extent to which the various factors such as geo-
graphic location, social class, and domestic situation influence school performance. The recent trend in research
terms has been away from such demographic evaluations
towards analyses at a sub-cultural level - exploring such
factors as parental attitudes and peer-group pressure.
Hargreaves's investigations into the causes of delinquent
behaviour amongst lower-stream secondary modern groups
is a good example of the latter style of approach, and one
that pinpointed the school's onus for working-class
failure. (2)

From personal experience I know that schools do offer a
lot to most pupils - but I know too that schools can actually
destroy a child's interest in education. One example will
suffice. At an evening performance of a play production
involving 'lower-band' third years, I had asked four girls
who were normally quite apathetic to involvement within the
school to help with the ushering of people to their seats and
with the interval sale of coffee. They arrived, beautifully
dressed, on time and in good humour, to be reduced to tears
within five minutes by a senior teacher who remonstrated
quite roughly with them for not appearing in school uniform.

Any teacher can recount such tales of mis-education, and
sadly they provide fuel for the de-schoolers or anti-school-
ers who want the school institution razed to the ground.
The arguments of the de-schoolers are supported by an impressive array of facts, but it would be naive to point the
finger of blame for working-class failure at any one single
institution or individual or set of organisational rules.
Certainly some young people are disenchanted with school
and in searching for causes of this disenchantment, it is
easy to lay blame. The press do it all the time: on parents
for inadequate supervision and concern for their offspring at
home; on schools for an irrelevant curriculum that distri-
butes second-hand knowledge through poorly qualified academics; on Local Education Authorities for bureaucratic
approaches that are unable to distinguish individuals from
group statistics; on the media that promote discontent
through glossy advertisements, and moral degeneration
through projections of sex and violence; and on peer-group
pressures that encourage deviance from the norms that society would generally wish to promote. At different times all
these factors have become the bogeymen for the blamers -
and sometimes with justification. But just laying the blame
doesn't actually produce a solution.

The de-schooling movement should at least be credited with highlighting the deficiencies of the existing system and articulating the discontent felt by many teachers about their roles and the management of the institutions in which they worked. How much the current militant attitude of some teachers is a product of the liberal atmosphere prevalent in the late 1960s when the free school movement gathered momentum, is impossible to estimate. Certainly, the writings of Illich and Reimer gave those who felt dissatisfied with the structure and content of schools immeasurable support plus a certain respectability.

As described in Chapter 2, the Scotland Road Free School, which opened in Liverpool in 1971, led to a mushrooming of similar projects in many large cities. For inspiration and philosophy they drew on the Summerhill model of 'freedom' and the writings of the apostles of de-schooling. All these urban free schools concentrated their efforts on the working-class children, who they regarded as the worst-hit victims of the unequal and inappropriate structure of statutory schooling.

That many of them were havens run by middle-class dropouts for working-class drop-out children is a harsh criticism, but one that contains an element of truth. Certainly in their early days the free school movement spawned a host of schools and projects where the emphasis on 'doing your own thing' soon proved an unworkable model in a long-term sense, and one guaranteed not to win LEA or trust support. The problems faced by the free schools has already been discussed. Those like the White Lion School, which continue to take an independent stance, are only kept alive by the personal commitment of all involved, particularly parents and teachers, who work for little financial reward. The trust fund money which supplements their own fund-raising efforts can only be a short-term reprieve. (3)

Another drawback to the approach of the early free schools was that, apart from being elitist in various ways, they were often counter-productive to the welfare of individual children, because they emphasised democracy and participation within their sphere of liberated education, without altering the basic structure of the society outside the school - where democracy is merely a gesture, and where work is not necessarily at all fulfilling. The free schoolers needed to recognise that their capacity for radical influence on society depended partly on an understanding of the political context in which they lived - which necessitated accepting historical and cultural perspectives as being relevant to the development of 'consciousness' amongst all involved, including the children. The success of the Black Power movement in the United States, spearheaded by Bobby Seale and Eldridge Cleaver, (4) testifies to the validity of this all-embracing 'consciousness' approach.

With direct reference to education this means that instead of viewing education as a commodity knowledge as it stands at present, and suggesting alternative curricula, it is necessary to understand first of all why it is viewed as commodity knowledge. We need to know how and why 'reality' comes to be structured in particular ways (for instance why maths is more important than music). To do this it is necessary to study the historical and cultural contexts by which the reality construction has been reached. The philosophy of the free schoolers, with a prevalent ideology that emphasised the abolition of authority and ideal of the free development of the child's personality, was too weak in its recognition of the influence of factors outside the existing educational structure.

If their hope was to change statutory provision, they needed to develop a realistic understanding of the relationship between school and society.

The literature on this subject is extensive. Bourdieu, for instance, with his concept of 'cultural capital' elaborates on the theme of how schools discriminate against working-class kids by neglecting to take into account the cultural inequalities between different social classes when children first arrive in the school. (5) And Bernstein has highlighted how teachers discriminate against working-class children by their unconscious choice of the middle-class language that they use in the classroom. (6)

This academic criticism of schools is pretty damning and when supported by rising vandalism (7) and truancy statistics, (8) it is hard not to concede that something must be wrong. The Behavioural Units that have mushroomed in the last decade are merely symptomatic of something more deep-rooted than the unruly attitude of a handful of kids. (9)

However, even if we accept the validity of the sociological critiques of schools, the question still remains unanswered about the most effective way of changing the situation. It is too easy to get caught up in an ideological debate about the legitimacy of such provision, when the possibilities for implementing change in the parent system are rather restricted. Whether these units are seen as a reasonable distribution of provision within a healthy status quo, or merely as cosmetic operations that disguise basic weaknesses and delay structural reform, is largely irrelevant.

What is important is what lessons they hold for general education provision. The question to ask now is: What can we learn from the operation of those special units that might improve the provision within schools? They do offer an opportunity to test out experimental ideas, both in terms of form and content. Given the degree of commitment from those staffing them, they do present a unique chance to grasp innovative ideas and ideals. Arguably they are the only part of the 'system' that can do this and in consequence comprehensive schools should be looking carefully at the processes going on in these 'special' units.

There are bound to be points of confrontation. The processes of operation of many special units challenge some of the basic assumptions under which schools operate. It would be sad if this challenge were regarded as merely threatening and dismissed out of hand without giving serious thought to its message.

But what are these basic assumptions that are under scrutiny?

1 That education is the prerogative of schools and teachers.
2 That learning is a process monopolised by classroom contacts and methods.
3 That the demands of the examination boards dictate the curriculum content of schooling.
4 That all children come equipped to cope with the learning/teaching situation as structured by the school hierarchy.
5 That parental and pupil involvement is a very secondary consideration.

Some of these assumptions have been openly and widely challenged by the Illich-inspired de-schoolers. Their critique about professionalism is hard for teachers to accept at any time, and at this particular point in time, when staff vacancies are not being advertised and there is a pervading atmosphere of cutbacks and retrenchment, it is no wonder that teachers are extremely sensitive and defensive about any suggestion which questions the legitimacy of their role.

But it doesn't need to be seen as a threat. With imaginative direction, the teacher's role could actually be enhanced by accepting the status of orchestrator - co-ordinating the efforts of interested people who would willingly join in the education process if they could be enabled to participate.

Ultimately the reality will have to be recognised. Teachers do distribute second-hand knowledge and though this is acceptable for purely academic information dissemination, it lacks realism when imparting practical information. There are plenty of other real people with relevant skills, like mechanics, cooks and builders, for instance, who could teach recognised school subjects much better than the certificated 'professionals'. First-hand contact with real people is as meaningful as bookish experience.

We know too that much learning takes place outside schools and that on the whole people learn very poorly through formal classroom instruction. Most of us learn the ropes by climbing them. We also learn better as willing participants. The haste to get kids into schools in this country is not paralleled in all other European countries ... and they don't seem to do too badly!

Of course, this response to the first two assumptions listed above is no more than those arguments delivered by the de-schooling brigade, but where I would part company with them is over their belief that school institutions/buildings can never become centres of learning for all kids. We don't have to dispense with them. Indeed, it seems to me that it would be foolish to destroy the edifice of such capital investment.

I am simply asking for a reappraisal of what goes on within the schools; and though to question the last three assumptions listed above is to challenge the very heart of the curriculum, a possible resolution doesn't necessarily require complete destruction of the present fabric.

They are, after all, self-evident truths.

A system dominated by exams must fail at least half of the school, and curriculum emphasis on academic learning is clearly inappropriate for unacademic kids.

Home situations and family tensions can obviously militate against learning for many youngsters. Schools cannot and do not always take into account what happens to kids outside of their precincts, and real involvement of parents is minimal - often restricted to the odd parent evening or open day. Of course, where the cultural values of home are the same as school it doesn't matter so much if there's little parental involvement; but otherwise it just simply reinforces the discrimination against working-class children. At an immediate and very practical level, the testimony of the pupils themselves is worth listening to.

The following is an extract from a conversation with
Lennox, one of our ex-pupils, about his thoughts on responsibility:

Q: How do you think you would encourage this sort of res-
    ponsibility in school?
L: If you stop treating children as children in primary
    school and treat them as kids, they'd grow up faster.
    If you stop treating kids as kids in the secondary and
    treat them as adults, with responsibility, they'd grow
    up faster.
Q: When can you start doing that in school?   Straight away
    or after a while?
L: In secondary school, as soon as they come in.   It's no
    good starting by treating them as children and then
    changing your attitude half way through.
Q: Could people - 11-year-olds - cope with that?   Think of
    yourself, for instance.   What does it mean to treat
    someone as an adult?
L: Well, it's how you approach people.   When they do some-
    thing wrong, don't go up and make an issue of it.
    Saying things like 'Stand outside boy' or 'Your
    parents'll hear of this' only makes people embarrassed,
    and when they're embarrassed people get aggressive
    back and then you've created another problem.   I began
    to hate a lot of teachers because they made me aggres-
    sive in this way.   I've seen a beautiful female teacher
    knifed because she embarrassed a guy.   Kids don't like
    being shamed.
Q: How could schools do more than that then - treating
    pupils as adults?
L: If everyone has a choice in deciding what to do for the
    next few weeks it helps.   If you've participated it
    makes a big difference.   It's asking a lot of course if
    you're not used to it.   I remember when I first came to
    Bayswater we were asked what we'd like to do and we
    all said 'go home'.   But then, after that, people made
    suggestions like going to a museum, going out, doing
    English, or running a play group, and it would be dis-
    cussed as a group.   It made you feel grown up because
    you were having to make decisions.

This is no more than the Danish girl Disse concluded in her
observations of what was the essential difference between
her own situation at Tvind and what she'd experienced when
she arrived early one day at the school in Bristol (p. 17).

Echoing Lennox and Disse, all the kids ask is for responsibility, for acceptance as individuals, and for time. None
of these are beyond the scope of a comprehensive school.
It is possible to devise a system – even one that has to
cater for a thousand-plus pupils, that allows all pupils a
measure of responsibility. If those administrating the
schools lead the way, the teachers at the chalk face could
follow. It means recognising responsibility as one of the
magic Rs. It is quite possible to organise a school to run
effectively without destroying individuality. Self-expression and determination don't necessarily have to occur at
the expense of social order. Rutter's evaluation of what
makes for a good or bad comprehensive school, even allowing for his emphasis on academic attainment as an indicator
of success, bears out this view. (10)

What is required is a recognition that teachers need time,
or pupils need time with teachers (or other adults), and this
time must be unfettered by curriculum demands. Creation
of such time will inevitably necessitate the involvement of
non-certificated personnel. There is no other way. One
ordinary teacher with a class of thirty children cannot possibly create the areas of space and time required single-
handed. The professionals have to accept and recognise
the contribution of others to complement their own specific
(and restricted) skill. It requires a reappraisal of the
hierarchical and often authoritarian structures within
school. If responsibility is to be given acceptable weighting, then teachers have to be given the time and the training
to cope with its demands.

It is tempting to try and present a doctrinaire blueprint of
how these Three Rs could actually be incorporated, but each
school and each class needs to define its own parameters and
approach. Some examples of how the requirements could be
met by interested class teachers may serve as a simple appe-
tiser. They are merely intended to be suggestive of a style
of approach.

Any form teacher could engage his pupils in a co-operative exercise that gave them a measure of Responsibility.
Right from the start of school, all children could be involved
in discussions about timetabling and lesson content. It is
perfectly possible to explain the purpose of their following
certain subjects and of doing homework. This approach may
of course expose the purposelessness of some curriculum
activity, but the honesty of such investigation can only highlight a crucial principle about values. In some instances

it may actually be necessary for a teacher to acknowledge
that particular group or class interests may override preordained curriculum slots.   There is value in taking
account of group dynamics and encouraging cohesion amongst
the members of the class, through visits and camps and
'group' work.   It is essential to ensure that all kids feel
involved, taking particular care to see that those on the
periphery have an acceptable role within the group.

By encouraging expression of their opinions, by involving
them in co-operative exercises that demand communication,
by simply talking with as opposed to at, aRticulation develops automatically.   But free talking and listening requires
time.   This necessitates initiative from those in the senior
posts to reinforce the attitude that the 'curriculum' isn't the
school god.   Digressions from it, interruptions of it, and
periods when it is completely discarded are not worthless
red herrings.   'Education is what happens when a good
teacher gets off the point' is sound advice.   Time just for
talking without anxiety feeling about curriculum requirement
has to be given a valued weighting, and this use of time has
to be seen as productive by all involved - an exercise which
may well require the presence of other adults.

By bringing other people from outside the school into the
classroom (and vice versa), the teacher can more nearly
maximise the contact with respected adults that is a crucial
element in the learning process.   If we think about our own
education, we must admit that the things of value we learnt
when young came from people we trusted, respected and with
whom we were friendly, most of whom certainly weren't
teachers!   And we learnt best when we understood the Relevance of what we were doing.

To implement even these few examples of applying the
Three Rs would require a fundamental reappraisal of form
and content within schools.   It is at this point that the en-
listed involvement of those working within special units
could prove invaluable.   Their experience and expertise
has much to offer mainstream education at a dynamic level
of involvement.

If there was a measured interchange of personnel between
the experimental units and mainstream education, ideas
about process and approach would begin to permeate the
school fabric.   The integration of teachers working in off-
site units, within the framework of consultative and advisory
bodies at school and local authority level, could provide a
valuable opportunity for evaluating the benefits of their ex-

perience, and possibly lead to the incorporation of useful
ideas within mainstream provision.   As innovators, experi-
menters and explorers they represent an as yet largely un-
tapped reserve of wisdom about what is critical in redefining
curriculum models.

Their experience needs to be shared.

Which is the purpose of writing this book.

Appendix 1

Pen portraits

The following are extracts from the referral agency reports concerning the individuals described in the group. Mainly they are derived from the social enquiry reports that are presented with the request for us to consider possible admission to the school.

The intention of reproducing them here is not to deride the accuracy of such reports because of their seeming inappropriateness to the subsequent behaviour of the youngsters in our setting. The very fact that the picutre painted by such reports (produced by professionals who knew what they were talking about) does often differ from the reality as we experience it, is what is really significant.

We would hope that it reinforces our argument about 'failure' and 'maladjustment' being socially constructed definitions. 'Thick' kids can become 'intelligent' merely by a change of environment. This argument is not intended as a contribution to the debate about whether intelligence is affected by inheritance or environment, because my belief is that no human being ever achieves the potential of his inherited intelligence and the degree to which he approaches this goal is determined largely by environmental factors!

Apart from the obvious change of name and the occasional transformation of particular characters to protect the innocent, these 'portraits' are an honest representation of the preliminary reports.

CLIVE

Clive first came to the attention of the police at the age of 12 when he was cautioned for being involved in taking and

driving away a vehicle. Eight months later, in January, for
non-attendance at school,he was made the subject of a two-
year supervision order. Ten months later, in November,
for a further joint offence of taking and driving away, a new
two-year supervision order was made. Five months later
in April he was remanded to an assessment centre for failing
to respond to supervision by not attending school. There he
was so disruptive that arrangements were made to transfer
him to a more strictly controlled institution. En route he
absconded, was found after four days and returned, where-
upon he immediately absconded again. A week later he returned voluntarily to the assessment centre and, at a court
appearance three weeks later, was made the subject of a
care order.

Clive appears to have lacked the support, stimulation and
guidance necessary for adequate emotional and social development. He has failed to find alternative gratification in
school in terms of social relationships and academic achievement. He continues to want the acceptance of peers and remains vulnerable to adverse influences. Clive represents
himself poorly, being untidy, lethargic and unco-operative,
and is initially resistant to adult direction. It is felt that
his hostile attitude reflects poor means of self-expression
(being severely retarded in verbal and computational skills)
and low self-esteem. Given his rather negative attitude
towards himself, he is in need of considerable help in raising his confidence and strengthening his character.

Since the Bayswater Centre has offered Clive a place, it
is recommended that he should be allowed to return home in
order to take this opportunity for alternative schooling.

JIM

Three months after starting secondary school Jim was referred to Child Guidance for poor school attendance. Already
in the remedial stream, progress was impossible because of
his frequent absences. Though he attended the special unit
regularly, subsequent return to school produced the original
erratic pattern of avoidance. In his third year of secondary
schooling he was made the subject of a care order and spent
a period of time at an assessment centre. He was diagnosed
as suffering from a neurotic dependence to the home and an
inability to cope with the transition from primary to secondary school; which situation only reinforced his existing

feelings of social and educational inadequacy.   It was considered that his dependence on the home stemmed from feelings of instability due to several family evictions and witnessing the physical removal of two brothers from home by
the police for various criminal offences.   The recommenda-
tion was for Jim to attend a day school for the maladjusted.

However, though Jim has a reading age of 7 or 8, he was
assessed as being above-average potential with outstanding
potential practical and creative abilities.   It is felt that the
maladjusted school recommended may not really be appropriate.   He desperately needs the stimulation of a small
group situation such as the Bayswater Centre is uniquely
placed to offer.

LESTER

Mid-way through his fourth year Lester was referred to
Child Guidance by the school, who were concerned about
his academic and social deterioration over the previous
year.   This was associated with the disruption of the family
due to parental separation and a hostile relationship between
Lester and his mother (with whom he stayed and from whom
he has occasionally stolen money and objects for pawning).
Lester's lack of self-esteem, his feeling of inadequacy and
his identity confusion, are reflected in his withdrawal from
school friendships, a 'don't care' attitude towards himself,
and increasing truancy.   It is felt that he is using the
truancy to call attention to his distress andhhe is desperately in need of a relationship with an accepting and trusting
male.   Lester's negative attitude to school is now so well
established that he could accomplish nothing, even were he
to attend, because there all his negative feelings are constantly re-inforced.   Unless alternative provision is found
he will be ill-equipped to cope with a job and independence
in one year from now.   A transfer to the Bayswater Centre
is strongly recommended – if a place is available there.

MARTIN

Martin was brought before the court in April of his third
year at secondary school for continued non-attendance.
Because of the home situation and a long history of truancy
in the family, a residential placement was recommended.

However Martin elected to return to school and was placed
on a supervision order. Failing to attend regularly, he
was admitted to the psychiatric ward of the Children's Hospital where he attended for over six months. His main
problem seems to be low self-esteem coupled with a feeling
of total lack of support from home. Basically his school
refusal is pure phobia, and beneath a surface bravado, he
is a neurotically anxious boy.

Applications for a transfer to other schools have been unsuccessful and it is felt that the best hope for Martin for the
remaining three terms of his school career would be the
support and stimulus he could gain from the Bayswater
Centre.

LIZ

At the beginning of her fourth year Liz was brought to court
for non-school attendance - following a family tradition of
truancy, where the example of three elder sisters was certainly not designed to encourage good attendance. Liz's
parents and Liz herself blamed the school for 'waging a ven-
detta' and victimising the children. Although the truth of
the situation was certainly not as one-sided as the family
suggested, there was no likelihood of Liz agreeing to return
to school. It was felt that a transfer of schools, which is
what the family wanted, would give Liz and the family a
chance to demonstrate their good intent. This recommenda-
tion was accepted by the court and a supervision order made
for two years, with the suggestion that if Liz failed to
attend the new school, then residential placement should be
considered. In the event, after an initial honeymoon
period, the original pattern of truancy reasserted itself,
and Liz came into conflict with various members of staff.
Having suspended her for breaches of discipline, the school
have no wish to accept Liz back and if a place for her cannot
be found at the Bayswater Centre it is very likely that Liz
will be taken into care.

SIMON

Simon's attendance has been poor ever since starting secondary school. A change of school at the beginning of the
fourth year did nothing to improve attendance and a mistake

made by his mother over his date of birth meant that he had
to remain at school a year longer than he'd always thought.
At the same time his elder brother was charged and committed to prison for sexual offences against little boys. Simon,
fearing victimisation (with some justification) from other
pupils because of his brother's well-known crime, gave this
as his reason for non-attendance. Whether this is a 'let-
out' is irrelevant, because Simon will certainly not return
to school.

Since he has less than a year of full-time education left,
it is essential that some provision be made for Simon. He
is severely limited in his literacy and numeracy ability, and
is lacking in many of the basic social skills he will need to
secure and hold down a job. Living alone with a neurotic
mother and one younger brother, he receives little support
from home and the hope is that a place at the Bayswater
Centre could give him the emergency social first aid that he
desperately needs.

DEBORAH

Soon after her fourth year began, Deborah ran away to
London after being charged with shoplifting in Bristol. She
committed a similar offence there and was brought back home
by the police. Though she did not talk in any detail about
her time in London, she was adamant that she will not repeat
the escapade. When Debbie appeared in court in connection
with the shoplifting offence, her poor attendance at school
was brought to notice and a supervision order for one year
was made. Unfortunately there seems to be an impasse in
relationships between Debbie and the school staff: she feels
they are prejudiced against her because she ran away from
home and the staff themselves feel unable to handle her
effectively. It is suggested that the Bayswater Centre may
be able to offer Debbie the secure base she needs.

ALEC

Alec was brought before the court six months into his fourth
year for non-school attendance. Having not been to his
local comprehensive school since the autumn term started, a
transfer to another school was attempted, but Alec stayed
there only thirty minutes. Referred to an assessment

centre, he settled in fairly well and opinion about him there
was divided between those who thought he was being pur-
posely unco-operative and magnifying small episodes in
order to avoid the trials that face many boys in a large institution, and those who thought he was genuinely frightened
and unable to alter his pattern of opting-out behaviour. A
placement in a third school has been considered but it is
felt that Alec's attitude to large institutions would militate
against success. The alternative to a care order and
placement away from home is a referral to the Bayswater
Centre.

JUDY

Her home is one of a small row of houses stuck out in the
middle of nowhere. There are no children of Judy's age in
the road and the buses are some distance away and very infrequent. Dad works fairly long hours and generally just
comes home to watch TV, with seemingly little communication between him and Judy's Mum, who is tied at home looking after the younger children.
   Judy has been attending poorly at school for most of her
secondary schooling. Since the beginning of the fourth
year her truanting grew worse, though Mum seemed to con-
nive with Judy about keeping Dad uninformed of her non-
attendance. Mum in fact depends a lot on Judy to look after
the children whenever she is ill or has to go out. She is a
friendly girl and gets on well with her peers, but there
seems no likelihood of her returning to a pattern of normal
attendance at school.
   Judy very much needs some form of educational provision
which would draw her out and exercise her mentally, thus
giving her more confidence to tackle difficult situations –
particularly since her lack of qualifications, her history of
irregular attendance and her rural isolation with the expense
of daily travel, will make it very difficult for her to find
employment when she can legally leave school. It is hoped
that a place could be offered her at the Bayswater Centre.

JOY

Joy's attendance at her comprehensive school has broken
down completely. She finds relationships with certain

members of staff very difficult, and has been involved in
many stormy scenes at school. She also feels that other
girls gang up against her and there is some evidence to
support this view. Since she is considered excellent 'O'-
level potential, and is anxious to prove she can achieve
positive results, it seems a real waste that no alternative
provision can be made for Joy. Her life history is somewhat unsettled, with parents separated and herself alternat-
ing between father (who allows her a lot of freedom and lives
in comparative luxury) and mother (whose financial situation
is much less opulent). It is felt that she is currently in
some 'moral danger' and the hope is that this attractive and
intelligent girl could be found a place at the Bayswater
Centre.

DIRK

Up to the end of his third year Dirk was no great problem in
school, although he sometimes was difficult to contain in a
classroom. During the fourth year, his behaviour grew
progressively worse: he became defiant and disruptive,
often truanted, and his attitude began to affect others in his
class. Eventually the school felt unable to cope with this
deliberate disruptiveness and defiance of school regulations
and he was suspended at the end of the Easter term of his
fourth year. Allowed to return to school after a promise of
good behaviour, he very soon reverted to his previous pattern of being rude and insolent to staff and truanting frequently. Consequently, towards the end of the summer
term, he was expelled from school.
   Attempts to find an alternative school placement failed because of his unco-operative attitude, and he was committed
to the care of the local authority, pending a court appearance for theft. Following a three-week period in the
assessment centre he was placed on a supervision order for
one year.
   It would seem that lack of support at home and problems
with older children in the family have made Dirk very insecure. He feels that what has gone wrong at school can be
partly attributed to the reputation of his brothers' failings
at the same school. Perhaps it is surprising that he has
not been involved in more acts of delinquency, and he would
certainly seem to be at risk unless he develops some interests which give him a sense of achievement and satisfaction.

It is unlikely that Dirk will settle again in a normal classroom setting but it is believed that he would gain a great
deal if he could be accepted by the Bayswater Centre.

Appendix 2

History and financing of the Bayswater Centre

The background development of the centre is described in detail in 'In and Out of School'. The parent ROSLA project from which it developed operates with similar sorts of youngsters to those described in this book: the main difference being in the case of the ROSLA link that the youngsters are still attending their neighbourhood comprehensive schools, albeit infrequently. They haven't yet reached the stage of school phobia or hard-core truancy. The aim of the ROSLA project link is not to provide an alternative model, but rather to offer an extension facility, which, as well as being educationally constructive itself, may also enable the youngsters to make more of their final school year.

   The Bayswater Centre, described in this book, sprang from the ROSLA project as an offshoot experiment which was ultimately itself responsible for the subsequent funding of both parts of the work. Below, is represented a brief chronological picture of the development of the school in terms of its funding, its staffing and its location.

October 1974   Begun as a privately funded off-shoot experiment from the ROSLA project, with six full-time pupils, referred from Education Welfare, probation service, Child Guidance and social services. Premises: disused church hall.

May 1975   The two teachers involved were appointed on to the Authority's staff. Number of pupils increased to twelve. The running costs for the unit still came from private sources, mostly charitable foundations. Premises: the crypt of the empty RC cathedral.

December 1975	The unit/school moved into the empty cathedral primary school, with no heating and very little equipment.
April 1976	A budget for running costs for the school was allocated by the local authority. Serious discussions were held about finding suitable alternative premises.
July 1977	The school had to move from the primary school base and took up temporary occupation of an empty caretaker's lodge 3 miles away, pending a final move to Bayswater Avenue.
July 1978	School moved into permanent base at Bayswater Avenue. Equipment and furniture provided from second-hand store. School meals service assisted with kitchen equipment. Since then pupils and staff have been involved in the redecoration and maintenance of the building.
August 1978	Hilary Workman, original co-organiser of the school, left and was replaced by Roger Newby.
January 1979	Third member of staff appointed on a one-year basis through the MSC Short Term Employment Programme.
March 1979	Secretarial assistant appointed on a one-year basis through MSC.
June 1979	The centre held its first 'Open Day' attended by a group of fifteen teachers (headmasters, deputy heads and senior staff) to discuss and evaluate the work of the unit. The intention was to try and identify features of the work that had implications for mainstream education.
May 1980	Half-time social work post initiated and funded by Child Guidance service.
June 1980	Re-allocation of 'home tuition' funds by LEA enabled us to advertise for a third teacher to join the centre.
September 1980	Additional staffing enabled the centre to increase its intake of pupils towards a maximum of 25.

Appendix 3

Conversation with Annie Lundgånd: June 1978

The following is the transcript of the interview with Annie – the teacher at Tvind, who was so generous with her time during our brief stay. Apart from four essential grammatical corrections to clarify the sense of her words (and a slight re-ordering of questions and answers to disguise our ineptitude as interviewers) it is a truthful representation of the tape-recorded conversation. Only the birdsong and sounds of various activities in the distance are deleted. Those who want further information about the school should write directly to:

Tvind Efterskole
6990 Ulfborg
Jylland
DENMARK

(and enclose £1 to cover the cost of the booklet and return postage).

Question: Annie, could you start by explaining the background to Tvind – something about its structure and how it is possible to set up a school like this in Denmark?

Annie: Surely.To start a school like this you have to have some money yourself, because you need to run for six months first without outside financial help. Then you have to have a curriculum the government will accept. There has to be a group of fifty people in the community who will support you and there has to be a headmaster the government can recognise. Then the government will assist you with 85 per cent of most of the expenditure, like teachers' salaries. The rest

of the money the pupils' parents will have to find
for themselves and they pay on average between
£20 and £40 a month for their children to stay
here.   It's a residential school but every third
weekend they go home to visit their families.
Half of the pupils come from Sealand – mostly
Copenhagen – and the rest are from Fyn and
Jylland.

It is possible for the pupils to take the ordinary state exams here, and the programme is
balanced between practical and theoretical work.
We feel that both aspects need to be developed.
We were famous when we first started because
our curriculum wasn't always based in a class
room.   We went out into society and the pupils
joined the practical workers in fields and the
factories and so on.   Our emphasis is on a balanced relationship between practical and theory.
In older days schools were based on theoretical
knowledge which was reasonable, because children at that time learnt their practical knowledge
at home.   But society has changed since then and
many things are ready-made at home, so though I
still think a school must be theoretical to an extent, it is important to be practical as well.   But
most schools haven't recognised that fact yet.
Today, you will find many young people who have
never really tried much practical work, but here
we think it's important that they do try.   In previous generations children had a job to do; they
could feel their necessity to the family, where
they had a definite part to play.   I'm not saying
we should revert to those days, but what we have
lost is a role for young people.   It is not just
true for youngsters; it is true for old people
too.   Society only has a real use for you if
you're between 25 and 40.   So we think here
that it's necessary to give young people responsibility for things that matter.   We don't have
cooks and cleaners – only teachers and pupils.
So we have to do the farming, the administrative
work and so on ourselves.   We have eight job
groups; each group being a mixture of ages and
sexes.   Each group is named according to the
job they do: cooks, clerks, printers, mechanics,

farmers, journalists, builders and energy technicians. They change round in these groups
four times a year. Mostly they stay a year or
two. In the farmers' group for instance, like
all the other groups, half the day is spent on
practical work- feeding the sheep, the pigs, the
hens. They have to take care of everything.
The other half of the day they work at theory.
This theoretical work has three elements: one we
call the 'everyday doses', one we call 'documen-
tation' and the other one we call 'visits'. Everyday doses includes recognised school subjects
like Danish, arithmetic and language. Documen-
tation means that we go to learn more about our
jobs. Farmers for instance can go to visit another farmer to learn about how he looks after his
pigs, what he does when things go wrong and so
on. The visit means going to a factory or something like that, just for a short time.

The aim is always to try and relate practical
and theoretical work together, and so when we do
Danish we have to ask what we need it for in our
job group, so that as far as possible they can see
a reason for doing it. We are concerned with
the reality. For example, the farming group
have made pamphlets about their visits to Danish
farms and about what to do when animals get ill.
In arithmetic they have to keep accounts of money
spent on seed and feed and income from sales of
food and animals. In between we have to do work
on elementary training, like grammar - which of
course is crucial for writing letters and such
like.

Another important thing is that they must make
their own decisions. They are so used to other
people - parents, teachers and so on deciding
for them; they are unused to having to take responsibility. We have a regular common meeting
for teachers and pupils where important decisions are taken and they learn very early on that
it's not just the teachers who decide things. If
they don't decide as well, then nothing will be
decided. Take the cooks, for instance, if they
don't want to make the food that day then no one
will get food, but you can be sure that the rest

will come to the cooks' group and demand 'What's
wrong - why haven't we got any food today?'
    We don't believe in forcing a change in people's
attitudes - you can't and shouldn't do that, but
you can give them the opportunity to decide for
themselves whether they want to change things.
It's important that you don't just have owners and
workers, like you do in capitalist factories,
where the owners decide everything. Everyone
must share in decisions. The situation here
must always be realistic.

Question: Annie, in your information sheets about Tvind you
say that the social mix of pupils here is 70 per
cent working class. Was that true to begin with?

Annie: No. In the beginning we just started taking
pupils on a first-come-first-served basis, but we
realised that if we didn't make such a rule, then
the middle-class people who plan ahead for their
children's education would swamp the school.
Working-class people don't plan ahead like that.
When a problem arises they solve it then, but not
before. So since we think here that the people
who need a new educational system most are those
children from working-class families, we decided
to make this 70:30 per cent rule.

Question: Annie, considering the mix here is as you say,
the remarkable thing is the different sort of
values and pattern of decision-making amongst
your pupils compared to any school in England.
Do you think to start such a school initially you
need pupils who are immediately sympathetic to
your aims, like middle-class children, who would
fit in more easily with your ideals about decision-making? So that you build up a pattern that
other kids fit into?

Annie: When we started this four years ago we had ideas
amongst the teachers about how it should be and
some ideas amongst 100 pupils about how it
should not be! And there was conflict of course.
And it was very hard work because there was
nothing concrete we could point to that had gone
before. We could only use words to describe our
ideals. But since then it has developed and it
now has a recognisable form and a structure.
When parents and children come to us now they

have some idea about how it works and what
happens, and every year some of the pupils will
be pupils from the year before. They are the
continuation of the school.

Question: So you rely on them?

Annie: No, not exactly, because now there are many
traditions associated with this school, so that
before they come pupils have expectations already.

Question: Was it very difficult in the beginning?

Annie: Yes, it was terrible. I don't want to think
about it! I was a teacher at the travelling high
school at the time and the others were in the
teacher training course. We didn't know much
about this age group who wanted to drink alcohol, to sleep a long time, to smoke hashish and
so on. It lasted six or seven weeks. We knew
we had to stop it, so we called a meeting with
everyone and the teachers said 'You must stop
this, we don't want to be teachers in a school
like this.' We told them what we thought the
school should do and if they didn't want to join in
they must leave, because it wasn't possible to
have a school like that - especially with pressure
from outside. This was a very famous meeting -
any pupil you meet now who was here then would
tell you about this meeting. It lasted five days;
we heard a lot of stories about what the kids had
been doing, and we made some really good decisions. We decided not to have alcohol in the
school, which was very good because these were
young people, like any others, who wanted to
drink. We made plans about what should go on
in their spare time, because this drinking and
stealing was happening then, when they had
nothing else to do. From then the foundation
was laid. We've had problems of course....

Question: Who enforced this rule?

Annie: They all did - pupils and teachers. At that
meeting they saw the reality, that if the school
was going to work, they had to be an important
part of it and that their consciousness mattered.

Question: Much of your ability to involve the pupils in this
decision-making process must be because you're
a residential community, where it's more possible for sanctions to be meaningfully enforced.

Annie: Yes, partly. I think it's very helpful that the pupils and the teachers are living here together, but I don't think it's the only way. It would be possible to do something in the state folk schools too.

Question: But when they leave the folk school at the end of the day, they go home to other friends and other pressures.

Annie: That's right. It's another situation. You can't transpose the whole model of this school, but you can use some of these things here in folk schools.

Question: But if you wanted to change folk schools it would be much harder to get pupils involved in the way you have here.

Annie: Surely. We have many more advantages. But I don't like saying it to teachers who then use that as an excuse for not doing anything in folk schools. It's wrong thinking. You may not be able to do the same, but you can still change some things. For instance, you can give pupils more responsibility and you can link theoretical work with practical work.

Question: Annie, can we ask you some more questions about the actual curriculum here? We are wondering how the practical learning is organised so that the theoretical work is linked to it. You need very good teachers, because people don't just learn theory by experience in practical situations. If each job group does 50 per cent theoretical and 50 per cent practical work, it would need a lot of careful thinking on the part of the teacher to link up the theory work.

Annie: You are correct. You have grasped one of the most difficult problems. We are not finished with thinking about that. I agree that it's not enough just to have practical experience – you need to provide clear links with the theory. One of the other problems too is that we are beginning to recognise that our qualifications as teachers should be better. When we're working in the groups as farmers or cooks we're not especially well qualified to do these things. We are only able to teach reading and writing because of our pedagogic training, so we must use some of our own time to learn these other skills. Only then

are we going to be equipped to cope with the basic
problems of linking theory to practice.

I could give you some examples how it is linked
at the moment. Let me use the clerks' group,
with which I am involved. As far as practical
work is concerned, they have responsibility for
the telephone and the post for the whole place.
Every morning they go to the village to collect
the post and distribute it back here. They have
to take care of all the new pupils who come here
to visit – they have to look after any guests and
they have to take responsibility for the money in
the office. That's the practical side. As far as
theory is concerned, they learn in arithmetic how
to budget, and to explain to the rest of the school
where the money is going. They have to work
out how much money the teachers should receive
every month, because the ministry has different
scales of pay according to background. That's
a lot of work, and on top of it they have to calcu-
late how much tax each teacher must pay. As
well as that everyone will pay 1200 kroner (£100)
a month but depending on circumstances the government will contribute between 30 per cent and
80 per cent of this. It's all worked out according to family income and in general most parents
don't pay much more than £40. Then the pupils
have to write to the parents and they know it's
got to be accurate – or they'll get angry parents
ringing up complaining! Now take Danish. They
need to learn to write, to read, to speak and to
listen. The latter two they learn trhough discussions here every day. Writing and reading we
approach in various ways. Firstly, since in the
clerks' group they all have to answer a lot of
questions from guests about the high school and
about the windmill and so on, they have to read
up about these so they can answer the questions.
Also they must read the newspapers so that any
articles about what we are doing can be reported
back to everyone in the school. They follow
these things. On top of that we receive a lot of
letters to answer every day from people wanting
information about Tvind, and naturally the pupils
can't write bad letters, so we correct them with
them.

Question: Annie, some of our youngsters have reading ages
of 7 or 8 or even less and to do the things you
suggest is impossible to begin with. Do you
have the same problem?

Annie: Sometimes yes. In Danish schools such children are put into special classes where they just
have to learn reading and writing and arithmetic
and nothing else. 'You must stay here till you
can do all these things first, you can't do languages or history or those things.' And of course
it doesn't work. When those pupils come here,
we say to them, 'OK perhaps you can't write, but
you're normal like everyone else, perhaps you
can do the agriculture – it's just as important
and you will learn reading and writing in that
group anyway.' We don't have special classes,
because it creates social problems.

We had a very good discussion just before
Christmas about this question, because at the
8th and 9th stage they're all mixed together, regardless of academic ability, but in the 10th
stage they're divided into a group that's taking
the 'real' exam and a group that's taking a less
difficult exam that everyone can pass. In other
aspects of the curriculum here the approach is
always that if they wanted to learn anything
practical – using the telephone, cooking and so
on, then of course they could, but in the case of
exams, we would say to some people that they
couldn't take them. There was an obvious dich-
otomy. But now that's changed. We say to
people 'Of course, if you want to take the exam
you can. The reason why you think you can't is
that people have told you for nine years that you
can't – but we don't believe them. We think you
can and that you should at least have the chance.'

So we decided that all those in the non–exam
group would join the exam class – all except two
who didn't want to. They didn't all pass of
course, but some of them passed, and those who
didn't learnt a lot anyway. For instance they
had studied languages, which they'd not done before, and naturally they couldn't be expected to
pass the exam in such a short time, but at least
they started to learn. Though they didn't get the

exam, at least they know it's more because they
haven't had the chance of doing language before,
rather than because they can't learn languages.

A good example was the girl who'd never learnt
English at all till she came here and she had six
months to go before the exam. But she went to
Ireland with one of the groups for a fortnight and
there she joined in with a class of 11- and 12-
year-olds at an Irish school. And because she
could only speak to them in English, she had to
learn the language. It helped her a lot.

Question: Going back to the question of relating practical
work to theory work, can you give an example of
this with the farming group?

Annie: Well, the farming group have made friends with a
similar group in Germany who are cultivating
land using organic methods and we know very
little about this. So we can learn from them and
we have exchanged many letters and visited their
school. That's one way we've linked theoretical
and practical.

Question: On an immediate practical level, who decides
what to grow and how to grow it?

Annie: That was decided after the group had visited
farmers roundabout to ask them about what they
grow in their fields. The neighbouring farmers
know much more about what to grow in our fields
than we do, so they gave us ideas in the beginning. Then the farming group made their own
plan and presented it to the farmers around to
see what they thought and finally they produced a
plan that they presented to the rest of the school.

Question: Annie, because you have an exam syllabus to
follow there must be things in it that it isn't possible to link with practical work - like calculus,
or much of geometry. Yet to pass the exam,
your pupils must learn these things. How do you
cope with that?

Annie: You've answered it yourself. There are many
theoretical things that you can link with practical
work and those things are good to learn. But
there are theoretical things that seem a waste of
time, yet are still required by the exam, so must
still be learnt. To the pupils it is quite clear.
'This we learn just because of the exam. We can't

see the reason but we must do it.' Mathematics
is a typical example of this. How we coped this
year is that we set three days aside in the autumn
to do it and we didn't combine it with anything.
The teachers didn't try to persuade the pupils it
was useful. They just said, 'You have to learn
it for the exam that is all.' And because everyone has agreed about the exam, they do it. We
try wherever possible to combine theory with
practical work but in the places where it's not,
we just say never mind we must still do it.

Question: But what if the pupils say, 'No, we won't do
this'? That is often our difficulty if we allow
people freedom to make their own choices.

Annie: But you see, these pupils have been here maybe
two years already by the time they reach the 10th
stage. If we put it to them at the 8th stage we
would have the same problem as you. We know
that when they leave here those with bits of paper
saying they've passed the exam will be in a much
better position. But it takes time for the pupils
to see the necessity and the ones who are leaving
in their 10th year know they can't put it off any
longer. But we must concentrate on developing
their consciousness, so that they can see the
point of taking the exam.

Question: Yes, but they still don't all pass do they? What
will happen to the ones who failed this year for
instance?

Annie: That's right. Five of them didn't pass, but we
know exactly what they're going to do. We have
followed them very closely.

Question: You knew they were going to fail?

Annie: Not definitely, but because of their work standard
we had a good idea. Out of those five, three are
continuing here for another year and they will
repeat the exam in several of the subjects. The
other two are leaving school: one has an apprenticeship and the other is going to a school of com-
merce, which one of the teachers here has helped
arrange.

Question: Suppose there are some pupils who you think will
fail, will you tell them?

Annie: Certainly, I don't agree with this protectiveness.
If I think they'll fail then I say it and we discuss

it from that starting point – whether or not they should try and improve. One of those kids who failed we discussed it with him some months before. We said we think you might fail, but you should try because you will learn more by trying. That's the plain, frank way of putting it.

Question: But that's different from actually saying you can't do this.

Annie: But the important thing is to encourage them to try all the same. In the case of this exam, it's not the boy who should be blamed for failing. The exam tests only a few small things of a human being's life.

Question: But if you tell people they may fail – that's not very encouraging, even if it's the truth. So we would hesitate to say the whole truth, because it might be non-motivational. If someone thinks you think they're going to fail, maybe they give up. If someone thinks that you have faith in their ability, they may be encouraged to pass; maybe they will try harder.

Annie: But don't you think that all their lives these people have met grown-ups who want to motivate them for something, and they get used to people who are lying and they hate their dishonesty. They look very closely at your motives for doing something or saying something. For example, the boy I just mentioned didn't pass the exam. When he'd taken two or three subjects he could see he wasn't going to pass and we discussed it and he went on through all the subjects. He got low marks, but he still wanted to go through the whole situation and learn what the others were learning. It wasn't a bad situation at all.

Question: Obviously you place emphasis on trying to help pupils pass exams and it's quite true that if you have qualifications you are in a better position to get a job, but in England as here there is much youth unemployment and qualifications don't necessarily lead to jobs. Also there's an attitude amongst young people – particularly working-class youngsters – that academic qualifications really aren't much practical use for many of the jobs they will do, and that the best way of actually learning is through doing the job itself. This

	takes away the motivation for doing exams. Is that so here?
Annie:	Yes it is so. But I will defend for a time yet the attitude that they should take exams, because this is still one passport into society. Of course you're right about unemployment, but one thing they learn here is to find out what they want to use their lives for. I can see that pupils who have left here are citizens in society, participating in it, and even though some don't have jobs, they don't lie in their beds all day and sleep. They're doing something active in the community where they're living. And that's important because it means they've realised that they are people who are able to change the situation they are living in.
Question:	Annie, what do the pupils do when they leave? Are their ideas about jobs and so on realistic?
Annie:	Naturally not always, but generally I think they are. What surprises me is that although unemployment is high in Denmark, nearly all the people who leave this school have a job. One thing they learn is not to give up. We had a boy who wanted to be an apprentice and he tried 80 factories before he finally got it. I think they learn to go on trying to get what they really want.
Question:	How do they learn not to give up?
Annie:	It's because they have responsibility here to find solutions to problems. If they are responsible for looking after the pigs and hens and so on then they have to solve any problems that arise themselves. They learn not to be so dependent on other people to make decisions for them.
	Let me give you some examples. Some of our pupils are living in Copenhagen, in the old part of the town, where they have been very active in organising the children and young people in sport and clubs. A lot of them are politically active over issues like re-housing people in the same area as they've lived for years. A lot of them are very active in the education world in the colleges they're at; a lot are involved with energy work at a town where they're trying to gather unemployed people.
Question:	These people weren't so political when they came here?

Annie: No, not at all. I think they learn it through the situations here where they have to take responsibility for a lot of things and they have to decide what they think about things. It's the first step in forming political opinions. We can't and shouldn't say what opinions, but they need to take part in political decisions in society, and you will find here a lot of political discussion – not necessarily about political parties, but about attitudes.

Question: Yes, Marianne (one of the girls) said she wasn't at all interested in politics – but in fact much of her talking is very political.

Annie: That's correct; that's how it is. But I understand what she means when she says she's not political, because the way that you look on politics is that it's to do with some far-off people in Copenhagen in the ministry. You wouldn't believe this, but when Marianne first came here she was very quiet. When she was at her folk school (in Aarhus) she was always quarrelling with teachers and they told her she was too silly to pass exams. Also, there were problems at home because her parents were divorced, so she left the home and the school and came here to a situation where the teachers didn't decide things for her; it was very much open to discussion and she began to take part in the school in a very responsible way. And she found out people were prepared to listen to her and to take her seriously. Very often grown-up people have an opinion about young people that they don't know very much. 'You're so young – wait till you're 20 and then we can discuss it.' But that's totally stupid, because young people aren't as spoiled as older people. In many ways they have a much clearer perspective. Grown-up people have so many attitudes to defend already.

Question: Can we ask a few questions about how you as teachers organise yourselves? You had a meeting last night, for instance. Do you have meetings like that very often – apart from the pupils?

Annie: Well, there are teachers at the high school, at the after-school, at the teacher training school, and there are teachers at other schools like this

in different parts of Denmark. The connection
between the three schools here is really only
through the teachers. We have a common economy you see. We meet every three or four
weeks for a weekend where we discuss pedagog-
ical questions.

We get a lot of experience from each others'
schools – which is why it is good to meet with
other continuation schools like Tvind. And at
these meetings we discuss how to start other
schools like this. A lot of teachers from here
will leave to start another school at the end of
this year. About five of us will be left to co-
operate with seven or eight new teachers. Out
of the ten leaving, seven are teachers who want
to start their own school, but they wanted first
to learn from us. So we said, very good, come
and join us and teach here for a year and get experience from us and then start your own school.

Question: What happens when teachers leave? How do you
decide on replacements – who would be suitable?

Annie: We suggest they speak with all the teachers first
of all, to discuss the work and the problems and
the conflicts, so that they really know what
they're letting themselves in for. If they still
want to, then we say OK come and work here for
a month and at the end of that we shall decide
whether it is working out. Then we make an
agreement for at least two years. We don't
think they should just stay for a year, because
there are so many new things to learn. After
that two-year period we leave it open for them to
stay or leave.

Question: Do you have a large turnover of staff?

Annie: Not many leave because they don't enjoy the work
– it's nearly always because they want to set up
other places. We discuss such things often at
our meetings here, when the teachers from the
three parts of Tvind get together every Thursday.
With guests we have some funny discussions,
sometimes when they ask 'Is it correct that you
have meetings where the pupils can't join in?
Surely, it's not democratic?' But we think it is
democratic. The teachers are discussing
things concerning the teachers. We don't use

our meetings to discuss the pupils. Naturally,
we have a lot of discussion which concerns the
school, but that's only natural. The pupils
expect that we should have the ideas. 'That's
your job, what else should do.' So naturally,
we make plans – that's our job!

Question: But you don't discuss the pupils, except with
them present?

Annie: Not now. We did when we first started, but it's
the wrong way to use the teachers. Their job is
to go ahead, to think about new developments.
If you start discussing a pupil, sometimes you've
got to involve them anyway to solve any problem.
And we think you should do it right from the
start.

Question: Does that hold true even when you feel that discussing, say, the problems at home, would make
it awkward for the person concerned?

Annie: No, I don't agree with doing it that way. OK
there may be problems, you might have some
problems at home, but why can't you speak openly
about them? It might be painful, but it's still
painful even if you don't talk about it. I think
it's better to be clear and that way you can help
each other. This weekend for example, the
parents will visit the school. It is well known
in some cases that this person has problems with
his mother – or another's father's in jail and so
on. But we speak openly about it and maybe the
person will say, 'My mother's coming, we must
not speak about so and so, we must not do this or
that,' and then we know how to handle it. Naturally, you can't do it without being able to trust
that other people will listen.

Take myself for example. When I was a child
I really had a big problem, because my father
was often drunk. I didn't want my friends to
know, so I didn't tell them or the teachers. I
tried to keep everything secret you know. Nobody made me face up to it. Nobody got me to
think why people like my father had this problem
or what could be done about it. I wouldn't have
liked it if anyone had done it, but it would have
helped.

Question: Before they came here, when they are problems

	at folk school – what happens? In England they may be sent to child psychologists, for instance. And they write reports and so on. Are you interested in any of that?
Annie:	No. We say keep your papers to yourself. If you read what they've written you have to laugh, because you wonder if it's the same person that they're talking about.
Question:	Annie, can we ask you two last questions? Firstly, whilst we've been talking with you this morning, several of the pupils kept coming up to ask you something, why is that?
Annie:	I am one of the two teachers with the clerks' group and one of us must always be in this building because of the telephone and the money. The two pupils who are taking care of the telephone may need to ask us something if they can't answer it themselves. About the money: if the pupils in the school want money they have to come to this building to get it and the pupils don't have the key to the money. It is a decision we've made.
Question:	They agreed to that system?
Annie:	Totally, because some of them know that they are tempted to take money if it's lying around, so therefore we have this system. No one has the chance to get hold of much money. If it's their own pocket money, they don't have much in their rooms because there are some who can't keep their hands off it.
Question:	And you talk about that? You know who they are?
Annie:	Yes, openly and frankly. If someone has stolen something we take it up at the common meeting and try to find out. It is quite open. Everyone will know you're the robber, but they won't look on you as a robber; rather they will try to find out ways of helping you stop stealing. We had a problem with one of the boys who'd stolen several times here and there. The common meeting decided he should spend time with people who had been in jail for a long time for robbery and he talked with these prisoners. He visited another prison and came back to relate it to the common meeting. Since that time he hasn't stolen anything yet. Perhaps he will, but at least he

Question:
Annie:

Question:

Annie:

realises a little better what his situation will be
if he goes on stealing.
Do the problems of stealing and crime affect the
neighbours locally?
No, nearly all the incidents of stealing have
taken place inside the school. We have had some
cases where things were taken from shops, but
the kids know that if they do it and we find them
out then they will have to take it back, pay for it,
and apologise. And there's a lot of respect for
that attitude.
Lastly, Annie, we realise that we are just two of
many thousands of visitors who come to Tvind
each year – to look at the windmill, or to look at
the school. But we know that if you observe
something very closely the thing you are observ-
ing begins to be affected. Isn't this a problem
here with your school for the pupils? You see
when we asked Marianne about this she said,
'We're used to people, it doesn't matter.' And
we wonder if that's true.
Well, of course it does. If you have guests,
you have to think about your own behaviour.
It's too easy to just do what you like and not to
think about how to behave to other people. But
when you have guests, you're in a new situation
and you have to behave differently; but it's a
good experience. There are a lot of young
people here who have come because they don't
want to be at home or at the school they went to.
There are a lot of things they don't want and now
they come here because there are things they
want to do, and it's very good for guests to meet
and talk with our pupils and learn from them.
Pupils coming here feel they have a mission:
they feel the school system must be changed.
When they were in ordinary folk schools it was
difficult for them to see what had to be changed,
but now they have got some ideas. Not that they
totally agree. But at least they are thinking
and talking about it. They help in the spread of
consciousness.

Footsteps behind us made us look up from the tape recorder,
resting so oddly out of place on the grass. Dorte smiled

down 'Må jeg få penge?' she asked Annie. ('Can I have some money please?') We had to laugh.

Appendix 4

Questionnaire sent out to students

Section One: How you regarded the centre with reference to the youngsters.

1 Did you feel the centre benefited any of the youngsters who came? (19 affirmatives)

2 If yes, could you say for what sort of youngsters it was most useful?
Those who are lonely, socially deprived and have difficulty forming relationships. (6)
Those lacking in self-confidence and expressive ability. (5)
Those with anti-authority attitudes. (3)
Those not easily pigeon-holed in school, who felt no one was interested in them and for whom welcome was a rarity. (3)
Those with little worldly experience. (2)
Those labelled useless.
The more mature ones.
The extroverts.

3 Did you feel the centre was harmful to any of the youngsters who came? (5 affirmatives)

4 If yes, could you say for what sorts of young people?
It rewarded and supported anti-social behaviour. (3)
It could be harmful for emotionally disturbed children or those who are very withdrawn, and the informality could be difficult to come to terms with. (3)

5 Did you notice any significant behavioural changes amongst the youngsters during the year? (19 affirmatives)
265

6 Increased confidence. (11)
  Increased awareness and ease in relationships. (10)
  Decrease in anti-social behaviour and increased respon-
  sibility. (4)
  Increased expressiveness. (2)
  The more morose cheered up.
  Increased understanding.
  Lessened inhibitions.

7 Could you list what you thought was most significant and
  beneficial for the youngsters about:
  (a) The content (i.e. what they did, or where they went,
  or who they met etc.).
  Outside visits. (12)
  Job guidance. (5)
  Visitors. (4)
  Their involvement in organising activities and expressing
  their views. (4)
  Knowledge of rights. (2)
  Making things.
  Making lunch together.
  Sex education.
  Favourable introduction to adult institutions.
  Equality of status with whom they met.
  (b) The structure (i.e. its atmosphere, the building, the
  staff, etc.).
  Friendly relaxed atmosphere. (8)
  Continuing staff support and acceptance. (6)
  Building not too 'posh' and pupils allowed some say in its
  decoration. (6)
  Small size group and high staff/pupil ratio. (4)
  Not like school. (3)
  Successful use of students.
  Humorous and patient staff.
  (c) The methodology (i.e. how we approached the young-
  sters and their 'education').
  Teaching by demonstration not coercion. (5)
  Continuous emphasis on responsibility and self-
  sufficiency. (3)
  Acceptance of kids' outlooks and problems as the starting
  point. (2)
  Positiveness and encouragement. (2)
  Presented adults as human.
  Developed awareness of each other in the group.
  Informality and mature approach.

Able to allow time for ideas to develop.
No continual correction or condemnation.

8 Could you list what you were most critical about concerning the centre's content and structure?
Not directive enough of youngsters. (4)
Sometimes too unplanned. (3)
Can't help very emotionally disturbed children in such a short time. (2)
Apathy of kids in a 'sin-bin'can be contagious.
Aggressive kids should be 'directed' more quickly into individual activities.
Difficult to balance 'freedom' with a structure the youngsters will accept.
No continuity of it during holidays.
Not supportive enough of students.
Not enough contact with homes.

9 If you were running the centre what would you change?
More work experience and careers guidance. (3)
More sport and outdoor activities. (2)
More literacy work. (2)
Develop more respect for surroundings.
More indoor board games.
More contact with regular school.
Widen age range.
More use of non-teachers to enable 1:1 for some work.
More community work.
More frequent assessment of work amongst staff.
More emphasis on self-improvement.

10 Could you add anything of personal relevance?
Helped with my awareness of adolescence and opened eyes to problems previously unknown. (3)
Kids' failure is partly their fault and not just dependent on background, so that caring staff attitude is crucial.
More discussion on home problems needed.
Social training important.
Kids eager to learn, once good relationships had developed.
Hard to make balance between acceptance and condoning anti-social behaviour.
Student volunteers need much support.
Important to return to smaller numbers in schools and classes.

Learnt value of sense of humour.
Learnt importance of trust.

Section Two: The value of placement at Bayswater Centre
with reference to yourself.

1 Did involvement at Bayswater alter your preconceptions
about adolescents, or ways of working with adolescents?
(19 affirmatives)

2 If so, could you elaborate further?
Had eyes opened to their insecurity and personal difficul-
ties. (4)
Any contact with adolescents would alter preconcep-
tions. (3)
Children surprisingly slow and ignorant, alienated and
suspicious. (2)
Hadn't realised how limited their experience is. (2)
Had to get on with the kids on their terms.
Confirmed established beliefs.
Saw youngsters initially as unfortunate, but then as
brave, since they had gone to a lot of trouble to avoid bad
schooling.
Had not met such kids before.
Expected too much.
Realised you need patience to work very gradually.
Realised individual interests and needs of such young-
sters.
Appreciated necessity for a sense of real purpose in
doing things.
Shed light on importance of backgrounds – kids seemed to
have matured too early in some ways.
Took away fear of meeting them in school.

3 Assuming you are working in a job which involves young
people,could you say whether participation at Bayswater
influenced:
(a) The kid of youngsters you opted to work with. (19
affirmatives)
Can you elaborate on your answer?
Chose relatively stable younger boys – as far as choice
allowed.
Would avoid teaching difficult kids in schools.
Prefer working with kids with individualistic tendencies.

No choice.
Made me more keen to work with kids of this kind.
Felt willing and able to work with older kids.
Chose socially and culturally deprived kids and adults.
(b) Your attitude to 'difficult' youngsters? (19 affirmatives)
Can you elaborate on your answer?
Became more tolerant because of a greater understanding of, and sympathy for, basic problems. (6)
Hard to do much in a rigid school structure.
Better to build a good relationship than thunder at kids.
Don't see any as difficult or abnormal now.
Won't get respect as a teacher if kid has none for parents.
Not as afraid. See aggression as part of their fears and insecurity.
More accepting and able to contact them in lessons.
Attracted to them.
Found it easy to get on with them at first, before usual discipline problems arose!
Can see reason behind their behaviour but am still incompetent to handle it.
(c) Your teaching style and lesson content. (7 affirmatives)
Can you elaborate on your answer?
See authoritarian teaching style as useless. (3)
More emphasis on group work - gives time for individuals.
Try to make lessons more orientated to what kids need.
Can see that for some kids motivation is more important than subject matter.
More relaxed and less worried about 'position'.
Put stress on socially relevant content.
Less willing to force low-ability 4th and 5th years to 'learn' subjects that are clearly irrelevant to them.
(d) Your approach to youngsters outside the classroom? (11 affirmatives)
Can you elaborate on your answer?
Feel more at ease with youngsters, more understanding. (3)
Try to treat them as responsible individuals.
Try to make them feel that I can accept them.
Increased awareness, sympathy and desire to help.
Try and see youngsters, who are difficult in lessons, outside the classroom.
Easier to get on with them.
See 'failures' in class as quite able to succeed outside.
Get on at their level - without being condescending.

(e) Your perception and handling of individual children amongst a group of thirty in a classroom? (7 affirmatives)
Can you elaborate on your answer?
More aware of youngsters with problems and their academic performance. (3)
Don't and wouldn't teach large classes.
Helped to alter practice, though hard to handle individuals and maintain a pottery properly.
(f) Your involvement in promoting any change within the school. (6 affirmatives)
Can you elaborate on your answer?
Not yet. (6)
Developing new syllabus for less able 4th and 5th years.
Have set up a school farm.
Run Duke of Edinburgh Award scheme and encouraged canoeing and mountaineering.
Involved in school discussions on changes for non-academic pupils.
In favour of altering exam system for bottom sets.
Involvement in community service opportunities.

4 Have you tried to influence other staff's attitude to 'difficult' pupils? (5 affirmatives)
If so, what?
Try to show that staff have responsibility for all children.
A little in conversation.
Try to use staff self-interest for pupil's benefit.
By mentioning the problems and the work of Bayswater Centre.
Discuss value of non-timetabled activities and more positive attitude.

5 Do you believe it is possible to alter the current curriculum content and structure of secondary schools? (12 affirmatives)
If so could you explain your ideas?
More practical lessons to develop social education.
More effort to develop basic English and maths.
Attitudes more important than content.
Make schools smaller and work more outside school.
Place more emphasis on personal relationships.
Need interdisciplinary co-operation for non-exam kids.
Classes must be made smaller and emphasise basic skills as priority.
Accept that non-academics actually exist, and provide for them.

Appendix 5

Attendance statistics

The following tables illustrate the attendance patterns for the two full terms that all the youngsters attended the school. They only have real significance when compared to their previous school attendance patterns. In the cases of Alec, Jim, Debbie, Clive and Simon these had been zero for some months before their referral to us. For all others, attendance patterns were below 30 per cent before referral to us.

After the second week of the spring term we abandoned the idea of meeting at Monday lunchtime, because it proved so divisive and disruptive, since only one member of staff could be present any earlier than one o'clock; which is why the maximum possible attendance each week became four sessions in effect.

Jim, Alec, Debbie, Clive and John had all left before the summer term started – and Maggie 'departed' before half term.

Christmas term attendance

Name	Week 1	2	3	4	5	6	7	8	9	10	11	12	13	14	Total attendance out of a possible 66
Jim	2/2	5/5	5/5	4/5	5/5	5/5	5/5	5/5	4/5	5/5	4/5	5/5	5/5	4/4	63
Martin	2/2	5/5	5/5	5/5	5/5	4/5	5/5	5/5	5/5	5/5	5/5	5/5	5/5	4/4	65
Alec	2/2	5/5	2/5	5/5	5/5	5/5	5/5	5/5	5/5	5/5	5/5	5/5	5/5	4/4	63
Clive	2/2	5/5	5/5	5/5	5/5	5/5	5/5	4/5	5/5	5/5	5/5	5/5	5/5	4/4	65
Debbie	1/2	4/5	3/5	5/5	4/5	3/5	5/5	5/5	1/5	2/5	4/5	0/5	0/5	0/4	37
Joy	1/2	3/5	2/5	4/5	2/5	5/5	5/5	3/5	1/5	4/5	3/5	2/5	4/5	4/4	43
Liz	X	5/5	5/5	5/5	5/5	5/5	5/5	4/5	5/5	5/5	5/5	5/5	5/5	4/4	63/64
Lester	X	1/1	3/5	4/5	5/5	5/5	3/5	4/5	5/5	5/5	5/5	5/5	5/5	4/4	55/60
Judy	Joined at half term							3/5	5/5	3/5	2/5	4/5	3/5	1/4	21/34
Dirk	Joined at half term								4/5	5/5	5/5	5/5	1/5	4/4	24/29
Angie	Joined after Christmas														
Simon	Joined after Christmas														

(Marginal annotations written vertically: "HALF TERM" between weeks 8 and 9, and "END OF TERM" at week 14.)

Spring term attendance

Name	Week 1	2	3	4	5	Week 6	7	8	9	10	11		Total attendance out of a possible 45
Jim	5/5	5/5	4/4	4/4	2/4	4/4	4/4	0/4	0/4	2/4	3/3	left	33
Martin	5/5	5/5	4/4	4/4	4/4	4/4	4/4	4/4	4/4	4/4	3/3	left M	45
Alec	5/5	2/5	1/4	2/4	2/4	1/4	2/4	0/4	0/4	0/4	0/3	left R	15
Clive	4/5	4/5	2/4	2/4	2/4 M	1/4	2/4	2/4	3/4	1/4	0/3	left E	23
Debbie	0/5	left	–	–	–	– R	–	–	–	–	–	left T	0
Joy	5/5	4/5	3/4	2/4	0/4 E	2/4	3/4	2/4	1/4	2/4	2/3		26
Liz	5/5	4/5	4/4	4/4	3/4 T	4/4	3/4	3/4	1/4	4/4	3/3	F	38
Lester	5/5	5/5	4/4	4/4	4/4 F	4/4	4/4	4/4	4/4	3/4	3/3	O	44
Judy	2/5	5/5	4/4	3/4	4/4 L	0/4	4/4	4/4	1/4	0/4	0/3		27
Dirk	4/5	5/5	3/4	4/4	2/4 A	4/4	4/4	4/4	4/4	4/4	3/3	D	41
Angie	X	X	X	4/4	4/4 V	4/4	4/4	4/4	4/4	4/4	3/3	N	31/31
Simon	X	X	X	X	X H	4/4	3/4	4/4	4/4	4/4	3/3	E	22/23

Summer term attendance

Name	Week							Total attendance out of
	1	2	3	4	5	6	7	a possible 28
Joy	0	4	4	4	2	3	2	19
Liz	4	4	3	4	3	3	4	25
Lester	3	4	3	3	4	3	4	24
Martin	4	4	4	4	4	4	4	28
Angie	4	3	4	4	4	4	4	27
Simon	4	3	4	4	4	4	4	27

Notes

CHAPTER 1 DANISH LESSONS IN PRACTICAL EDUCATION

1 'Fact sheet on Denmark – Education', published by Cultural Relations Department and Ministry of Foreign Affairs of Denmark and obtainable from the Danish Embassy in London, 1978.
2 'Danish Folk High Schools', published by the Danish Institute in Copenhagen, 1972
3 Julius Nyerere, 'Education for Self-Reliance', Government Printer, Dar-es-Salaam, 1967.
4 See the articles in Aarhus newspaper 'Information' on 12 May and 27–29 May 1978 for a detailed critique of the Tvind complex by opponents of the school, who regard the process as one of 'indoctrination'.
5 See the article Tvind Windmill by Marshall Merriam in 'Resurgence', July 1966.
6 See particularly 'Subsistence Education' by David Woollcomb available from: 6 Regent's Park Road, London NW1, the 'Times Educational Supplement' article Time for a Change by Peter Newell (29 September 1978), and All the Skills in the World by Margaret Murray in the 'Times Educational Supplement', 22 March 1976.

CHAPTER 2 ALTERNATIVE PROVISION IN BRITAIN

1 John Holt, 'Instead of Education', Penguin, 1970.
2 'How to Set Up a Free School', available from 57 White Lion Street, London N1.
3 Figures taken from the 'Public and Preparatory Schools Year Book', 1979.

4   W.A.C. Stewart, 'Progressives and Radicals in English Education 1750–1970', Macmillan, 1972.
5   See Leila Berg, 'Risinghill: Death of a Comprehensive', Penguin, 1969.
6   Ivan Illich, 'De-Schooling Society', Penguin, 1971.
7   See 'Pedagogy of the Oppressed', Penguin, 1972 and 'Education: the Practice of Freedom', Writers and Readers Press Co-operative, 1976, both by Paulo Freire.
8   See 'How to Set Up a Free School', p. 35, section on 'White Lion School costs'.
9   'Behavioural Units' report by DES, available from Elizabeth House, York Road, London SE1 (published 1978).
10 See article Playing Hookey is Legal by Malcolm Dean in 'Education Guardian', 31 July 1979.
11 Michael Rutter et al., 'Fifteen Thousand Hours', Open Books, 1979.
12 Rob Grunsell, 'Born to be Invisible', MacMillan Education, 1978.
13 'White Lion School Bulletins', nos 1–4 from 57 White Lion Street, London N1.
14 See 'White Lion Bulletin' no. 3
15 R.F. Mackenzie, 'State School', Penguin, 1970.
16 See Special Units: Some Educational Issues, by Mike Golby in 'Socialsim and Education', vol. 6, no. 2, summer 1979.
17 See S. Bowles and H. Gintis, 'Schooling in Capitalist America', Routledge & Kegan Paul, 1976, p. 263.

CHAPTER 3 A TALE OF TWO CLASSROOMS: THE Rs THAT COUNT

1   See Toward Contemporary Issues: Youth, Chapter 6 in Erik Erikson, 'Identity: Youth and Crisis', Faber & Faber, 1968, particularly pp. 243–5.
2   See Roger White and David Brockington, 'In and Out of School', Routledge & Kegan Paul, 1978.
3   D.H. Hargreaves, 'Social Relations in a Secondary School', Routledge & Kegan Paul, 1967.
4   See Paul Willis, 'Learning to Labour', Saxon House, 1977, for a broader discussion of the reality of the job prospects for working-class youngsters.
5   Hargreaves, 'Social Relations in a Secondary School'.

6   See the Prologue in Erik Erikson, 'Identity: Youth and Crisis', for a discussion about identity formation.
7   See D.T. Leach and E.C. Raybould, 'Learning and Behaviour Difficulties in School', Open Books, 1977.

CHAPTER 4   SCHOOL PHOBIAS: THE MYTH OF LABELLING

1   Dennis Marsden and Brian Jackson, 'Education and the Working Class', Penguin, 1963.
2   See statistics presented by Jean Floud in Social Class Factors in Educational Achievement, Chapter 2 of 'Family, Class and Education', ed. Maurice Craft, Longman, 1970.
3   See D.H. Hargreaves, 'Social Relations in a Secondary School', Routledge & Kegan Paul, 1967.
4   See Erich Fromm, 'A Sane Society', Routledge & Kegan Paul, 1957.
5   C.M. Fleming, 'Adolescence: its Social Psychology', Routledge & Kegan Paul, 1948.
6   See Helen Keller, 'The Story of My Life', Hodder & Stoughton, 1958.
7   See Joey Deacon, 'Tongue Tied', published by the National Society for Mentally Handicapped Children, 1974, and available from the NSMHC Bookshop, Pembridge Hall, Cambridge Square, London W2.

CHAPTER 5   AUTUMN TERM

1   See Michael Rutter, Barbara Maughan, Peter Mortimore and Janet Ouston, 'Fifteen Thousand Hours', Open Books, 1979, p. 196.
2   See Erik Erikson, 'Identity, Youth and Crisis', Faber & Faber, 1968, p. 244.
3   See Race Aces Course Cures Car-crazy Joy-riders, article by Harvey Elliott in the 'Daily Mail', Tuesday 4 July 1978.
4   See Roger White and David Brockington, 'In and Out of School', Routledge & Kegan Paul, 1978, Chapter 6 on Self Sufficiency.
5   See Peter Shaffer, 'Equus', Samuel French, 1974.
6   See 'Fifteen Thousand Hours', p. 196, section on Shared Activities between Staff and Pupils.

CHAPTER 6 ANCILLARY FACTORS: RESOURCEFULNESS, THE FOURTH R

1 'Behavioural Units', DES booklet published in December 1978, see particularly Section 4, Issues Arising from the Survey - Accommodation, Equipment and Finances.
2 'Loving Us', by Howard Case, available from the author at Ladywell, Westhorpe, Stowmarket, Suffolk (published 1978).
3 See 'Socialism and Education', vol. 6, no. 2, summer 1979: article by Mike Golby on Special Units.
4 See Frank Field, 'Free School Meals: the Humiliation Continues', CPAG, 1977.

CHAPTER 7 SPRING TERM

1 See C.M. Fleming, 'Adolescence: its Social Psychology', Routledge & Kegan Paul, 1948.
2 See 'Daily Mail', Tuesday 4 July 1978, Race Aces Course Cures Car-crazy Joy-riders, by Harvey Elliot.

CHAPTER 8 SELF-ANALYSIS

1 See G. Atkinson, The Highfield Experiment, 'New Behaviour', 10 July 1975.
2 See Masud Hoghughi, 'Troubled and Troublesome', Burnett Books, 1978.
3 Michael Burn, 'Mr Lyward's Answer', Hamish Hamilton, 1956; see particularly pp. 283-5.
4 See C.M. Fleming, 'Adolescence: its Social Psychology', Routledge & Kegan Paul, 1948.
5 See text of speech delivered by Professor W.D. Wall to a conference entitled 'Working with Schools', at Bristol University on 4 May 1978.

CHAPTER 9 LEAVING SCHOOL: THE FINAL TERM

1 Paul Willis, 'Learning to Labour', Saxon-House Press, 1977.
2 Everett Reimer, 'School is Dead', Penguin 1971.
3 This year six out of the original group stayed on for

four months after the statutory leaving date to pursue their 'educational' interests.

4 'Loving Us', by Howard Case, available from the author at Ladywell, Westhorpe, Stowmarket, Suffolk, p. 148.

5 Intermediate Treatment Centre, Bethnal Green, Annual Report 1976, available from the Crypt, St Johns Church, Roman Road, London E2.

CHAPTER 10 STUDENT INVOLVEMENT

1 See Roger White and Dave Brockington, 'In and Out of School', Routledge & Kegan Paul, 1978, particularly Part Two: Towards a Survival Curriculum, and Appendix One: Section on Survival Skills.

2 See Pierre Bourdieu, The School as a Conservative Force: Scholastic and Cultural Inequalities, in 'Schooling and Capitalism' ed. Roger Dale, Routledge & Kegan Paul, 1976.

3 See 'In and Out of School', Chapter 9, A Programme for Teacher and Social Worker Training.

4 See Bruno Bettelheim, 'Children of the Dream', Thames & Hudson, 1969.

5 Masud Hoghughi, 'Troubled and Troublesome', Burnett Books, 1978.

6 DES Press notice 10 July 1979 entitled 'DES Supports Research into School Changes'.

7 With acknowledgments to Kevin Smith for allowing me to use this journal extract.

8 See E.F. Schumacher, 'Small is Beautiful', Blond & Briggs, 1976.

9 With acknowledgments to Paul Greenhalgh for allowing me to use this journal extract.

10 With acknowledgments to Kevin Smith for allowing me to use this journal extract.

CHAPTER 11 METAMORPHOSIS OF A SCHOOL: THREE Rs

1 See Michael Rutter et al., 'Fifteen Thousand Hours', Open Books, 1979, particularly Chapter 7 on School Processes: Association with Outcome.

CHAPTER 12 CONCLUSION: IMPLICATIONS FOR MAIN-
STREAM EDUCATION

1   See Maurice Craft, 'Family, Class and Education',
    Longmans, 1970.
2   See D. Hargreaves, 'Social Relations in a Secondary
    School', Routledge & Kegan Paul, 1967.
3   See 'How to Set Up a Free School', section on White
    Lion Street Costs, p. 35, available from the school,
    57 White Lion Street, London N1.
4   See Bobby Seale, 'Seize the Time', Panther, 1969 and
    Eldridge Cleaver, 'Soul on Ice', Jonathan Cape, 1969.
5   Pierre Bourdieu, The School as a Conservative Force,
    in Roger Dale, Geoff Esland and Madeleine MacDonald,
    eds, 'Schooling and Capitalism', Chapter 12, Routledge
    & Kegan Paul, 1976.
6   B. Bernstein, 'Class Codes and Control', volume 3,
    Routledge & Kegan Paul, 1975.
7   See L.F. Lowenstein, 'Violence in Schools', NASM
    Pamphlet, 1972, and 'Discipline in Schools', NUT
    Pamphlet, 1976.
8   See article Playing Hookey is Legal in 'Education
    Guardian', 31 July 1979. 'No one knows how wide-
    spread truancy has become, but a major study in Scot-
    land found poor schools reporting a 10 per cent group
    of persistent truants.'
9   See 'Behavioural Units', published by the DES in
    December 1978 and available from Elizabeth House,
    York Road, London SE1.
10 Michael Rutter et al., 'Fifteen Thousand Hours', Open
    Books, 1979. See particularly Chapter 10, Conclu-
    sions: Speculations and Implications.

Bibliography

ATKINSON, G., The Highfield Experiment, 'New Behaviour', 10 July 1975.

BERG, L., 'Risinghill: Death of a Comprehensive', Penguin 1968.

BERNSTEIN, B., 'Class Codes and Control', vol. 3, Routledge & Kegan Paul, 1975.

BETTELHEIM, B., 'Children of the Dream', Thames & Hudson, 1969.

BOURDIEU, P., The School as a Conservative Force, in 'Schooling and Capitalism', eds Roger Dale, Geoff Esland and Madeleine MacDonald, Routledge & Kegan Paul, 1976.

BOWLES, S. and GINTIS, H., 'Schooling in Capitalist America', Routledge & Kegan Paul, 1976.

BURN, M., 'Mr Lyward's Answer', Hamish Hamilton, 1965.

CASE, H., 'Loving Us', available from the author at Ladywell, Westhorpe, Stowmarket, Suffolk; published 1978.

CHANAN, G. and GILCHRIST, L., 'What School is For', Methuen, 1974.

CLEAVER, E., 'Soul on Ice', Jonathan Cape, 1969.

CRAFT, M., 'Family, Class and Education', Longman, 1970.

DES, 'Behavioural Units', December 1978.

DEACON, JOEY, 'Tongue Tied', NSMHC, 1974.

EISSLER, E., 'Searchlights on Delinquency', New York, 1949.

ERIKSON, E., 'Identity: Youth and Crisis', Faber & Faber, 1968.

FINGARETTE, H., 'Self in Transformation', Harper & Row, 1965.

FLEMING, C.M., 'Adolescence: its Social Psychology', Routledge & Kegan Paul, 1948.

281

FLOUD, J., Social Class Factors in Educational Achievement, Chapter 2 of 'Family, Class and Education', Longman, 1970.

FREIRE, P., 'Pedagogy of the Oppressed', Penguin, 1972.

FREIRE, P., 'Education: the Practice of Freedom', WRPC, 1976.

FROMM, ERICH, 'A Sane Society', Routledge & Kegan Paul, 1957.

GRUNSELL, R., 'Born to be Invisible', Macmillan, 1978.

HARGREAVES, D., 'Social Relations in a Secondary School', Routledge & Kegan Paul, 1967.

HOGHUGHI, MASUD, 'Troubled and Troublesome', Burnett Books, 1978.

HOLT, JOHN, 'Instead of Education', Penguin, 1970.

ILLICH, IVAN, 'Deschooling Society', Penguin, 1971.

ILLICH, IVAN, 'Celebration of Awareness', Penguin 1973.

ILLICH, IVAN, 'After De-schooling, What?', WRPC, 1974.

JACKSON, BRIAN and MARSDEN, DENNIS, 'Education and the Working Class', Penguin, 1963.

JOHNSON, RICHARD, Notes on the Schooling of the English Working Class 1780-1850, in ed. Roger Dale et al., 'Schooling and Capitalism', Routledge & Kegan Paul, 1976.

KELLER, HELEN, 'The Story of My Life', Hodder & Stoughton, 1958.

KOHLBERG, L., 'Vita Humana', 1963, vol. 6, pp. 11-33.

LEACH, D.J. and RAYBOULD, E.C., 'Learning and Behaviour Difficulties in School', Open Books, 1977.

LISTER, IAN, 'De-Schooling Revisited', WRPC, 1976.

LISTER, IAN, Getting There from Here, Chapter 2 in 'Education Without Schools', ed. Peter Buckman, Souvenir Press, 1973.

MACKENZIE, R.F., 'State School', Penguin, 1971.

MILLIBAND, R., 'The State in Capitalist Society', Weidenfeld & Nicolson, 1969.

NYERERE, JULIUS, 'Education for Self Reliance', Government Printer, Dar-es-Salaam, 1967.

OWEN, ROBERT, 'A New View of Society', London, 1813-14.

PIAGET, J., 'The Moral Judgement of the Child', Routledge & Kegan Paul, 1932.

RUTTER, MICHAEL et al., 'Fifteen Thousand Hours', Open Books, 1979.

SCHUMACHER, E.F., 'Small is Beautiful', Blond & Briggs, 1976.

SEALE, BOBBY, 'Seize the Time', Panther, 1969.

SHAFFER, PETER, 'Equus', Samuel French, 1974.
STEWART, W., 'Progressives and Radicals in English
Education', Macmillan, 1972.
TAPPER, T. and SALTER, B., 'Education and the Politi-
cal Order', Macmillan, 1978.
WARDLE, D., 'English Popular Education 1750-1970',
Cambridge University Press, 1970.
WHITE, ROGER and BROCKINGTON, DAVID, 'In and Out
of School', Routledge & Kegan Paul, 1978.
WILLIS, PAUL, 'Learning to Labour', Saxon House Press,
1977.
WOOLLCOMB, DAVID, 'Subsistence Education', published
by the author at 6 Regent's Park Road, London NW1.
YOUNG, M. and WHITTY, G., 'Society, State and School-
ing', Falmer Press, 1977.

Schools, centres and units consulted or visited

V = Visited

Albany Alternative Education Project, Creek Road, London SE8.
Barrowfield Community School, 1 St Marnock Street, Glasgow.
Bermondsey Lamp Post School, 184 Long Lane, London SE1.
Bridge Centre, Allcock Street, Deritend, Birmingham 9 (V).
Centre 525, Fairmuir School, Dundee.
Coventry City Centre Project, Tudor House, 14 Span Street, Coventry.
Cowley St James Tutorial Unit, Beauchamp Lane, Cowley, Oxford (V).
Durdham Park Free School, Durdham Down, Redland, Bristol (V).
Douglas Inch Centre, 2 Woodside Terrace, Glasgow.
Freightliner Farm, 9 York Way, London N7.
Govan Project, Broomloon Road, Govan, Glasgow.
Hammersmith Teenage Project, 58 Bulmer Street, Shepherds Bush, London W12 (V).
Intermediate Education Centre, The Crypt, St Johns Road, Bethnal Green, London E2 (V).
Kenton Lodge Residential School, Newcastle on Tyne (V).
Kettering Intermediate Treatment Project, Kettering Social Services, Kettering, Northamptonshire.
Key Centre, Ladywood, Birmingham 16 (V).
Manchester Free School, 28 Brundretts Road, Manchester 21 (V).
Maudsley Hospital Special Unit, Camberwell, London SE5 (V).
Mearns Centre, Greenock, Strathclyde.

Midland Adventurers, 29 Trinity Road, Aston, Birming-
ham (V).
North Kensington Education Project, 92 Tavistock Road,
London W1.
Norwich Tutorial Unit, Norwich.
149 Centre, Surrey Road, Reading, Berkshire (V).
Panmure House, Canongate, Edinburgh (V).
Portobello Project, 49 Portobello Road, London W2.
Rainer Foundation, 89a Blackheath Road, London SE10.
Riverside Truancy School, Bath, Avon(V).
St Paul's Community School, Balsall Heath, Birmingham (V).
Salamanca House, Randel Road, London SE11.
Tvind School, Ulfborg, Jutland, Denmark (V).
Watford Social Education Project, 15 Harwoods Road,
Watford.
White Lion Free School, 57 White Lion Street, London N1 (V).

DATE DUE

JUN. 1 8 1982			
JUN 2 8 1982			
MAY 3 '89			
MAY 2 4 '89			
JUN 1 4 '89			
FEB 2 7 1996			
MAY 1 6 2005			
GAYLORD			PRINTED IN U.S.A.

COLUMBUS COLLEGE LIBRARY

LB 3081 .W45   sscc,circ

Absent with cause :

3 7337 00144 6056

LB
3081   White, Roger
.W45   Absent with cause

COLUMBUS COLLEGE LIBRARY
COLUMBUS, GEORGIA